LAND
OF THE
SNOW LION

BY THE SAME AUTHOR

The Windhorse
(with Julie Donnelly)

LAND
OF THE
SNOW LION

Elaine Brook

JONATHAN CAPE
THIRTY-TWO BEDFORD SQUARE
LONDON

For my mother

First published 1987
First published in paperback 1989

Jonathan Cape Ltd, 32 Bedford Square, London WC1B 3SG

A CIP catalogue record for this book
is available from the British Library

ISBN 0-224-02732-8

Photoset by Butler & Tanner Ltd, Frome and London
Printed in Great Britain by
Mackays of Chatham PLC, Chatham, Kent

Contents

High mountains and glaciers are the realm of the legendary *seng-ge*, or snow lion, symbol of Tibet. White, with turquoise mane and tail, it leaps from peak to peak without touching the snow.

Illustrations

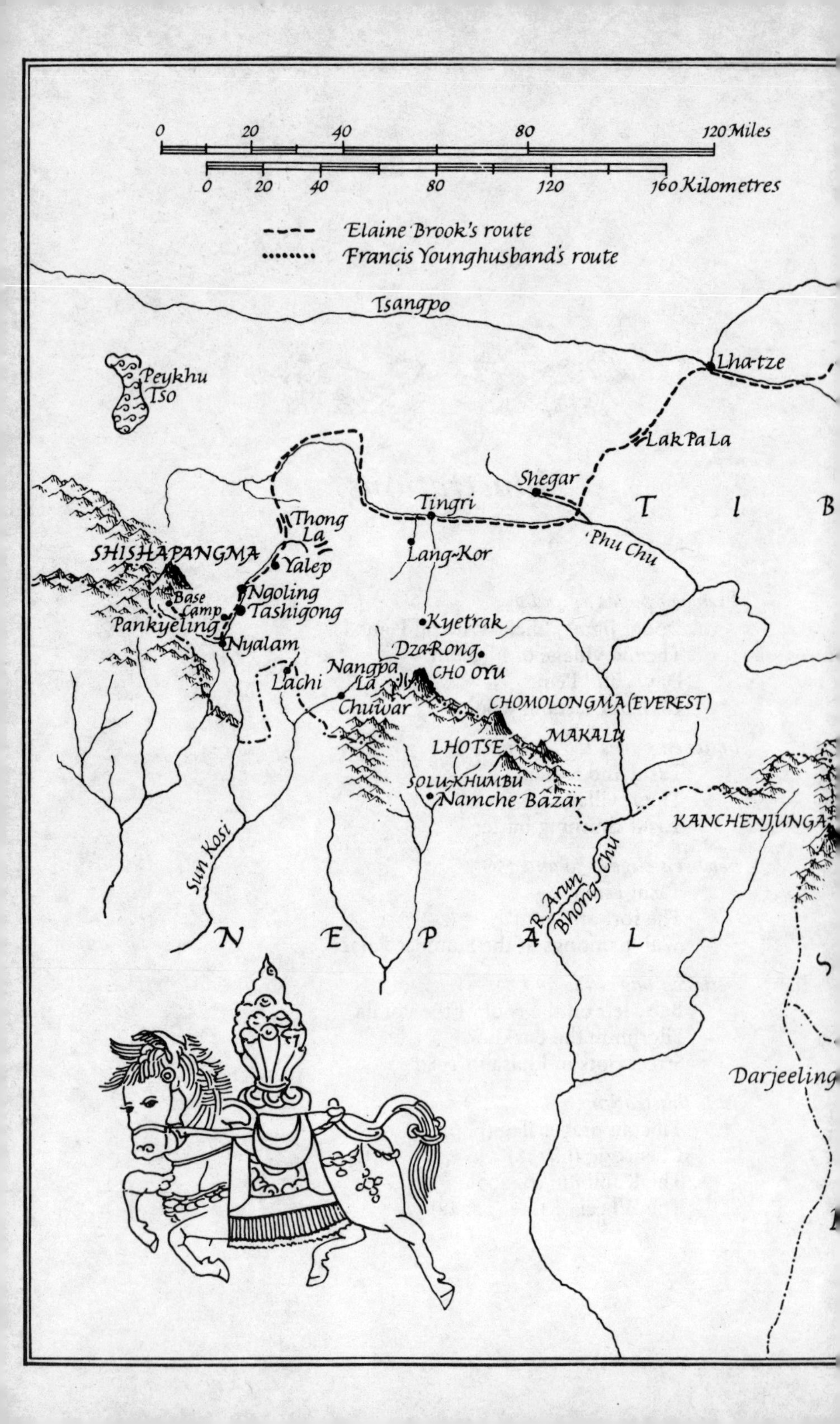

0 20 40 80 120 Miles
0 20 40 80 120 160 Kilometres
Elaine Brook's route
Francis Younghusband's route
Tsangpo
Peykhu Tso
Lha-tze
Lak Pa La
Shegar
Tingri
T I B
Phu Chu
Thong La
Lang-Kor
SHISHAPANGMA
Yalep
Ngoling
Base Camp
Tashigong
Pankyeling
Kyetrak
Nyalam
Dza Rong
Nangpa La
CHO OYU
Lachi
Chuwar
CHOMOLONGMA (EVEREST)
MAKALU
LHOTSE
SOLU-KHUMBU
Namche Bazar
KANCHENJUNGA
Sun Kosi
Bhong Chu
R. Arun
N E P A L
Darjeeling

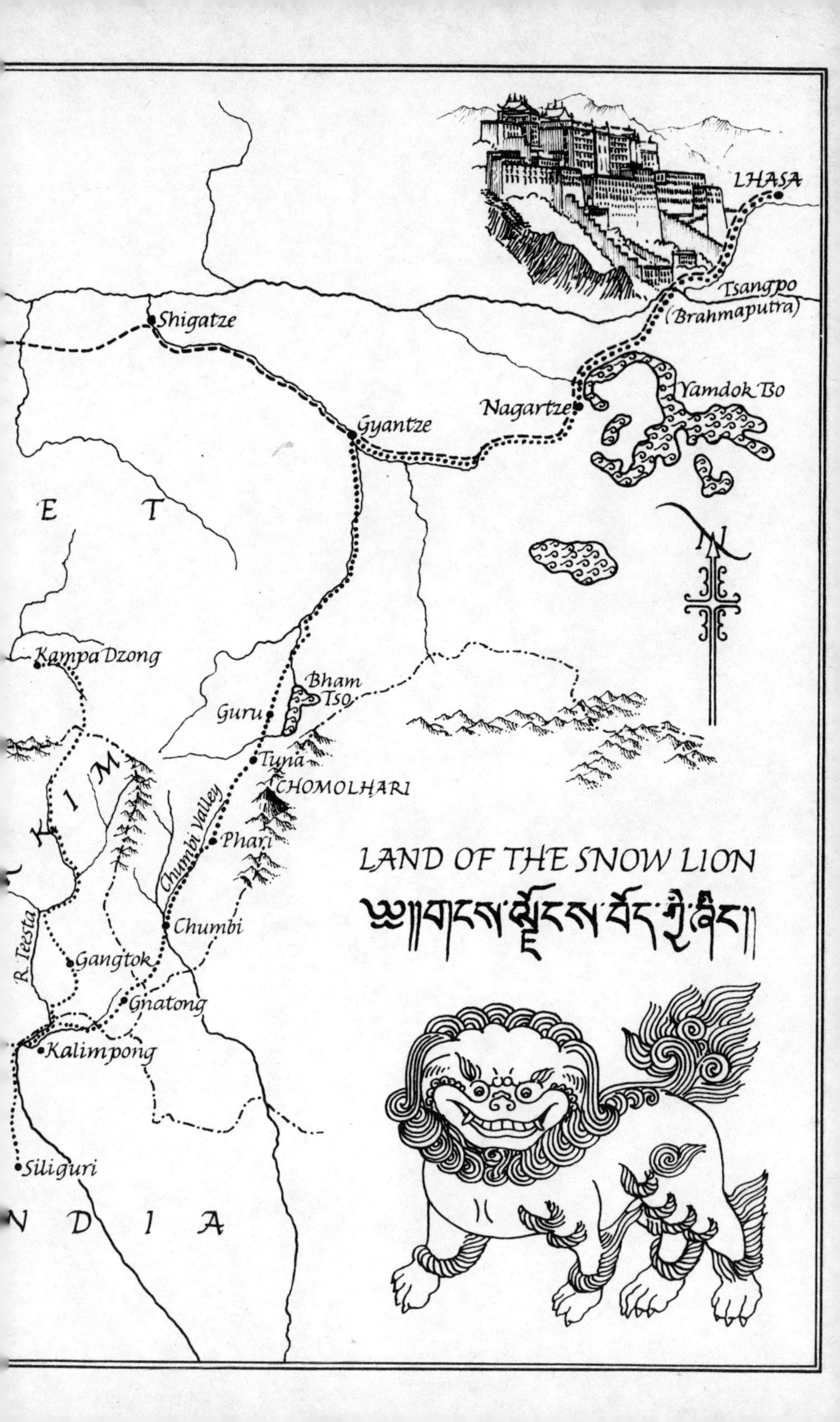

LHASA
Tsangpo
(Brahmaputra)
Shigatze
Yamdok Tso
Nagartze
Gyantze
E T
N
Kampa Dzong
Bham Tso
Guru
Tuna
CHOMOLHARI
K I M
Chumbi Valley
Phari
LAND OF THE SNOW LION
Chumbi
R. Teesta
Gangtok
Gnatong
Kalimpong
Siliguri
N D I A

Tibetan Prayer Flag

PART ONE

The Mountain

Do you remember Sisyphus? He was doomed for ever to push a great stone to the top of a mountain, whereupon it would roll back down, and he would have to push it to the summit all over again.

A climber is like Sisyphus. But a climber is his own stone.

Reinhold Messner

I

Into the Unknown

The spacious marble hall of the airport was empty but for a group of crop-haired officials lined up to greet us, crisp navy-blue 'Mao' suits as uniform as their polite smiles. I wondered what, on first sight, they made of Doug, a head taller than most of them and sporting for the occasion a carefully chosen 'Mao' cap, from which his long greying hair flowed out.

Everything was a model of crisp efficiency compared with our chaotic progress so far. The officials handed out check-lists of equipment and a number of forms to fill in before we and all our luggage were whisked away into a waiting minibus.

We joined the orderly column of cyclists, horse-drawn carts and the few other sleek new minibuses which comprised the only traffic on the long, straight road into the city of Peking. The sun streamed between the slender trunks of the trees on either side of us. Every tree had a little wall of mud around it, provided in order to collect what little rain fell in this part of China. A shepherd watched over a small flock of sheep grazing sparse blades of grass in the dappled shadows of the woodland. The trees ended abruptly in an area of ploughed earth. Presumably the workers had gone home for the night, leaving the mature trees for replanting where they had unloaded them, lying on the ground, their roots wrapped in earth and bound carefully with rope. These groves, it appeared, did not sprout up here naturally; they were transported and erected on the chosen site like so many flagpoles.

As we reached the flat outskirts of the city, the evening sun flickered between chunky, heavily laden electricity pylons until it was blocked out completely by concrete apartment buildings, five-storey cubes standing in ranks either side of the road. Groups clad in denim-blue and khaki-green were exercising or chatting on the dusty grass outside. Further into the city the density of cyclists increased, until the minibus was nosing through a sea of grey-blue movement.

Our hotel was one of a number of solid, municipal-style buildings which looked as if they had been borrowed from the Russians in the 1950s. The streets were wide and straight, and the overall impression was of a city which had all been built at the same time, and largely on an austerity budget.

We were allotted five minutes for a wash before our escort shepherded us down to a plain and functional dining room with seating at table for about three hundred. It was almost empty. The food was tasty and the waitress pretty under her shapeless blue denim. She wore a name badge bearing a number.

Our escort was apologising for Tibet.

'It is a very backward place, people still work with their hands. And they *still* have religion.'

'Do you believe in God, Mr Su?'

'No, I believe in being happy and working for the State.'

I rose early the next morning to photograph the sunrise from my hotel window. After twenty minutes, the orange disk emerged from the pollution haze above the factories. I recalled a friend quoting a Chinese he had met: 'Give our industry another ten years and we will have overtaken you in the West ...' As I looked across at the billowing black smoke I felt saddened that the energy and vision which had inspired a nation to the Great Leap Forward, and brought thousands from destitution, should end in a repetition of all the mistakes we had made in our own Industrial Revolution.

Doug and I went for a walk in early-morning Peking. The wide streets were packed with people going to work, either jammed into rush-hour buses or as part of the flowing tide of cyclists. Private cars were scarcely to be seen and were, we had been told, only for the use of high-ranking government and Party officials. Along the broad pavements groups were moving in unison to the traditional patterns of T'ai Chi. Despite the drab, shapeless clothes, still bulky with winter quilting, their movements were beautifully graceful and controlled, their concentration turned inwards, a centring of mind and body according to an ancient formula which had somehow survived the restructuring of an entire culture. Other groups were practising in the People's Park, moving slowly on grass almost worn away by the passing of thousands of black-slippered feet. People on park benches were reading or singing to the songbirds in cages that hung from the trees. A girl by the park gate whirled and stabbed the air with a slender wooden sword, her face as expressionless as the thousands clicking past on bicycles.

I wanted to understand what I was seeing and realised I did not. My Western upbringing had conditioned me to search for a spark of individuality within these conforming masses, but the Chinese do not show their emotions. The blank faces gave nothing away.

Breakfast was at seven forty-five sharp, and a meeting with the Chinese Mountaineering Association was scheduled for nine. We too were expected to conform with the System. It was not easy for such a ragbag of disorganised individualists, whose anarchic tendencies had drawn them to the insane sport of climbing in the first place. We managed to assemble at the proper time for breakfast and all turned up for the first of the meetings, but then aroused acute anxiety among our hosts by arriving late, in disorderly ones and twos, for lunch. During the days of negotiation that followed, I seemed to slip even further from any understanding of what the Chinese were really thinking and feeling.

The cause of these protracted discussions was money – or, more precisely, their outrageously high prices and our miserably inadequate budget. Compared to expedition extravaganzas of the previous year, it appeared that our charisma and ability to attract wealthy sponsors fell woefully short of Chinese expectation. Why could we not produce the affluence of the Chris Bonington team, which had just been dispatched so smoothly (with two of my old friends, Pete Boardman and Joe Tasker) to Everest with the full financial backing of a large industrial company in Hong Kong? While the Chinese expected their charges to be met, we had arrived in Peking in the belief that a small gap in our budget could be bridged with a little bargaining and compromise. The System did not allow for fluctuations, however, and certainly not for the existence of a decadent Westerner without plenty of money. If we were to consume their package, they expected to be paid the asking price without question.

I found my attention wandering from the heated exchanges to the dreary conference room and the orderly grey concrete vista beyond the window. This was far from the romantic image of distant Tibet which had come to mind when Doug's phone-call lured me from the indulgence of sunny American ski slopes . . .

Colorado has some of the best skiing in the world, and my skis were waxed and waiting for a fresh fall of snow. Even though March was almost gone, the icy mountain air promised the light, cold powder we were waiting for. By first light, nine inches of it blanketed untracked slopes under a blue sky.

The telephone rang.

'Elaine, I guess it's for you. It's that guy with the weird accent I can't understand . . .'

I put down my skis and picked up the phone. Doug Scott's unmistakable Nottingham accent crackled over the transatlantic line.

'Eh-up duck. How y'doing?' He wasted little time at two pounds a minute, and went straight to the point. 'Do you want to go to Tibet? Georges has dropped out, so there's a place on our expedition to Shishapangma. It'll cost you fifteen hundred. The rest's covered by sponsorship.'

I said yes automatically, even though it would devastate my

savings and put an end to the ski season even before it had begun.

'Well, you'd better get on a plane then, because we're going next week.'

My mind filled with thoughts and images. I had always wanted to visit Tibet, of all the countries in the world the most mysterious and the least known. I had even struggled to learn some Tibetan, with the aid of a solid and dog-eared Tibetan grammar. But was I ready to travel again? I had flown out from England only a few days earlier with the intention of settling down for a while. A nomadic and homeless existence is exciting, but sometimes tiring. The romantic images of Tibet crowded back: fluttering prayer flags in a windswept desert, yak caravans and wild nomads. The eleventh-century poet Milarepa had spent legendary years meditating in caves in the mountains around Shishapangma. Maybe I could find the caves and traces of the legend, even in these days of Chinese occupation.

My only doubt revolved around the idea of being tacked on to the end of a team of world-class climbers who were intent on tackling a huge, unknown Himalayan face. Two members of the expedition with whom I was already acquainted, Roger Baxter-Jones and Paul Braithwaite, had climbed with Doug many times before. Paul played a leading role in the Everest expedition which put Doug on the summit in 1975, and then developed a lung allergy on K2 which kept him away from the Himalaya for a year or two. Alex MacIntyre was of a younger generation of ambitious climbers, but was already well-known for his fast ascents of technically difficult routes in the Alps and the Himalaya. These four would have little patience with someone who got in the way of their achieving the 26,291-foot summit of Shishapangma by the hitherto unclimbed South-West Face. So why were they inviting me to join them? Doug knew as well as I did that, for all our past adventures together, this great mountain wall was beyond my ability. It was also beyond my ambitions. My question drew from Doug only vague suggestions about the role I was to play.

'Well, Georges was planning to climb Shishapangma by an easier route with Nick ... Nick Prescott's the bloke who's organising the trip, but he won't be coming with the four of us on the main climb. You could always come with us while we're acclimatising . . . You can either climb with Nick or go and look round Tibet. . .'

The thought of tagging along with these highly accomplished climbers on short acclimatisation ascents made me nervous enough; the whole idea of tackling an 8,000-metre peak, even by an 'easy' route, with an unknown partner, produced a stab of real alarm. Especially as Doug's tone had implied already that this Nick fellow was a bit of an eccentric, with more confidence than experience.

I was quick to point out that one needed tried and trusted partners for ambitious climbs. It was Tibet, not the mountain, that held my interest. If he was suggesting that I might use the expedition as a means of getting into an otherwise closed country, and at the same time fill the £1,500 gap left by Georges, then I was more than willing. If they were looking for a replacement partner for Nick Prescott, they would have to look elsewhere.

Doug was encouraging and persuasive. He too was interested in Tibet, and was eager to have a companion who shared that interest, as he felt sure the others were going just for the climbing. Perhaps I would be able to interpret for him when we found ourselves in Tibetan villages . . .

Five days later I was back in England.

Doug's house was in the familiar chaos of expedition preparation. Boxes and duffles, already half packed with crampons, down suits, packets of dried food and other paraphernalia, littered the downstairs rooms. Doug was out somewhere collecting more climbing gear. His wife Jan was fielding the stream of phone-calls, stepping serenely over the piles of equipment spread across the floor.

'It's always the same, everything left until the last minute. But he'll have it all under control by the time he has to leave. He always does . . . So you decided to go on another one, after what happened on the Makalu trip?' She laughed. 'You're brave!'

I had not forgotten Makalu. Doug had invited me to join

him, and a party of his family and friends, which included his climbing partner Reinhold Messner, on the four-week walk-in through the foothills of the Nepal Himalaya to Makalu Base Camp. Doug had always tried to avoid a structured expedition organisation in which everyone has set tasks under the direction of an official leader, preferring instead the more informal approach whereby a group of individuals learn how to work together through awareness of themselves and each other. It was not a happy journey.

From the start, it appeared that he did not want me along after all. Before long he was accusing me of every sort of negativity, and became enraged by almost anything I said. Although I was not the sole target, I found the experience depressing. I knew well enough from the past how Doug's open enthusiasm and his gentleness had a way of swinging unpredictably into outbursts of blinding rage, and that any attempt to talk things through simply provided fuel for another explosion. On the way to Makalu I kept out of Doug's way as much as I could and sought the company of Reinhold, when he was not striding out ahead of the group. Reinhold was preoccupied at the time with the first draft of an account of his solo ascent of Everest from the Tibetan side. He would read passages to me and ask for my opinion. It was difficult to penetrate the complex personal symbolism of his writing, but Reinhold appeared content to remain obscured by his own mystique. Perhaps it was his way of maintaining a shred of privacy under the cloak of fame while being open and friendly with everyone he met. His stories of adventures in Tibet stirred my own desire to go there, if ever the chance arose.

Later, Doug explained his reasons for being in such a contrary mood, and I felt, or at least hoped, that his invitation to Tibet implied a tacit agreement that there would be no repeat performance. All the same, I could not help wondering why he would consider taking me along with this tough climbing expedition. Was it simply Doug's impulsive generosity, or was there something else? He was not short of friends or contacts among the climbing élite. I broached the subject with Jan.

She paused, smoothing the blond curls of the sleepy three-year-old on her lap.

'Well, I hope you're not counting on going up the South-West Face with them. Doug's made it pretty clear that it's just the four of them doing that. And I don't know about you climbing with Nick either. Paul was saying the other day' – she laughed again – 'he didn't fancy the idea of having to interrupt the main climb to go to the rescue of a couple of noddies stumbling around elsewhere on an eight thousand metre peak. Doug might have time to take you and Nick up something while he's acclimatising, but you shouldn't expect him to do anything that might interfere with the real climbing.'

Her words made me feel superfluous. I had no wish to be *taken climbing* by anyone. Doug's invitation had bubbled with enthusiasm; there had been no hint of begrudged time. The hesitation was all on my part. I was surprised he had not mentioned my plans either to Jan or to Paul. I had agreed to go along for the sake of the entry permit and their expedition budget, and would then go off to look at Tibet once they were launched up the mountain. It would all work out in the end, I thought, without stirring it up now, so I said no more about it. I did not want to lose the opportunity of going to Tibet altogether, just as we were setting off. At least Nick had seemed to accept my attitude when he met my plane at Heathrow.

Nick Prescott was taller and broader than I had expected of someone with a full-time office job which severely limited his mountaineering activities. His blond hair and gold-rimmed spectacles, combined with his agitated and enthusiastic manner, created an impression more youthful than his actual years. I liked him, although I found his blinkered determination to climb in Tibet decidedly unnerving. Clearly Doug had said nothing to Nick either about my climbing intentions, and I found it hard to break the news to him.

It was due entirely to Nick's remarkable prescience that we were going into Tibet at all. He had first written to the Chinese government in 1979 for permission to climb in the northern Himalaya, where no Westerner had travelled since the Chinese take-over in Tibet in 1951. In that time the country had been through a border war with India, an abortive uprising and the Cultural Revolution, and had seen the departure of its spiritual leader, the Dalai Lama, who had been forced to flee into exile. No Westerner had ventured Mallory and Irvine's northern route up Everest and very few had witnessed first-hand the change in lifestyle that the Tibetan people had undergone.

Meanwhile, neighbouring and independent Nepal enjoyed a flourishing Himalayan tourism. I had visited Nepal in 1981 to reconnoitre for a women's climbing expedition in the Khumbu region, but instead found myself wandering from village to village, off the beaten track, where the Sherpa people had settled after crossing from Tibet five centuries ago. No doubt conscious of the foreign currency being earned by their neighbours from climbing permits and trekking tours, the Chinese decided to open the Tibetan door a crack and issued their first climbing permit to the West in 1980. In March that year Nick received his invitation to apply formally to the Chinese Mountaineering Association for either Everest or Shishapangma, the only two peaks on offer at the time.

Nick decided to go for what he thought of as the less ambitious of the two. (As it turned out, Chris Bonington was given the Everest permit.) The Chinese had first climbed Shishapangma in 1964, by a route on its much less steep northern side, but Nick's application for one of the two northern routes resulted in a permit to tackle the mountain on its unclimbed southern side in 1982. He had thrown in this alternative only because there were three spaces on the application form and on the map he had spotted a convenient valley which wound round the southern face.

The cost of an expedition the size of ours could be as much as £50,000. So began Nick's dogged determination to gather together a team, raise some finance and see the project through.

A group of climbers assembled and then faded away again; China was unknown and expensive, and the rules were confusing. The following April, Nick telephoned Doug Scott to try to revive his project. Doug was very interested, having heard nothing in response to his own application for Shishapangma, and he set about gathering my expedition companions from among his climbing friends. It took them almost a year to raise from sponsors most of the budget, and only twenty-four hours before boarding the plane the expedition was finally declared solvent.

Wedged into the tiny space remaining free from gear in Doug's Cortina, I watched the grey view from the M1 roll past and wondered what Tibet would be like. Winter was hanging on in England as March turned to April. How much snow, I wondered, would still be lying, or indeed falling, on the windy Tibetan plateau at 14,000 feet?

Doug was looking tired. He drove in silence after a sleepless night spent packing, lips puckered round a squashed hand-rolled cigarette, his enormous restless energy temporarily in abeyance. He mumbled something about the team's plan for a fast, lightweight 'Alpine-style' ascent, without the lifeline of fixed ropes linking them to the ground. Nothing was known of the south side of the mountain and the maps at our disposal were less informative than the few photographs we had acquired, taken from summits across the border in Nepal. None of us had experience of the Chinese System. Guesswork and uncertainty were going to be the hallmarks of this enterprise.

We extricated ourselves from the car outside a neat house on a tidy estate, where expedition paraphernalia lay strewn across Nick's trim lawn.

'Better late than never,' yelled a voice from among the assembled packers.

'*Ma chérie*!'

I heard the mimicked French accent and was immediately engulfed in Roger's bear-hug. He worked as an Alpine guide in Chamonix, and had driven to England only two days before. Nick smiled and waved a cheerful hello. Alex went on with the packing. Paul would meet us at the airport, where his loud greeting in a broad Manchester accent would be bound to announce his presence in the bedlam long before we spotted his tall lean frame and thinning hair.

Within a few frantic hours I was standing beside a mountain of assorted baggage which had been transferred from Nick's lawn to the weighing-in desk at Heathrow. Doug was going through his fast-talking routine as he homed in on airline officials while passing to the rest of us ever-increasing amounts of 'hand luggage', taking complete command of the situation by sheer force of personality. Alex provided back-up with aggressive vitality, his small frame and mop of unruly curly hair in almost comic contrast to Doug's shambling bulk. I was relieved to find we were in the aircraft's upper cabin, away from the annoyance of other passengers. The lack of alcohol on Pakistan Airways did nothing to inconvenience our expedition, which had brought plenty of its own. After a hot and humid stopover in Islamabad, we staggered with our preposterous hand luggage into the cavernous marble hall that constitutes Peking airport.

The Chinese Mountaineering Association fielded several representatives at our meetings, including Mr Shi Zanchun, the Vice-Chairman, and Mr Chen San, the Protocol Officer, who was also a very experienced mountaineer, although Chinese reserve and the State directive against individual glorification precluded many reminiscences. Our chief contact in the discussions was Mr Wu Ming, a small and shy but shrewd man, with horn-rimmed spectacles and an immaculately crisp Mao suit.

Nick had produced estimates based on staying in 'budget-rate' hotels, as outlined in the protocol. What was not outlined until we reached Peking was that 'budget-rate' applied only to accredited students; we did not qualify. The deficit widened when we were informed that the authorities in Lhasa were not allowing camping this year. We would have to stay in the Tourist Hotel there, at a cost of 210 *yuan* (about £70) per person per night. The food supplies we were expecting had not been ordered yet, and it seemed we would be required to air-freight them to Lhasa at even more expense. Our hosts were polite, sympathetic and inscrutable: it was unfortunate, yes, that we had not fully understood the protocol; it was unfortunate that we had arrived without sufficient funds, but then, we could always cancel and return home. It did not seem to matter what we did so long as the regulations were not contravened in any way. We were playing on their home ground and according to their rules – rules of which we had a totally inadequate grasp.

A certain mistrust began to enter the talks. Difficulties were exacerbated by the fact that, while the Chinese were coordinated and unanimous in their attitude and response, our team enjoyed no such rapport. We were six individuals, each trying to press home his or her own point.

Doug and Alex, our chief spokesmen, displayed a fine disregard for the Chinese way of conducting business. Polite smiles and assurances of Chinese–British friendship from our hosts would be met with angry tirades and shouts of protest. To their credit, not one of the CMA representatives flinched or raised a voice in the face of this barrage during the whole fourteen hours of negotiations. I shared in the frustration produced by the flow of meaningless pleasantries from the other side, yet I felt embarrassed by our vulgar display of manners. During a break for tea I suggested to Alex that we might try conforming to local custom. He was defensive.

'Look, Elaine, you've got fifteen hundred tied up in this as well. You can't just sit back and say nothing.'

Nick was catching the blame for his over-optimistic budget, and our united front crumbled still further.

'Your accountancy is screwing up because you've made assumptions that don't fit a third world system.'

'It's lack of expedition experience . . .'

'Bloody hell, Nick.'

My exasperation began to extend to my own side. It was easy to be wise after the event. Still, having organised expeditions of my own, I knew that criticism from the sidelines is no help at all. I decided to skip the next meeting.

It was hard to tell when things began to turn in our favour. Perhaps the Chinese finally accepted that we really did not possess the vast funds they imagined we were trying to hide. Maybe it would be better for profits and Chinese–British friendship if some economies were worked out and we were allowed to pay with the money we did have.

'How much did you intend to spend in China?'

Nick peered at his notes through gold-rimmed spectacles.

'Fifty thousand nine hundred and sixty *yuan*.'

There were a few more tense moments as each side tried to reconcile the other's figures. Twenty per cent of the total estimate had already been deposited. At last, Mr Wu Ming announced his 'honourable-face-saving-with-a-view-to-cooperation' proposal to help us out of our financial difficulties and allow us to continue with the expedition, now that we had already arrived in China. Telephone calls were made to Lhasa, essential food supplies were bought and delivered, and arrangements were made for us to buy more food in bulk at our stopover in Chengdu. Suddenly the regulations were all on our side. Our frustration turned into admiration for the speed and efficiency with which difficulties could be overcome, even if the smiles and handshakes were cool and distant, marking a convenient cooperation rather than any close friendship.

The Chinese have a special relationship, known as *guan-shi*, which they form with certain friends. Within the family and this reciprocal relationship, no effort is spared to help one another. Outside this tight circle, everyone is a stranger. Why should a Chinese spare any of his effort for a stranger?

The system for taking care of foreign tourists is a recent offshoot of the Communist administration, but it reflects an approach to outsiders which is far older than the present regime. We had our own set of tour guides and interpreters, our own hotels set aside for foreigners, even our own money, specially printed Chinese *yuan*, which could be spent only in the Chinese Friendship Stores for consumer goods, expensive handicrafts and luxury foods. Although nominally of the same value as ordinary *yuan*, the tourist money fetched an inflated rate of exchange on the black market. But we were escorted everywhere by our Chinese guides and had no opportunity to experiment in monetary trading, even had we dared to risk offending our hosts by doing so.

The expedition interpreter turned out to be a thin and nervous young man from southern China by the name of Wu. He immediately became the subject of Paul's robust sense of humour.

'Well, Mr Wu, we'll 'ave to fatten you up a bit before we get up in all that snow . . .'

Our entourage of guides shepherded us off to the Great Wall, a large section of which was renovated as the obligatory tourist monument, as we might show off the Tower of London to a visiting Chinese as proof of a great and glorious past.

Despite the tenacity of our escort, we each took a turn at going missing in the few days of rest that remained to us before our departure from Peking. Roger even managed to miss a banquet given by the CMA in our honour by going out jogging and losing his way in the grid of identical streets, lined by almost identical rows of buildings. The others gave him a gleeful account of the amount of alcohol they had consumed.

'What no woman in it this time, Roger?'

'I'm not like that!' Roger protested.

'Yeah, irresistibly charming to women. Wouldn't you agree, Elaine?'

I grinned. 'Wine, women and a phoney French accent.'

Roger stared at me as the others howled with laughter. My sense of humour was becoming as abrasive as theirs.

We managed a 100 per cent attendance at a reception at the British Embassy. In the true spirit of the Revolution, absent was the ornate building full of antique furniture and luxurious carpets. The place was, however, cheerful and friendly despite the standard concrete walls and tubular metal chairs, which gave it the appearance of a works canteen. There we heard the news that Argentina had invaded the Falkland Islands. It was strange to realise that we were about to set off into the unknown, to a region in which none of our fellow Britons had set foot, and would be out of touch with home for three months in these turbulent times.

2

The Way through Tibet

It was 8 April when we flew to Chengdu. The hotel was almost identical to the one we had left in Peking, but there was in Szechwan a marked contrast in both the province and the people. Humidity hung in the air like a green haze; here was an ideal place for growing vegetables. We went down to the market to stock up on expedition rations. The inhabitants of Chengdu were a lively bunch, crowding round us with grins and curiosity. The clothing and housing were as drab as in Peking, but the atmosphere was animated and full of fun. There was little segregation of foreigners in this market as we were jostled and teased all along the rows of stalls. A plump woman no higher than my shoulder brought us nuts and little china bowls of local liquor. She and her friends followed me round the market, encouraging me to sample everything that was for sale. When I tasted the powdered chillies it seemed as if the whole market joined in the laughter.

Doug bought three hundred eggs and was looking for a basket to transport them from here to Base Camp. I admired his optimism. So, apparently, did the locals, as we were shown an impressive array of hand-woven baskets. They were now convinced we had completely taken leave of our senses. I was finally extricated from the market, clutching a bunch of freesias, by a frantic Wu who was convinced we would be late for supper.

Poor Wu was finding it impossible to get all six of us moving in the same direction at one time, so as to arrive punctually at our next scheduled stop. In Peking he had resorted to constant phone-calls to our hotel to ask whoever answered where the others were. Before our departure for Chengdu he had woken us in the middle of the night to remind us to pack. The following morning he relented a little, until he realised that Paul was still wallowing in the bathtub.

'Hoh, my god!'

Clutching his forehead, Wu raced back down the corridor, and I could hear him beseeching Paul to try not to be late for breakfast, just this once.

The weight of baggage we had accumulated seemed more alarming when I saw the age of the plane, but everything managed to rattle its way into the air and we began the climb from the humid plains to the mountainous plateau of Tibet. From horizon to horizon below were white and blue-black mountains, with a few snow-dusted forested valleys between. I wondered how the Chinese army had ever got into Tibet.

'Makes a bit of a mockery of peak-bagging, don't it youth?'

'Which one's Namche Barwa?'

'Wouldn't mind a permit to go there, it's one of the highest unclimbed peaks in the world.'

'They won't issue permits until the Chinese have climbed it.'

I wondered why these mountains had not begun to entice me to think again about climbing. I had to admit that whatever it was I had been seeking over the last ten years in the headlong pursuit of higher summits and harder rock pitches, I had not been finding it. There was no denying the sharpening of awareness that comes from risk and concentration on a technical challenge, but where was it all leading? A glimpse of higher awareness is meaningless if it fades, only to be recaptured on another mountain with yet more effort and risk. That way could only lead to pushing the risk too far in the end. It was easy to confuse the goal with the technique, and imbue climbing with some kind of spiritual mystique. To me, the goals of climbing were too deeply rooted in military-style conquest and personal glorification. If I was, after all, searching for some inner purpose, I had to break out of these layers of self-justification and explore in other directions.

The mountains were behind us, and we were flying over the glacier-fed River Tsangpo and a small, dusty village at the base of an alluvial fan. The blue Tsangpo flowed through a brown desert, eastwards to Namche Barwa, then south to become the Brahmaputra of India. Its source, the sacred Mount Kailash, far to the west, is also the source of the Indus and the Sutlej, which flow into a different ocean.

Lhasa airport is well out of the city, in empty desert. Two Tibetans, Pemba, our Liaison Officer, and Drolma, the tourist guide, were there to meet us with a smart new minibus. By the time they managed to get us aboard they almost certainly wished they had been assigned to the immaculate Japanese expedition which had disappeared with tidy efficiency in the direction of Lhasa about fifteen minutes earlier.

The dusty road passed a forty-foot Buddha figure painted and carved in relief on the cliff face, and a little further on the bus stopped outside a small monastery. Drolma explained that the monastery was closed because the monk had gone to Lhasa for the day. The place looked as if it had not been used for a while, but I made no comment and went off in pursuit of photographs. I returned in time to witness the arrival of a German tour group. They turned out of their minibus, threw sweets to the local children in order to film the resulting scrimmage, then packed themselves back on board and disappeared in a cloud of dust. I turned away in disgust. Surely with all these rules and regulations the Chinese could spare one to protect their own people from uncivilised Westerners? Perhaps they didn't consider Tibetans to be their own people yet.

Doug was interested in oracles.

'Did the Tibetans have any advance warning that the Chinese were about to invade?'

There was a trace of a wry smile on Drolma's lined face as she answered. 'Oh, yes. Two days before, by radio from Peking.' She worked for the government now; she wore Chinese clothes and could speak Chinese. There were no oracles in New Tibet.

I had read much about the awe-inspiring sight of the golden roofs of the Potala Palace – the first buildings to be seen as one enters Lhasa. I was pressed up against the window, determined not to miss it. The building of the huge Drepung monastery towered on the hillside above us, and I caught a fleeting glimpse of the Potala on its hill before it disappeared behind an enormous cement factory belching black smoke.

As we drove into the city, I could see why they needed so much cement. There was little of the original city to be seen, the buildings having been replaced with concrete army baracks and blocks of civilian accommodation. I found it difficult to tell the difference between the two. The sunlight reflecting from the corrugated iron roofs competed with the golden rays shining from the roof of the distant Potala.

The CMA headquarters in Lhasa are housed in one of these new compounds, and it was here that negotiations were resumed over our arranged economies, such as spending only one night in Lhasa and travelling in the equipment truck, thus saving £4,000 for minibus hire. We had abandoned the idea of visiting Chris, Pete, Joe and the rest of the Everest team in their Base Camp on being told the detour would cost an extra £2,000!

We very quickly learned two things: *mayo*, the Chinese word for 'no', 'there isn't any' or 'not possible', and the sullen and uncooperative disposition of our Liaison Officer. It was clear he was out to make a profit from this expedition: he wanted the minibus for his own comfort and the opportunities it afforded for trading; he was also put out when he discovered we were hiring equipment for him instead of presenting him with expensive gifts. As far as he was concerned, if we were not prepared to buy his favour then we might as well go home. It was also clear he was inventing regulations to suit himself.

'It is forbidden for foreign tourists to ride in trucks.'

'It is not possible to be ready to leave Lhasa tomorrow.'

I walked away from the shouting match to wander round the CMA compound. I was tired of this arguing. All I wanted was to get out of this succession of hotels and meeting-rooms so that I could explore. I began chatting to a group of navy-clad Tibetans in a corner of the courtyard. When my unpractised

Tibetan ran out, they called over a friend who spoke English. His name was Jigme, and he had been a national football coach before working for the CMA. He had been educated in Darjeeling, where he had learned English, but had returned in the early Sixties, full of youthful idealism, to help build the New Tibet. His voice was clear and slow, as if he were hiding some great sadness. I found myself pouring out all our problems to him as if I had known him for years. To my surprise he offered more than sympathy. Within minutes he was talking to the people in the main office, who then checked through the messages sent from Peking. Yes, we could cancel the minibus, and they would even help us to pack. Some of the local administrators, at least, were prepared to be helpful. Back in the minibus, I dared not look at Pemba, but I could see him in my mind's eye, snarling in his corner like a beaten dog.

The team was temporarily jubilant. The economies had been accepted, but investigation of the Thomas Cook Lhasa cache revealed, in addition to the tents and stoves they had kindly agreed to lend us, a pile of vegetables stored under some dry earth and ten crates of Budweiser beer left behind by an affluent American expedition. The Chinese were asking a price appropriate to such rarities, but it was paid without argument. I wondered how convincing were assertions of poverty now we had shown we could easily afford luxuries like canned beer.

Almost immediately a heavy debate broke out with the bus driver who was producing regulations that he had to be paid an extra 20 *yuan* cash if we wanted him to take us to the old city. The climbers, still clutching their beer, protested that we could not possibly afford this. We were very much at the driver's mercy because the Tourist Hotel is almost five miles outside Lhasa and commuting on foot would take time – time that we did not have. Eventually he relented and we set off towards the Potala. I was beginning to wonder if every movement during the next three months would entail such a hassle.

As soon as we stepped out into the old city, every other thought vanished from my mind. Pilgrims thronged the Barkhor, circumambulating the great temple of Lhasa, the Jokhang. Other pilgrims were prostrating their bodies full-length on the ground before the temple. It was hard to realise that only four years earlier the penalty for so doing was to be machine-gunned on the spot. The authorities had allowed a measure of religious freedom again after the twenty-year ban introduced by the 'Gang of Four'. Not surprisingly, the relaxation of restraints had coincided with the opening of Tibet to tourism. Perhaps the authorities thought that religious belief had been safely obliterated from Tibet. For some, at least, the lure of material gain and consumer goods was a poor exchange for spiritual wealth, and they had once more gravitated to the few temples that remained, lighting butter lamps before the statues, spinning prayer wheels, counting mantras on their rosaries. These acts, performed with a devotional state of mind, are intended to build up spiritual merit.

Traders had set up their stalls at the side of the street and jostled with the crowds as they walked or prostrated. Nomads from the desert flashed brilliant smiles from sun-darkened, weathered faces. Chunks of coral, turquoise and amber gleamed around their necks and were strung in their ears and hair. Boisterous and vibrant, they were grubbily beautiful in their patched homespun and oily leather, their long hair braided with deep red wool. Where did their energy and spirit come from? One would never think these were people who had seen their country changed beyond recognition, leaving only a few small corners where the minority like themselves could gather. I felt as if I had awoken from a blue-grey expressionless dream, and remembered why I had come here. I wanted to spend more time with these wild-looking people, perhaps learn where they found their inner resilience and strength.

The driver and Wu were complaining about our late arrival for supper. I didn't give a damn about supper, I wanted to stay here. As appearance at supper was obligatory, whether or not one felt hungry, we were all too soon locked into the System again. To be fair, concern that visitors are fed regularly and punctually – and, incidentally, in very large quantity – is probably greatly appreciated by most normal tourists who do not share my natural aversion to regimentation of any kind.

Over supper we talked to a Tibetan who was returning to his

country again after twenty years in exile in India and Germany. Tibetans travelling on refugee papers are granted a visa if they sign a declaration that they are Chinese citizens residing abroad. The visitor shrugged.

'They are building up their case that Tibet is a part of China. Many Tibetans refuse to sign, but you know how it is, I want to see my family again.'*

He also said that Heinrich Harrer had returned for the first time after his famous seven years in Old Tibet – and had been granted a stay of seven days in New Tibet.

I asked him if Lhasa had changed much in twenty years.

'There is hardly any of it left. Everywhere I look, the old buildings have been replaced by new ones. Tibetans were not allowed to maintain their houses, so a lot of them fell into a state of disrepair and were then pulled down and replaced.'

The hotel itself was a modern Chinese building, or rather, a single-storey complex set around three dusty courtyards. The concrete walls and corrugated-iron roofs were plain and unadorned, as were the beds and tables within. The emphasis seemed to be on keeping it as clean and functional as possible, with the printed flowers on the bedcovers and the vacuum flasks of hot water in the rooms adding a welcome splash of colour. We were told there were only three Tourist Hotels in Tibet; the other two – in Shigatze and Shegar – were scheduled stops on the drive to the mountains. These were somewhat less expensive than the Lhasa hotel, at only £40 per night. I wondered if these too would be without heating. In the freezing Tibetan night, the concrete dining hall took on the aspect of a vault.

The food served in the Tourist Hotel came from China in packets or cans. It was of a higher standard than was normally available, but the processing rendered it devoid of taste. Paul, whose gourmet palate belied his lean and bony frame, peered suspiciously at the platters on offer.

'No, don't fancy any of that. Tried it last time. God, what's this? Looks like Thomas's arse just after he's had a shit!'

---

* Some Tibetans compromise with the Chinese requirement by previously depositing a signed statement with the Tibetan government in Dharamsala that although they were signing the Chinese statement in order to see their families, their allegiance was still to the Dalai Lama.

He poked the canned meat dubiously with a chopstick. He was missing his favourite horse, Thomas, almost as much as his wife's home cooking.

The expedition equipment was delivered from the airport with remarkable efficiency and, true to their word, people from the CMA were helping to load it into the Liberation Army truck whose battered green hulk would transport us for three days across the Tibetan plateau. There were more arguments with Pemba, whose bullish determination to be as awkward as possible aroused the animosity of the whole team. Mild little Wu had the unenviable task of translating the slanging that frequently erupted between Pemba and Doug, who alone of the climbing zealots was determined to see something of Tibet on the way.

There was no water supply in the hotel that night. Everyone was tired, and Drolma looked grey and exhausted after a day of our demands. I wondered when last she had had a holiday. Before turning in, I went round to her room. As she turned, her eyes said, oh, not another problem, but her voice was controlled.

'Can I help you?'

I gave her the freesias.

The lines of strain relaxed. I thought she was going to cry. She took the flowers and turned away. They might have been the only flowers in dusty Lhasa.

We left before dawn under a full moon. It was cold in the back of the truck, perched on top of the food and equipment. In the moonlight we looked like bandits in some bizarre western, with silk scarves tied over our faces to filter the clouds of yellow dust billowing up from the dry dirt road. Paul had brought an industrial mask in the hope of protecting his lungs from the all-pervading dust. He was making an effort to be jolly in spite of the discomfort.

'Oh, Mr *Wu*, what can we do with *you*? You're looking cold, Mr Wu, you need warming up! Come on, Elaine, get into the sleeping bag an' rub his chest for him.'

I gave Paul a furious glare, but it was lost in the gloom. It made me angry to be referred to as if I were the expedition groupie. He did not mean it spitefully, but when it came down to it, none of them could conceive of a woman on this sort of trip in any other context. Doug had confided quite cheerfully to me that both he and Alex had discussed my presence with their respective ladies. They had given their assurances that they would not sleep with me during the trip – as if it was their decision, not mine! Few men seem able to accept women climbing on equal terms. Women are there 'to soften the atmosphere for men . . . ' Long ago I had learned from pub talk after a day's rock-climbing that women are of three types: wives are 'hags', single girls are 'tarts' and good climbers are 'dykes'. God, I thought, they're probably expecting me to be their cook and potwasher for three months. Then I reminded myself that to take these attitudes seriously was as ridiculous as having the attitudes in the first place.

I began to notice that Nick's attitude differed from that of the others. Although he was often vying with them in his accounts of adventures and narrow escapes, he avoided verbal muscle-flexing. When he spoke of his wife it was with affection and respect. I felt relaxed in his company, even if communication between us remained superficial. We got along well but were unlikely to become friends.

For all that the others were egocentric and quarrelsome, they were alive with a love of adventure and displayed a sense of humour with which I could readily identify. So why not leave them to their gamesmanship and just enjoy their company?

The sun burst over the brown hills to the east, dust-shimmering fingers of light probing the cold darkness of the dry valley. Roger beat on the roof of the cab, and the truck screamed to a stop in the middle of the bridge over the Tsangpo. We erupted from the back, stretching cold limbs and running around looking for vantage points for photographs. The guards on the bridge ran towards us, waving their machine-guns and shouting. Wu translated that it was forbidden to take photographs. It was useless to try to persuade them we had no interest in the bridge, only the sunrise. It was probably the quickest we had ever managed to board a vehicle.

The sun rose higher over a parched and barren desert of softly brilliant colour, ochre sand and rock casting deep red-brown shadows under an expanse of cloudless blue sky. In the thin air the sun's rays burned hot on exposed skin, yet patches of shadow still held a frosty chill. There were small cairns with prayer flags at the top of the first high pass, reminders that other humans lived and moved in these arid hills. On the far side of the pass a lake mirrored the deep blue of the sky, and beyond the lake was a small village of flat-roofed adobe houses.

The truck stopped briefly, and swarms of curious children scrambled up to check out the strange-looking people piled on it. They examined everything within reach, including the Walkman cassette players, but without showing any inclination to help themselves. A group of adults came towards us, carrying sooty kettles of chang, the local barley beer – welcome to parched, dust-clogged throats. They would take no payments for their offering; it was just a spontaneous gesture of welcome to travellers passing through, although children were happy to accept our chocolate. Within two or three minutes Pemba was shouting angrily that we had stayed too long, and the driver was grinding his gears into action.

It was a frustrating routine. As soon as we stopped anywhere interesting, such as the town of Gyantze, where Sir Francis Younghusband had spent three months with his expedition in 1904, Pemba would almost immediately start hustling us back on board again. To make matters worse, the dust had clogged not only our throats but the fuel system of the truck as well, and it was breaking down with increasing frequency, always in the middle of the empty desert. Fumes were wafting up to our perch from a leak in the petrol tank, and it was a sorry and grumpy team that finally staggered into the hotel at Shigatze at one a.m. – nineteen hours after leaving Lhasa.

Pemba was informed that nobody was leaving Shigatze until the truck was in running order again. Wu was beginning to show signs of strain from being middle-man in so many heated discussions. We decided to take advantage of our day's respite by seeing as much of the town as possible, taking Wu with us and leaving Pemba to deal with the truck. We were assigned a tour guide from the Shigatze Tourist Office, a smart young Chinese by the name of Cho. What a contrast in character to our sincere and harassed Wu! Cho was possessed of a supercilious manner and an utter disdain for all things Tibetan. He reluctantly accompanied us to the Summer Palace of the Panchen Lama, about a mile out of town, assuring us it would be closed. It was, but we managed to get a glimpse over the wall at the building, which was in the throes of renovation and repainting. Later, Doug, Roger and I managed to evade Cho and set off for the Tashi Lhunpo monastery, perched on a little hill above the city.

Outside the walls a group of people were sitting and talking together among the stumps of what had once been a grove of trees. They were brewing salt tea in a huge, soot-blackened pot over a twig fire. I recognised one of the tea-drinkers as the young nomad I had spoken to in the market earlier that morning. He smiled at us, and beckoned us over. I had never been among people whose hospitality and welcome to complete strangers was as expansive and unguarded as the local people we were meeting in Tibet. Even the Sherpas of Nepal, whose traditions stem from the same Tibetan roots, have come to putting price tags on their tea and foodstuffs in the face of a growing tide of foreigners, which now outnumbers them two to one. I wondered whether the same thing would one day happen here if the Chinese continued to increase their tourist programme. We were soon well ensconced around the fire, clutching china bowls of tea, while our host brought us handfuls of tsampa, ground roasted barley grains, to mix with the brew. Contrary to most of the accounts I had read about Tibet and its supposedly dreadful tea made with rancid butter, I had no objections to this brew, which to my mind tasted like a thin bouillon. The butter was not rancid, although it was very rich, being made from the milk of *dri* (female yaks).

The nomads had left their herd of yaks and *dri* parked up on the hillside above the town, under the care of the rest of their party. Six of the group had come down to spend a few days making pilgrimage to the shrines at the monastery. They were also hoping to spend some time talking with the monks. This information took some time to impart as I was still learning how to apply the Tibetan I had learned to actual conversation. In addition, these nomads were Khampas, originally from Kham in Eastern Tibet, and they spoke with an accent which differed somewhat from the conventional Lhasa dialect. They were typical Khampas, taller than most Tibetans, wild and strong-looking. They were handsome despite the dust matted in their long pigtails, with high cheekbones and confident, sunburned smiles. Their clothing, like their personalities, was colourful and flamboyant, black homespun edged with silver, or an oily sheepskin jacket set off by a battered velvet cap of uncertain age.

As well as ourselves, there were two monks being entertained to tea at the fire. They too were Khampas, and were wandering practitioners of the Nyingmapa, the oldest sect of Buddhism in Tibet. Their appearance and manners were as unconventional as those of their lay friends, and they took delight in teasing us about our enthusiasm for taking photographs. The older of the two, a handsome, humorous character with a fringe of white beard and a dark red sheepskin-lined robe, held our attention the longest. He would pose motionless for a few minutes, then break into laughter and make faces at the cameras. At one point he leaned over and invited Roger to drink from his cup – the top of a human skull. This was an unorthodox use for a ritual object formerly kept by monks in Tibet as reminders of the impermanence of all things, including human life. He clearly had no objections to being photographed. In spite of his antics I could see that his appraisal of us was shrewd, and missed little. How I wished I could stay here longer, to be able to talk with him at length!

Government regulations did not allow foreign tourists into the monastery itself without a Chinese guide, so we returned the following morning with Cho. He looked bored with the whole place and his commentary of facts and figures was sporadic.

'This monastery was built in the fourteenth century by the

first Dalai Lama. It covers an area of thirty thousand square feet and is big enough to house three thousand monks. At present there are six hundred in residence. I will tell you about Buddhism. It is called Lamaism. This is the Yellow sect . . .'

Somehow these were not the answers to the dozens of questions that were in my mind, but I noticed that when I asked Cho to translate a question to the monk who was showing us around, the Tibetan would turn his head away and mumble the answer. During a brief minute when Cho's attention was elsewhere I managed to ask a question myself, and found the monk more than willing to talk to me directly. However, Cho was marshalling us to go into the main temple. His instructions were quite clear: any photography inside the building would cost the equivalent of £200 per room, payable to the Chinese government, through him. For a moment I thought Doug, in his enthusiasm for Tibet and photography, was going to pay the fee. Shouts of horror and protest from Alex and Roger reminded him of the expedition's lean funds.

Inside the main temple, about seventy monks were gathered, sitting crosslegged on low cushions, chanting in unison. We stood listening, the whole group silent for once, as the sound swelled and filled the hall with a resonance that for me seemed strange, yet strangely familiar. All my reading and intellectually-acquired knowledge had not prepared me for anything like this. I knew that what I was hearing and seeing bore a deeper significance than I could perceive; I knew this instinctively, and for a moment I felt as if I were about to break through the barrier of unknowing and understand it all.

Then the moment passed and I was back in the dark hall with a group of foreigners and seventy Tibetans. The chanting ceased, and the monks stood up, folding the heavy woollen ochre-coloured cloaks from their shoulders and placing them on the cushions. I felt suddenly embarrassed that we had all trampled into the temple with our shoes on. One of the monks looked straight at me, his eyes slowly focusing as if he had just become aware of his surroundings and my presence. Then he smiled, a broad, unselfconscious grin of sheer delight. He turned, and walked barefoot from the hall.

Pemba was in a fury because the truck had been ready before we were. I could hear the shouting long before we reached him. But still we lingered, deep in conversation with two young men, one Canadian and one English, who had managed to hitch-hike to Tibet from mainland China. Someone in Inner Mongolia had mistakenly given out a few Lhasa permits, and although the arrival of a scattering of unescorted Westerners had aroused some surprise among the local authorities, there was as yet no definite policy for sending them back to Peking. Meanwhile, they were making the most of the opportunity, and were travelling around paying local rates in the hotels – 1·50 *yuan* in Lhasa, where we had paid 210. This news was a great encouragement to me, as I was beginning to wonder how I would ever be able to break away from all this supervision and explore Tibet in my own way. Now there was a hope that I could simply wander off, as these two had done, and take a look around while officials tried to decide what to do with me.

We settled ourselves for another dusty day in the back of the bouncing truck. Pemba managed to tread on the basket of eggs and was more unpopular than ever. Doug had bought a cassette of Tibetan music at the hotel; I plugged in an extra pair of headphones and listened in. It was the *Lhamo*, a kind of historical opera performed by lay people at festivals such as the Tibetan New Year. Women's and men's voices alternated in wavering cadences which seemed to echo the vast emptiness of the land through which we were travelling. It was almost as if the rhythmic syllables within the song contained sounds basic to any language, for as I listened, lulled half-asleep by the movement of the truck, it seemed that the voices were speaking to me in French and other languages I understood. Doug said afterwards he was hearing English.

We stopped for lunch by an isolated grove of spindly willow trees, the first things to raise their heads above the rock-strewn ground since Shigatze, apart from the telephone lines raised to just above yak-height on stocky mud-and-stone pillars.

A scattering of houses, hardly a village, stood beyond the trees. It was difficult to find a sheltered spot where the ever-present dust did not blow into the food. A man and his wife appeared through the trees and stood watching us for a moment. They were cheerful and strong-limbed, their sooty clothing almost in rags. Even though I had seen plenty of Tibetans since arriving in Lhasa, I was still very aware of their obvious poverty. Tibetan friends in Nepal were so comfortably off compared to these people, even though they had fled with almost nothing into exile twenty years before.

The couple realised what our problem was, for the man beckoned, and showed us to a wind-free gulley behind the trees. His wife reappeared with a large kettle of chang.

'*Shea, shea*!'

We drank, as directed. After two cupfuls I was protesting.

'I can't drink it all!'

'*Shea*. I've got plenty more at home.'

'Where do you live?'

'Over there. Come and look.'

It was a small, stone-built, single-roomed house. There was not much light coming through the small window, and the interior was blackened with soot from the fire. I couldn't see much. Neither, evidently, could Nick, who had followed me in through the low door and then straightened his back and the rest of his six-foot frame. His head hit the ceiling with a loud thump.

'Oops, sorry, I'm breaking your roof.'

Our hosts were greatly entertained by his size.

'*Chen-po du*'!'

There were angry shouts from outside. Pemba had decided we had overstayed our allotted time. Our hosts' guard dog went into action, yapping and snarling ferociously. It was gratifying to watch Pemba back off hurriedly. When we left, the two Tibetans held the dog down as we passed, as they had done on the way in.

The town of Shegar stands at an elevation of 4,280 metres (about 14,000 feet), and we could justify a rest-and-exploration day because we needed the acclimatisation. Above the town the ruins of the dzong, or fort, caught the sun's rays, red against a deep blue sky. This would provide a good viewpoint, as well as a chance to gain a little extra altitude. We left Pemba at the dusty barrack-hotel and began the climb.

The walls and turrets of the fort were built into the crumbly rock of the pinnacle on which it stood. Even in destruction it was impressive, built with nothing but bare hands and an instinctive knowledge of stone and balance. The Red Guards had had to resort to dynamite to bring it down when their artillery failed. I wondered if the technology that destroyed it could ever succeed in building something comparable. The red-painted ruins of the monastery stood part-way down the rock pinnacle below the fort.

Stretching away to the distant Himalaya on the horizon were barren brown and purple hills split by the flat river valley. From this vantage point I could see the changing living patterns of Tibet spread out below like a map. The old town clustered around the foot of the rock below the monastery. Each house had its own high-walled courtyard and outbuildings in one compact unit. These walls formed a maze of narrow interlocking streets which effectively blocked the dust-laden winds that swept down from the Himalaya. The new commune and barrack buildings of Shegar spread out beyond the old community in an open-plan grid pattern, like an American frontier town. The wide, straight streets funnelled the wind against the buildings. No wonder the inhabitants were all walking around with dust masks over their faces like a strange parody of hospital surgeons. The new sprawl also used up a large part of the alluvial valley floor, precious as the only agricultural land to be found in the country. I felt the architects would have done better to look to traditional Tibetan ideas for inspiration, rather than to American colonial ones. I commented on the changes to Roger, but he saw things differently.

'You can't expect people to stay in a medieval way of life just because it looks pretty to you. Now they've got hospitals and schools, and machinery to cultivate their land more easily.'

'But less of it to cultivate,' I put in. 'And I get the impression that a lot of people still feel that the religious education they had before was preferable to what they have now. And they all want the Dalai Lama back.'

'Yes, well, I'm sure a lot of old ladies down our way would love it if the Pope moved in next door. They've got a lot more things now than they had before. You can't stop progress.'

I walked on up the slope in silence. Would I be prepared to live without the material ease and comfort bestowed by a technological society? As Roger implied, it is very easy to take all that for granted and extol the virtues of simple living without experiencing or understanding the realities of a harsh existence. One has only to look at the mad scramble for comforts and consumer goods that is taking place in all the developing nations – from capitalist India to communist China – to see that those actually living the simple life can't wait to get cluttered up with Western decadence. Personally, I felt I could give up a lot of material comfort if it would buy freedom from the threat of pollution and nuclear war. But then I had not sampled the life of a Tibetan peasant, and nowhere in the world was safe from the nuclear threat these days. Certainly not Tibet, which was now a strategic site for China's major missile bases.

Back in the town, I stopped to talk to a group of women mixing concrete on a building site. They seemed quite concerned that I should go to see a stranger who was in the hospital, but I could not follow their directions clearly. In the end, one of the women took me there. In a small concrete room at the end of a long corridor a white-coated Chinese doctor was tending to his patient. He saw me in the doorway and beckoned me over. I stepped over a puddle of water and piles of bloody bandages to reach the bed, and found myself looking down into the frightened eyes of a young, dark-skinned Indian. The woman explained that the patient had been found in a state of collapse a few days ago, somewhere near Tingri. He had crossed the Himalaya barefoot and had suffered frostbite.

'They took off his legs yesterday.'

To emphasise the point, the doctor flipped back the covers to reveal bandaged stumps below the knee. I wondered what would happen to him now, in a country whose language he did not understand. He had the long hair and lean look of a *sanny-*

asin, a Hindu pilgrim on his way to holy places in the Himalaya. I wanted to offer help, but the doctor spoke only Chinese. I went to find Wu. He and Doug came over with antibiotics from the expedition supplies. The doctor thanked us, but assured us he had plenty at the hospital. Despite the very limited conditions he seemed dedicated, cheerful and confident that the young man would recover.

Doug and I had originally hoped to camp in the village of Tingri on the following day, but what with Pemba and high prices it was beginning to look unlikely. Moreover, Alex, Roger and Paul were pushing to get to the mountain as fast as possible, and were in favour of driving straight through to Nyalam. From there we would set off for Base Camp on foot. In the echoing concrete dining room of the hotel, the breakfast discussion became polarised on this issue. As if there wasn't enough arguing when Pemba was around. I decided it was a good time to pack.

'Hang on, Elaine, you can't just walk off like that. You've got to say what you think.'

I felt like reminding Alex that no one would listen anyway, but managed to stifle it in time.

'It doesn't really concern me. What I don't see of Tibet now I can see while you climb your Face.'

Roger said, 'But we thought you'd be climbing with Nick while we were on the Face.'

Having discussed the possibilities for exploring Tibet at some length with Doug, I was surprised to find he had communicated nothing of this to the others. The response to Nick's climbing plans made it clear enough that the presence of anyone outside the four Face climbers was unwelcome.

'Nick, you're an idiot. You don't know what you're talking about.'

'You can't expect to climb with us if you haven't got the experience.'

'You'll just slow everybody down.'

The best approach seemed to be to say nothing and wait until it was time to leave. Now that I had my entry permit and they had my contribution to the budget, it remained only for them to start climbing. They would be happy enough to have me out from under their feet.

Back in the truck, Doug began talking to Nick and me again about climbing with him while he acclimatised on the smaller, easier peaks around Shishapangma itself. At first I thought he was trying to ease Nick's disappointment, but such was the strength of his personality and enthusiasm I found myself recalling all the good times I had spent climbing in the past. What was the use of attempting to justify them in my present frame of mind? Perhaps just one small climb would be fun after all ... I could always postpone the decision until Base Camp.

The truck rumbled past the village of Tingri, perched on a little hill standing alone in a broad plain. Beyond stretched the Himalaya – Everest, Cho Oyu and the Nangpa La Pass to Solu-Khumbu in Nepal. I had listened to the stories of Sherpa friends about the trading journeys they made to Tingri over the 18,000-foot pass, and was hoping to spend time in the village on my return.

In this region were many of the places where the Tibetan saint Milarepa had lived and meditated; now I was looking at one of them, and I could begin to forge a link between the actual present and the legendary past, putting flesh on a character who had hitherto seemed distant, almost mythical. History leaves us facts, but it takes a deeper search to discover the personality behind them.

I knew that Milarepa remained one of the Tibetans' most popular saints. He was not born to wealth or princedom, but as a poverty-stricken peasant who became a black magician and murderer. By the power of regret, hardship and devotion to his teacher, he managed to atone for his crimes and, after years of meditation, to reach the ultimate spiritual goal of enlightenment.

Milarepa, in turn, became a great teacher, and caves where he had meditated became enshrined as places of pilgrimage by his followers, although how many of these shrines had survived the destructive onslaught of the Red Guards in Mao's Cultural Revolution of 1965 I had yet to discover.

During his years of meditation in mountain caves, Milarepa

had survived on a diet of nettles. One day, he was on his way to stay in a cave at Chuwar, two days south of Tingri.

> When I arrived in Tingri, by the Chuwar road, going through Peykhu, I sat down by the side of the road and watched what was going on. Some pretty young girls passed and, seeing my emaciated body, one of them said, 'Look, what misery! May I never be reborn as such a creature.'
>
> I said, 'Listen to my song . . .'
>
> You proud young girls, my sisters, and I Milarepa of Gunthang,
> We are disturbing to each other.
> In the eyes of these beautiful girls
> The handsome man is preferred, the hermit ignored.
> In the ears of these young girls
> This brief song sounds pleasant, the profound Dharma unpleasant.
> Unfortunate girls, you have faith only in ordinary life.
> Your self-esteem and wrong perception burn like fire . . .
> Hypocrites are praised more than gold
> And the faithful are rejected like stones on the road.

The more I thought about it, the more I, too, found Milarepa of Gunthang somewhat disturbing. What was it this man had seen that, by comparison, produced in him such disdain for 'ordinary life'? What was it that made years of caves and nettles a delight instead of the uncomfortable boredom which was all I could visualise? Even I felt this was taking the 'simple life' too far. And yet there had been times, wandering alone in the barren wastes of the mountains with no ambitions or summits to worry about, when a kind of exhilaration and peace had pervaded my whole being, leaving no thoughts of the cold and discomfort I was experiencing. Was it, then, possible to train and control the mind to the point where far more severe conditions could be overcome for a whole lifetime? I had to admit I was curious. I wondered if insights into this kind of heightened perception still remained in New Tibet.

3

On the Edge

The truck ground its way up the 18,000-foot Thong La Pass, the summit of which had only recently been dug out of the winter snow, which lay heaped on either side of the road. Suddenly the aptness of the traditional description of Tibet as 'the roof of the world' became apparent. We were on the top of the watershed; from here the Po Chu river flowed south, cutting a gorge right through the barrier of the Himalaya, to become the Bhote Kosi of Nepal. It was as if we were looking down on the mighty Himalaya. Although the mountain summits were at a higher elevation than this pass, their roots began in the valley which dropped away beneath our feet. This was not the only contrast to the southern side of the range. The deep and humid valleys of Nepal are thickly forested with pine and rhododendron, while the undulating, high Tibetan plateau is in the rain shadow of the mountains, allowing only a sprinkling of the monsoon rain past to water the spiky, high-altitude grass.

We also got our first glimpse of Shishapangma, to the west, a plume of cloud blowing from the summit. During the previous two years a handful of expeditions had been allowed beyond Lhasa to climb Everest and the north side of Shishapangma, but we were now entering a part of Tibet that had not seen a Westerner since the Chinese takeover nearly thirty years before.

From here the road followed the valley down, through the gorge, to cross the border and continue to Kathmandu. Many Tibetans had fled from the Chinese along this route, seeking sanctuary in Nepal. We descended for almost 6,000 feet to the village of Nyalam, where we would leave the road and set out on foot.

Our first view of the village was not encouraging. The evening dusk and a dank mist creeping up the gorge brought a heavy chill to the air, while the day's melt from the snow, still piled up in corners, had produced a thick mud in the streets which was now beginning to freeze over. Pemba had disappeared, leaving us to search around the concrete and corrugated-iron buildings which comprised the village housing, teashop and makeshift cinema for someone who could tell us where we were supposed to camp. We had been told in Peking that Nyalam was a military border area, out of bounds to foreigners, and that we would have to camp outside the village. The place was deserted, everybody being in the cinema.

The little I had read about Nyalam, or Nyenang, was a warning by a prince to Milarepa on the inadvisability of going there: 'The land of Nyenang is full of fear, a paradise for bandits and murderers. Lepers are there in crowds . . .' To this, Milarepa replied, 'Although Nyenang is of bad repute, the people there are candid and ingenious.'

It seemed they had lost little of their ingenuity since the eleventh century. When we finally tracked down the village dignitaries, and Pemba, we were assured that we would be staying in the comfort of the tin-and-concrete 'conference room' – at the rate of twenty *yuan* per person per night, cash. We protested that we could not afford so much. Besides, we had been told that we were not permitted to stay in the village. They argued that local regulations did not permit camping. I was beginning to develop a picture of a country full of people quoting endless and conflicting regulations to each other – and making most of them up as they went along.

The Commune Leader, a toothy and cheerful Chinese, was a friendly and sincere man who seemed to be doing his best to help us within the limitations of following the crowd and remaining as inconspicuous as possible. This, of course, meant going along with what our Liaison Officer wanted. It was obvious that Pemba was behind this move to keep us in the village, for reasons best known to himself.

In the end we had to resign ourselves to three expensive days in Nyalam waiting for the promised yaks to arrive to transport the equipment up to Base Camp. This delay, it appeared, was due to the yaks having been sent to meet us at the north side of Shishapangma – because the locals were of the opinion that it was not possible to get to Shishapangma from Nyalam. It took a good deal of arguing, and brandishing our permit to climb from the south side only, to persuade them that this was the way we meant to go.

Nyalam was not an endearing place in which to spend three days of one's life. The corrugated-iron roof of our accommodation provided little insulation from the penetrating night chill, while the interior became hot and stuffy as soon as the sun heated the roof. Outside, muddy streets were bordered by barrack-like buildings, truck tyres or barbed wire. It was necessary only to follow one's nose to find the single lavatory that served the whole commune – a small shed with a row of sloping holes leading to an open drain. In the absence of water and an adequate slope, the holes were filled to overflowing with decomposing excreta already producing enough of its own heat to be buzzing with flies despite the cold outside.

We were awakened each day by Patriotic Songs of the Revolution blaring out from the loudspeakers at every street corner, whereupon the entire population of Nyalam would empty into the streets for community exercises. At least, that was what it sounded like. At five in the morning I was in no mood to go and see for myself. As usual, great care was taken to ensure that we were brought three large meals a day. The food enjoyed the distinction of uniting the whole team in agreement: it was the worst that any of us had ever endured. Perfectly healthy eggs, spinach, flour and rice would disappear into the commune kitchen, to be boiled in large vats until they became a grey, greasy, glutinous mass to be served up to the population. All we wanted in Nyalam was to leave it.

Nick was suffering from a cough and a cold, probably induced by the dust and exhaustion of unaccustomed truck travel. Alex was delivering lengthy lectures about looking after himself better and not being stupid enough to walk on cement floors in his bare feet. Soon Paul and Roger joined in the criticising and Nick retired to bed, mumbling defensively.

The pecking order was beginning to establish itself. Since we left London, it had manifested itself in proportion to the amount of discomfort and frustration being experienced by the team at that time. Alex's bullying tactics made me feel uncomfortable, yet I was more annoyed with Nick for allowing it to happen. Alex was probably just compensating for the fact that, being small, he had no doubt already endured years in the role of victim. I was waiting for him to start on me. As the only woman and non-climber, I was an obvious target! Perhaps it was Alex's very chauvinism that made him too gentlemanly to pick on a woman, or else he sensed that I was ready for him. So far we seemed to have an unspoken agreement discreetly to avoid each other wherever possible.

With Nick in retreat, Alex's attention turned to Wu.

'Have you got a girlfriend, Wu?'

'No, I have no girlfriend. I am busy with my studies, and the State does not encourage such distractions for students.'

'But how can you manage without a girlfriend? Aren't you normal? I couldn't manage without a girlfriend. I need *sex*.'

'*Six*?' Wu's amazement was genuine. When the ensuing laughter had subsided, Alex's tone was concessionary.

'Well, six would be nice, but I can manage with one.'

The yaks arrived, late, at ten o'clock on our third day in Nyalam. With them were two unlikely-looking denim-clad yak boys, both of whom looked remarkably unenthusiastic about the prospect of accompanying us for the next few days. Their initial estimate for reaching Base Camp was two journeys of ten days each, which brought shouts of protest from the expeditionaries who had based their estimates on approaches in Nepal, where a full quota of standard-performance yaks would cover the distance in a single run of three days. Doug was demanding of the Commune Leader an explanation as to why his communist yaks performed so poorly compared with the capitalist yaks a few miles away over the border. In the end, we were given a reluctant promise to try to reach Base Camp in two or three days. As only eight yaks healthy enough to make the journey could be found and caught, it was decided that they would take half the equipment and then return for the rest.

We should have recognised it as a bad omen when the yak boys proved incapable of loading their animals without the help of all the expedition members and a few helpful locals from the village who had wandered over to watch. The Sherpas and Tibetans who ran the yak trains on the Nepal side would have had everything loaded and on the road within the hour. We took considerably longer, as inexperienced hands tried unsuccessfully to prevent the half-trained yaks from jumping around just at the crucial moment when the loads were being counterbalanced on either side of their backs. Add to this disarray the fact that yaks have long horns and weigh nearly half a ton, and it is not really surprising that the day was half over by the time everything was moving up the trail behind Nyalam.

Trouble was not long in coming. We passed the small hydroelectric plant on the river, but then, not far beyond the last cultivated field, one of the yaks lay down and refused to continue. It was obviously sick, with mucus running from its mouth and nostrils. If these were supposed to be the healthy yaks, those that had been rejected must have been in a sorry condition. There was a small stone hut nearby in which the abandoned equipment was stored, and the sick yak was left in the adjacent field. Less than twenty minutes further up we encountered the first patches of wet snow lying on the narrow track which crossed the steep, tussocky hillside. The yaks ran amok, shedding their loads, one of which rolled and bounced down towards the river at the bottom. Whether it went in and sank or not we failed to discover, for it was never found. Then one of the yak boys was discovered sitting behind a rock smoking a cigarette and laughing at the chaos. Paul hauled him to his feet and told him to get on with his job, whereupon the boy burst into tears and sat on the rock sobbing pathetically for the next hour while the rest of us attempted to retrieve the supplies and equipment – and the yaks – from a wide area of mountainside.

The afternoon mist had crept up the valley from humid Nepal, bringing with it wet snow and a miserable dampness. Doug and I ploughed ahead through the wet whiteness and caught up with two of the unladen yaks. I recognised one, trailing a braided rope from its nose-ring. It had been nicknamed Thomas by Paul, after his horse. The other had to be lassooed before we could start to drag them back down the trail to where they had shed their loads. Wu was supposed to slap them on the rear to keep them moving, but he was nervous of their horns and wary of getting too close. Alex loomed through the mist, encased in a blue Goretex rainsuit. He helped out with a bit of rump-thumping, but was twitchy and nervous too, and spent most of his time shouting orders. I handed him Thomas's rope and went back to try to get Doug's yak to move. The next thing I heard was Alex yelling at me to come back and watch the animal, which he had hastily tied to a rather inadequate bush.

I sloshed over to him through the soggy snow.

'Okay, Alex, calm down a bit.'

'You stupid woman!' he exploded. 'Can't you see there are yaks and bags all over the place?' He turned and strode off down the valley.

Doug tethered his yak, came over to sit on a wet rock, and rolled a cigarette.

'You were going to take him on then, weren't you. The little vixen coming out.'

I shook my head.

'Not really. There wasn't any point. He was just scared of the yaks, that's all, and he didn't like it that I noticed.'

'Hm. He was hopping out of their way a bit, wasn't he.'

We sat in silence for a while, watching the snow blow across the valley, while the yaks munched at the scrub placidly, as if nothing had happened. It was ten minutes later that I suddenly remembered the flash of anger, the indignation of being shouted at and the welling up of all the nasty things I could have screamed back at Alex. Then, in the next instant, it had gone, as logic insisted it would be a complete waste of time, and would add the extra complication of having to make peace later. What surprised me was how quickly I had forgotten all about it. How many other pieces of my mind did I lose track of during the course of a day? How can any of us really call our minds our own unless we are in complete control, wholly aware of all of it, all the time?

Fascinating though the idea was, I was unable to pursue the train of thought further, as the need to reassemble this expedition before nightfall was going to require all personnel to work overtime while daylight lasted.

Camp and supper was a damp and hasty affair put together in the blizzard. All the loads had been retrieved except the one which had disappeared towards the river, and the yaks had wandered off to graze, ruminating, perhaps, on the futility of expeditions and the absurdity of carting such a large amount of Western junk up an uninhabited valley.

So many parallels still exist between climbing expeditions and the military expeditions on which they were originally modelled. Our current efforts to mobilise equipment up to Base Camp recalled a comment by a staff-officer of Younghusband's expeditionary force during efforts to move the British Army over the Himalaya from India to Tibet at the turn of the century: 'Transport has completely broken down, and the supply depots are a mass of chaos . . .' Their situation was considerably more complicated than ours; in addition to Nepalese and Tibetan yaks, they were using mules, bullocks, buffaloes, ponies and even half a dozen camels – a total of 19,608 animals.

The Tibetans we had met so far had shown no more understanding of, or indeed interest in, the objectives of our climbing expedition than had their forebears towards the objectives of the military expedition of 1904. The expeditionaries displayed a corresponding failure to question the relative value of these objectives, dismissing those who did not share their attitudes as ignorant and inept. I wondered what kind of romantic stories those soldiers had brought home with them? I myself had listened avidly to the tales of climbers returning from the Nepal Himalaya, and had built up a picture of intrepid explorers thrashing their way through untracked, leech-infested jungles and raging mountain torrents to reach their chosen mountain. For a while I had remained convinced that I was just not tough enough to venture into this world of strong men, intrigued though I was by their accounts of pristine mountains and by the hints of their meaningful conversations with the mystical hill people they met on their way. What a contrast my first-hand experience had been! I discovered that climbers are treated to five-star tourist service all the way along the well-travelled trails to well-populated base camps with Western comforts and Western food cooked for them. The most fluent Nepali I had ever heard from mountaineers was *chini* (sugar), the 'meaningful conversations' thus being limited to how much of it they wanted in the tea brought to their beds in the mornings.

Our foray into Tibet without an attentive and well-trained staff waiting on our every need was perhaps the most obvious way in which our expedition differed from its predecessors on either side of the border. Even the lure of this previously unexplored valley seemed less enticing now I thought about it realistically; Tibetan herders had been grazing their yaks all over it for generations. It was only Westerners who had not been here before.

Nick was coughing violently and made straight for his sleeping bag. Paul was sympathetic.

'Poor old Nick. Come on Elaine, why don't you jump in with him and rub 'is chest with something nice?'

There he goes again. Oh Paul, dear old Paul, I wish you wouldn't, 'cause one of these days I'm gonna punch your nose ... I pelted him with the peapods I had just stripped for supper, and eventually he shut up.

Next day we returned to Nyalam leaving Nick and Roger to watch the camp. It took just an hour.

The Commune Leader was sympathetic, dismissed accusations by the yak boy that Paul had attacked him, dismissed the yak boy and found a replacement. As there were now only five yaks left disposed to continue, he promised to find another five and send them on with more gear as soon as possible. He seemed to be earnestly and sincerely trying to help us; we almost began to hope he would be able to make things happen.

The weather did not improve over the next two days; neither did the performance of the yaks and their handlers. Roger and I were feeling out of sorts with sore throats, and it seemed that everything was conspiring to hinder our progress.

Alex put tremendous energy into herding and controlling the yaks. He did not have to prove anything to anyone – except, perhaps, to himself – but his attitude gradually mellowed, as if he was satisfied that a possible weakness had been overcome. I almost began to like him. Certainly I admired the will that insisted he be good at everything, forcing him to face any fears and overcome them. With a rural background, I had few qualms about large bovine animals, but I knew I was becoming increasingly aware of the dangers involved in climbing mountains. I was beginning to doubt that I could find the necessary determination to face and overcome that fear. I wondered if part of the reason that Alex climbed was a reassertion that he could do just that, despite his declared motivation being one of calculating ambition. He claimed he wanted to continue to be a brilliant climber for the next few years, become famous and live on his reputation for the rest of his life. His aggressiveness and drive supported this argument, but sometimes I felt there was more to Alex than just that.

At the foot of the moraine on the north side of the river was a deserted stone hut. I pushed open the makeshift door and smelled the wet soot and the traces of butter and yak-hair blankets. The little earth gardens beside the door had nothing in them but a pair of worn-out Chinese shoes. Inside, snow still lay in piles where it had blown in through holes in the mud roof, a white contrast to the soot-blackened interior. I wondered how long it had been since yak-herders had lived here.

Doug, Alex and Roger had climbed the moraine the previous day and returned with news of a good campsite just beyond the ridge. I started to climb, encouraging Nyima, our new yak boy, to follow me with the yaks. Half-way up, he turned and saw Doug and Alex reach the stone hut and stop for a snack. He lacked confidence without his partner, and was unwilling to continue, half convinced that the rest of the team were going to camp at the hut. I was unable to persuade him to move again until Alex caught us up and marched on ahead. Reluctantly, Nyima heaved himself to his feet again and persuaded the even more reluctant yaks to do the same. The sound of yak bells coming from the valley made me turn, and there below us plodded a line of five more laden yaks, driven by an older man who obviously could understand his animals and control them easily. As he caught us up, his face broke into a mischievous grin at Nyima's erratic progress. He and his yaks had just come straight from the village in a little over two hours. The yaks were healthy and plodded steadily up the slope after the lead yak. Namgyal, the old man, followed, controlling them with a series of shrill whistles, walking with that bandy-legged gait peculiar to older Tibetans wearing the traditional felt-and-leather boots.

Next morning, despite tea and breakfast in bed, none of the three Tibetans showed any inclination to move until the sun reached the camp. They were probably being paid the same as if they had stayed in the commune, and so perhaps were working out their own compensations for being up here in the snow and mist. To compound the difficulty, there is a State directive to the effect that, in the interests of National Unity, all China is on Peking Time. Peking being far to the east, everyone's watch was registering eleven o'clock here in Tibet when, according to the sun, eight o'clock would have been more appropriate. This brought a feeling of failure when, at supposedly eleven o'clock, loads were still not packed. However, we managed to move everything to a camp further along the ridge, while Doug and Alex went on ahead to scout for a site for Base Camp.

The camp kitchen was a cramped and miserable affair squeezed under an old tarpaulin draped over one side of a rock. There never seemed to be enough time at the end of the day to re-erect it satisfactorily before the dire need for hot drinks and food pushed all other priorities aside. Then it was a case of trying to produce enough food for everyone on a spluttering primus cooled by the icy wind ripping through the holes and gaps in the tarpaulin.

Most of our food comprised dried beans and noodles, with a limited amount of fresh vegetables, eggs and canned fish. No doubt weight and expense partly governed the choice, though I suspected it also had to do with Doug's preferences, a vegetarian diet having improved his arthritis. Still, having bought the stuff, he was demonstrating remarkable skill in avoiding cooking any of it. Although I had no interest in becoming an unpaid camp cook for the duration of the expedition, I found myself making tea and cooking meals on most days after leaving Nyalam. Nobody insisted, but it was obviously what they all expected, and for the time being it seemed the least hassle to go along with it. Camp kitchen had the added advantage of being out of the way of the constant arguments with the yak boys. I had hoped the atmosphere would mellow a little once we left Pemba in Nyalam, supposedly guarding the remainder of the stores, but it was beginning to look as if the mood was set for the trip whoever was with us.

Complaints about the food reached a peak in Nyalam, and Paul, with his gourmet tastes, hoped for something better as soon as we left the village. This was misplaced hope in the circumstances, and he was soon joined by Alex and Roger in bemoaning the absence of meat in our supplies. All invective was invariably aimed at Doug, not me, but I was beginning to find it rather wearing. I absented myself from the cooktent a few times and let them cook for themselves.

That evening I discovered Doug perusing the *Whole Earth Cookbook* for bean recipes and muttering under his breath. There had been another argument in the kitchen.

I could not resist pointing out the futility of the situation.

'It's guaranteed to cause problems. There aren't enough of the things they like to last the trip. You'll either have to buy meat or let them cook their own food and figure it out for themselves. It's just becoming an excuse for more arguments.'

Doug glared defensively at me over the top of the book.

'It's not arguing. It's just a normal sense of humour. Better out in the open than going off in *moods* all the time.'

'I can just imagine how you lot would react if *I* started yelling at people.'

There was nothing more to say without provoking a quarrel of our own. I had no wish to spend long hours listening to them wrangle over meat, schedules, Nick's climbing ability or anything else. I preferred my own company and my studies, especially as I still had a lot of Tibetan to learn. There was no 'mood' involved, although obviously there was the implication that I preferred my books to their company. I figured that if they were thick-skinned enough to enjoy arguing then they should be able to avoid taking offence. But Doug obviously had done so already; his sharp tone made that quite clear. What was he worried about? Did he want to go home and pretend it had all been jolly and happy? If he was content with the atmosphere as it was, why did it need my approval? He himself had already complained about Alex's aggressiveness. I knew instinctively that if I joined in the shouting they would all be horrified. Perhaps by the same token I was seen as different enough for any criticism, implied or otherwise, to be taken more seriously.

Doug was not speaking to me next morning. All attempts at conversation fell dead. In the end I tried the direct approach.

'What's bothering you?'

I was surprised by the violence of his outburst.

'Everything you say is just false – there's no love there! I can feel the hate coming out off you, in black waves . . .'

He turned and stomped off through the snow after Namgyal and the yaks. Only Doug and Alex were going to Base Camp. The rest of us were to stay where we were and organise loads for the final carry the following day.

I spent the day feeling depressed. I knew from the past that there was no solution once Doug was like this. It was beginning to look like Makalu all over again. Doug's swings of mood were unpredictable at the best of times, the black ones being as all-pervading and powerful as the enthusiasm and generosity that were their natural counterpart. On the Makalu expedition it had got out of control because, as Doug had explained afterwards, someone had been intent on persuading him to spend less time with me. This time I knew it was Alex who had been stirring him up. Any attempt at conciliation would only make matters worse. I wasn't going to make the same mistake again. We would reach Base Camp tomorrow, and then I would leave.

It was late by the time Doug and Alex returned from Base Camp. I heard the yak bells in the darkness and ran up to the cooktent to put on some tea. Inside, chaos reigned. The rest of the team were already in there, each trying to make his own cup of coffee. How were these people ever going to work together to climb a mountain? Somehow a meal and a brew took shape. I was surprised and relieved to find Doug in a much better frame of mind now Base Camp was established, in spite of disagreements with Namgyal, who had insisted that they should be climbing the mountain from the other side. He confided the substance of his discussions with Alex, who had had plenty to say about women on expeditions. Quite apart from hindering the climbing team, he said, I was simply not pulling my weight.

'But I think his opinion of you improved when you got up and cooked his breakfast this morning.'

I was indignant.

'I already do more cooking than the others. What's all this other work everyone else is supposed to be doing?'

Doug switched to the role of mediator, persuading me not to get angry with Alex. I still felt uneasy, less because of Alex himself than the effect he was having on Doug. Apart from Nick, whose plans I discounted as being too dangerous, Doug was the only person who had really encouraged me to come up here in the first place. Now I was here, he had suddenly decided to listen to the opposition after all. Why was he so easily influenced by every skilful talker to bend his ear? I knew another outburst could come at any time. More than anything I was disappointed in myself. I had taken great care to stay out of trouble spots and ensure a peaceful time while I was with the expedition, and yet here I was embroiled in problems anyway.

Next morning dawned cold, crisp and clear. We had established a temporary peace, the mountains were beautiful and I was *not* going to get diverted into petty bickering. Time up here was too precious to waste on that. I walked with Namgyal, watching the way he controlled the yaks with his shouts and whistles, and the occasional pebble which always hit the load and not the yak. He seemed to find my desire to learn Tibetan as amusing as the spectacle of all this paraphernalia being so earnestly hauled up this remote slope. He was still convinced it was the wrong valley anyway, and assured me we would do much better to go back to Nyalam and wait a month. Then, he said, the weather would be sunny every day, the deep wet snow would have melted and the grass would be tall and green. Much better for the yaks, much better for climbing. Perhaps he was right. I remembered Reinhold saying he had found the climbing very good in Tibet in the summer, in contrast to Nepal which has its heavy monsoon rains at that time of year. It seemed ridiculous to try and explain to Namgyal that there was a piece of paper somewhere in an office in Peking which said we had to climb now, not later.

There were tracks in the snow, criss-crossing the line of the ridge we were following.

'Namgyal, what made these tracks?'

'*Jangu*.'

I tried to look suitably puzzled. That one was not in my book of Tibetan grammar and vocabulary. Namgyal demonstrated graphically with ferocious snarling and clawing, saying that the creature was big, fierce and brown.

'*And it eats yaks...*'

My mental image of a gigantic carnivore prowling the range diminished in size when I remembered Wu translating for the yak boys a few days ago, saying that the sick yaks could not be left unattended in the valley because of the danger of wolves.

Namgyal had a sharp, witty intelligence which enabled him to bridge the gaps in my vocabulary, and to teach me new words as we went along. He told me he was a farmer and had a house, a wife and a twenty-year-old son. Tibetans are allowed to own up to three yaks, the rest belonging to the local commune. Namgyal had been friendly with the Lama of Pankyeling Gompa when he was a young man. During the troubles of the Cultural Revolution the Lama had fled across the Himalaya to Nepal, and Namgyal had not heard from his friend since. Had I met the Lama while I had been in Nepal? I told the old man that there were many Tibetans now in Nepal, both lay and ordained. Perhaps his friend was among them. Pankyeling was a small village a few miles up the Po Chu valley above Nyalam. I wondered if it might be the site of Dopa-puhk, the 'stomach-like-cave' where Milarepa had recounted his life-story to his followers, shortly before his death.

We stopped for lunch. Namgyal pulled out a small leather pouch full of tsampa, mixed it with a little snow-melt and moulded it into small cakes. He handed one to me. It was plain and unsweetened, sugar being an imported luxury in cold Tibet, but it was wholesome and far more appetising than the food in Nyalam. He examined the offered half of my grain bar and chocolate carefully before eating them.

We caught up with Nyima at the edge of a snow-filled valley, where he was unsuccessfully trying to persuade his five yaks to cross. I headed off a couple that had broken away from the group, but had no more success than Nyima at persuading them to plunge into belly-deep snow. Namgyal left his yaks and walked across to me, with an amused smile that said, 'Just step aside and I'll show you how it's done.' A few whistles later, all the laden yaks were ploughing their way down the steep slope, dragging their legs laboriously through the porridge-like mush. One had cut a hoof and was leaving a splotch of red in the deep footprints.

We reached Base Camp and pitched tents in the afternoon blizzard. The kitchen tarpaulin did not go up so well, and ended in a drunken lurch against its rock. Making tea involved first scraping a mixture of sooty petrol and snow from the damp and unwilling primus, and then seeing to it that none of the nauseating flavour got into the tea. I managed to locate some potatoes in the chaos of stores which Nyima and Namgyal were unloading and returned to the cooktent to find Doug in residence, clutching a pot of rice and fiercely defending its existence from the protests of the other three. The scene was utterly comical, yet exasperating. Did they expect me to try to cook in the middle of all this? Perhaps Doug was right. Perhaps the only way was to join in the scrapping.

'For goodness' sake! This is ridiculous. Let them get on with it themselves.'

Doug's anger swung round through a hundred and eighty degrees and focused itself on me.

'There was no problem till you interfered. If you didn't have so many hang-ups about yourself you wouldn't take everything so personally.'

Evidently it was not considered my place to join in the scrapping. I decided to take my own advice and beat a hasty retreat. As if it wasn't enough being stuck with a bunch of grumpy climbers, Doug had to start blaming me for the squabbles, either for joining in or not joining in!

Doug came over later to conciliate.

'What's upsetting you?'

'All this aggro is really starting to get me down. I suppose I'm just not used to it. The other trips I've been on weren't like this.'

'You shouldn't take it personally. It's just the lads' boisterous behaviour. It's just a stage in the game. It'll be okay once we start climbing.'

Unfortunately it was the climbing that was worrying me. The others had reluctantly agreed to Doug's suggestion that I come along on the first climb, less because they wanted me on the mountain than to ensure that I was too busy to go exploring and perhaps get into trouble with the authorities. If that happened, they feared it would reflect on them, and perhaps result in the expedition being called off. Now Doug was an unknown quantity. His sudden outbursts of temper could occur again at any time, and on the mountain that would be not only unpleasant but also dangerous. He might even interpret altitude sickness as yet another bad mood, and become angry again. It was this that concerned me, but it was difficult to confront him with it directly. I found myself speaking generally, as a metaphor for what concerned him personally, and trying to work the conversation round to the reasons for his fury of the previous day. Whenever we got too close to the subject his anger would rise again, confirming my fears that I would be climbing with a human time-bomb. I realised I was only making things worse by trying to discuss the problem. So I backed off, saying I was just depressed by the aggressive atmosphere.

Doug seemed comfortable with the role of mediator between myself and the others, persuading me that it was only my own neuroses which made me perceive such lighthearted banter as aggressive, and that I was the only one who did not think this was a really happy trip. I could see he was largely right about that. The atmosphere had been the same for the last three weeks, and although I had preferred to avoid it, I had not found it particularly threatening. It was only since falling foul of Doug's temper that my neuroses had been having a field day. So long as I agreed with him, Doug was reassuring, now his usual comfortable self again. Perhaps he would relax once the climbing started.

He went back to the kitchen and once again I could hear raised voices in the distance.

More and more, I was longing to leave and explore on my own. I felt trapped by the group's insistence that I had to stay here until they had started the Face and were safely out of reach of the authorities. Even retreat to the peace of my books and studies brought complaints of uncooperativeness from Alex and of moodiness from Doug. I knew that my refusal to become camp cook and dishwasher left me no role here that would satisfy any of them. My fears about climbing could easily have been solved by staying in Base Camp until I was allowed to leave, but added to my dislike of this dismal place was the feeling that I should not give in to my fears so easily.

Although I found the aggressive atmosphere depressing when I was in the midst of it, from a safe distance I found it quite interesting. Perhaps it was the inevitable result of having more than one prima donna in a single camp. Individually they were used to dominating those around by force of personality, and this was inevitably causing friction as each jockeyed for position in the pecking order. Experienced mountaineers like Doug were inevitably a little sensitive to younger, dynamic climbers challenging their authority and wanting to do things their own way. Usually Doug automatically took control, because of his experience and forceful personality. On occasion, however, other forceful personalities would emerge, and things would not be so simple. It was clear that Alex was measuring himself against Doug, testing his strength and experience against those of a man fourteen years older. The arguments began to sound not unlike the clash of antlers in the contest for the leadership of the herd.

4

High Altitude

Doug went down to Nyalam with Wu to organise delivery of the rest of the stores and to buy meat. The rest of us ferried up a cache of stores dumped further down the ridge when two of the yaks had refused to continue. It was interesting to note that all the beer had already been carried up – only food and climbing equipment remained. Gear stashed, Paul, Alex and I settled in to make quantities of tea. I looked around.

'Where's Roger?'

'In his tent. He's in love, missing his girlfriend.'

Alex was impatient.

'He's always moping off on his own. He ought to get his head together if he wants to go climbing. You can't be in two places at once.'

As usual, Alex's comments were abrasive but to the point. I, too, was experiencing the unsettled feeling of wanting to be elsewhere. I hoped they would get the acclimatisation climb over quickly, so that I could leave. I took Roger a cup of tea and we chatted for a while until he joined us in the cooktent. The conversation switched to Nick, who was out for a walk.

Paul was stirring his tea.

'He's a headbanger, that bloke.'

Alex was more basic. 'Well, I don't want to be lumbered with him on a rope. Doug says he'll do it, but his ropework isn't safe.'

Roger grinned. 'I'll do it. I'm used to it. The problems will probably sort themselves out as we get higher.'

'He's not acclimatising well down here at sixteen thousand feet. He's always tripping, and cutting his fingers. Up there you can't get away with clumsiness. There are knife-edge ridges and long stretches of snow over blue ice. It's dangerous.'

I wondered if Nick was really as oblivious of the risks he would be running as he seemed, or if it was simply bravado in an attempt to hold his own with the rest of the group.

The conversation turned to the subject of equipment. There had been a general free-for-all before they had left London and most of the gear was now divided up.

Roger asked, 'Who's going to keep what at the end of the trip?'

'I'm keeping the camera,' said Alex.

Paul suggested, 'Why not put a price on everything and divvy it up that way?'

'No, that's no good. I haven't got any money.'

'Well I'd like a tent out of it.'

'No, you can't. I'm keeping the tents for Annapurna in the autumn.'

Roger interrupted. 'Hey, Alex, don't forget you've put in five hundred less than anyone else.'

'Tough. I wouldn't have come otherwise. You're lucky to have me!'

Nothing was agreed. Everyone knew it would be solved by the democratic scrimmage at the end of the expedition.

Next morning Alex organised Paul and Roger to join him on a carry of equipment to an Advance Base at the foot of Shishapangma. I walked round the flank of the mountain, to a valley leading away to the east, in the hope of finding a short cut to Pankyeling. It proved an uninviting route. The way ahead was barred by a steep rock wall, beyond which I could see just a little of the shimmering gold and brown of the desert with blue sky above, like the light at the end of a tunnel of swirling black cloud. There had been so much bad weather since we had been in Base Camp. Noticing that my water-bottle was leaking on to the down jacket in my pack, I quickly drank what I could, and poured the rest out before my emergency gear became soaked and useless.

Next morning, tea and breakfast wouldn't stay down. I remembered not eating last night's supper either. Was it a stomach upset or dehydration, due to going without water for most of yesterday? Either way, I felt awful and went back to bed.

Doug had returned and was getting ready to make another carry to Advance Base with the others.

'You coming, Elaine?'

'Not sure. I'll see how I feel in a little while.'

I could hear Roger outside asking Doug if I was coming along, and was shocked by the reply.

'Best to leave her. She's off in one of her moods again.'

This was unfair and getting out of hand, I told myself peevishly. How could anyone be so wrapped up in his own ego as to react in this way every time he failed to get the response he wanted? Then doubts crept in. If I was so annoyed about a stupid comment, perhaps it *was* just moodiness. I packed my rucksack and stomped outside. If only everything would keep still while I looked at it. Roger peered at me.

'Are you okay?'

'I think it's just dehydration. I'll take a water-bottle and keep drinking.'

Doug lent me his water-bottle and we set off. I found it difficult to keep up with the others. Alex was waiting for me at the top of the first steep moraine.

'Are you okay? It's a long way you know.'

'I feel very sick, but I'll go back if I can't make it.'

He shrugged and caught up with the others. They all stopped about an hour later to try out some rock-climbing moves on a large boulder. It was good to sit down and have a drink, but as soon as I did so I began to shiver violently. The icy water felt like a cold rock in my stomach. I wandered away in search of some rocks, wanting to be sick in private. I waited for a while, but the others did not pass me. When I went back to the boulder they had gone. The snowstorm had increased, and although only a few minutes had elapsed, I was unable to see them in the tangled mass of moraines and swirling flakes. The snow had already obliterated their tracks and the wind drowned out my voice.

It was hard to tell when my ability to make the right decisions had become seriously impaired – possibly when I had decided to come along that morning. Certainly I could have returned to the camp quite easily from the boulder, but for some reason I decided it was too early in the day to give up, and set off in the direction I thought the others had gone hoping to pick up their tracks. I have no idea how long I spent stumbling around in those moraines, and with the combination of blizzard outside and dizziness and nausea inside, I had even less idea in which direction I was going, or where I was. The next thing I clearly remember was sitting propped against a rock, listening to an argument going on somewhere inside me. There was a calm, assured voice saying that everything would be all right if only I could pull myself together, while a whimpering, snivelling voice was protesting that it was hopeless, I was too weak, and I was lost anyway. A third part of my awareness seemed to be listening to all this with an impartial curiosity. The weak voice pointed out, quite rightly, that I no longer had the faintest idea where the camp was, or how far. The calm voice replied that it did not matter '*... only trust me. I know.*' So I let it take control, and walked into the swirling whiteness. The exhaustion and dizziness seemed to fade away, and although my rational mind had no idea which way I was going, somehow I *knew* that I was being guided in the right direction. I saw no landmarks that I recognised, and had lost all track of time. Then I found myself at the top of the moraine slope, looking down on the camp. Everything was transformed by the thick snow. The weak voice surfaced, bleating on about the snow and the cold, and my soaking wet clothes. Immediately the nausea returned, my exhausted legs crumpled under me, and I found myself sitting in the wet snow, unable to move. It was a while before the calm returned, and then I walked easily down the last slope as if in a trance.

The others were in the cooktent drinking beer. Doug lumbered over to meet me.

'Eh-up me duck. How're you doing? We were about to come out and look for you.'

I pushed him away. If I stopped now I would never make it the last few yards to my tent. He came over later with a mug of hot orange juice and large helpings of sympathy. I was appalled to learn that it was past five-thirty, and that they had been back for an hour and a half, after going up to the Advance Base. Where had I been all day? The voices I had heard now seemed no more than hallucinations. . . but surely hallucinations do not guide you home? I was too tired to think about it. I tried to tell Doug what had happened, but it was difficult to put into words. Doug talked about his trip down to Nyalam and his discussions with Pemba and the Commune Leader. He also mentioned that on the way down he and Wu had become separated in the fog, and Wu had nearly drowned trying to cross the river alone. Doug had gone back up the valley to search for him, but Wu had in the meantime found his own way to Nyalam to dry out and recover.

The story only served to increase my feeling of vulnerability. It would not occur to Doug that Wu had never been in mountains before and might be unable to keep up with him in the fog and rough terrain. He did not feel he had left Wu behind, only that they had become inexplicably separated, almost as if some third party was involved. Would I be left behind like that on the climb? It was certain that the others could easily outpace me.

Doug wanted to know what had been happening in camp while he was away. I related the conversations about Nick's prospects on the mountain.

Doug asked, 'Where was Nick at the time?'

'Out for a walk.' I paused. 'I'm not very comfortable about the way Alex talks about people behind their backs.'

I was thinking of myself rather than Nick. Exhaustion and dehydration were catching up with me, bringing a heavy depression of body and mind. I was fed up with the lot of them. They cared about nothing but themselves, and had invited me in the first place only because they needed my contribution to expenses. Now they just wanted me out of the way, yet would not let me go. Suddenly I hated Alex. What right had he to go stirring up trouble behind my back? Even in the confusion of conflicting emotions, I knew I was angry with Alex because these underhand tactics were out of character, and therefore far more difficult to deal with than his natural abrasive honesty.

Doug interrupted my complaints by asking, 'What did they say about me?'

If I had not been so exhausted and depressed I would have laughed. Here we all were, totally wrapped up in our individual selves, each intent on preserving a fragile separate ego from damage! Now I was cornered. Either I had to lie to Doug, or else provoke him by refusing to tell him what had been said.

'They said your rope technique wasn't good enough.'

I could tell he was angry, so I said no more.

Next morning, I slept late. I woke to hear Doug outside, talking to Roger.

'Elaine says there's too much backbiting going on in this group.'

I was furious. Of all the underhand tricks, to go sympathising with someone who is sick and depressed and then spread her whinings around everyone else – as if *he* had not been complaining too. If only Doug knew when to keep *quiet*. I stomped outside and yelled at him to shut up. Doug yelled back that I was a stupid bitch. We stood there shouting at each other while Roger stirred the breakfast porridge, amused by the whole performance. When the non-sequiturs got out of phase he would wave the porridge spoon as if umpiring a match and make us go back and start again. Eventually we ran out of insults and breath, and felt much better. Even as contestants we had been forced to see the funny side of the match, and were content to concede a draw. Doug went back to his tent while I set about washing the breakfast pots. Several layers of gloom had been lifted from my view of the world. Alex wandered over.

'Maybe we should have a talk.'

'Maybe we should. It's too dangerous to go climbing with these undercurrents going on.'

'You're the one causing problems, putting Doug in a bad mood.'

'So why have you been making things worse by stirring it up?'

Alex shrugged. 'Of course I've been trying to separate you and Doug. You're distracting him. He's here to climb a mountain, not go wandering off round Tibet. I need him for the Face, and everything that stands between me and the Face has to be got out of the way. The team comes first.'

'Yes, but whether you like it or not, I'm part of the team until I leave. You can't suddenly decide to turn parts of the team against each other as it suits you. Where would it all end?'

I expected an angry outburst at the criticism. To my surprise, he thought for a moment and then nodded assent. It was a relief to talk to someone so logical and pragmatic. I knew that from now on Alex would say what he thought directly to me. I also knew this meant receiving the sharp end of his tongue, but I didn't mind. It was not long coming.

'It's you that's the problem on this trip. A woman who can't take it in a man's world.'

I could only agree with him. This was no place for someone who was not totally committed to climbing the Face. I reminded him that I was here to see Tibet and was hoping to leave as soon as possible.

'Well you can't go off too soon, and risk dropping us in the shit with the authorities. In the meantime, I don't want Doug in a bad mood and not in the right space for climbing the Face. It's you who gets him going. It's like having a lovers' quarrel erupting all the time.'

I looked at him sharply. That kind of suggestion could cause all sorts of problems. Alex hastily qualified the statement.

'Of course, I don't mean it literally. But there's the same kind of irrationality about it.'

Again I could see his incisive perception was right. Doug always related to men as men and to women as women. One of his favourite maxims was 'man hunter, woman nest-builder'. I tended to relate to people as people and found nothing unusual in having 'climbing only' friendships with men. I could see I was being as insensitive to Doug's attitude as he was to mine, yet I was still too stubborn to accept the 'nest-builder' role of camp domestic.

Alex was being provocative again.

'It's been the same ever since we left London. You've been following Doug around like a puppy. Is that all you've come here for?'

'I haven't been following him anywhere. I'm the one who speaks Tibetan, and I'm interested in the country. Doug is the only other one interested, so it's inevitable we should finish up in the same places a lot of the time.'

But if I went climbing I *would* be following Doug, and I did not feel comfortable about that. Strangely enough, there was no sting in Alex's insults, now that he had been completely open about their purpose. He saw Doug's interest in Tibet as a threat to their success on the mountain, and my presence as heightening that interest. I tried to reassure him that it had always been my intention to travel round Tibet alone. It was my way of doing things, and I had no thought of encouraging Doug to come with me. Alex looked surprised and not altogether convinced.

Next day we left Paul and Roger in camp, recovering from stomach upsets, and carried supplies up to the Advance Base. It was a lazy, relaxed walk, with the sun shining on the snow peaks that surrounded us. This is what climbing is about, I thought, as I leaned against a rock munching a bar of chocolate. Then I reminded myself that this was not *entirely* what climbing was about. Higher up, where the real climbing started, there was a good deal of risk and hard work as well.

The tension of the last few days seemed to have gone, and Doug was his usual cheerful self again. He kept a cautious eye on me in case I relapsed into dehydration. It seemed ironic that the air had been cleared by plunging into the sort of slanging match I had been trying so hard to avoid. I knew, of course, that Doug would remember it as the only argument of an otherwise peaceful trip. Woman's place was to be supportive of man, not to express opinions of her own.

I remembered taking part in American expeditions where the

inability to get along amicably with one's fellows had been considered a greater failure than any inability to get one's body up the mountain. Yet I could see that to succeed in getting to the top of this remote, unclimbed face – among the ten highest in the world – and then safely down again required a certain single-minded ruthless ambition. It was not unlike any other glamorous enterprise in the business world. Looking at it in that way, was it appropriate to expect that we should all be experiencing the kind of heightened awareness Doug was hoping for? Doug himself was struggling to reconcile such interests with his own ambitions for success and recognition. Clearly so much of the wrangling arose from two strong views of what we were doing: Alex was focused on achieving the summit while Doug wanted to explore his own mind on the way. They could avoid a direct confrontation so long as I was there to absorb the anger each felt when either of them saw a personal ambition threatened.

Having recognised the situation, why did I still feel trapped by it? I longed to extricate myself from between them. I wanted to see Tibet and be free of the mental gamesmanship that, by trying to withdraw from it, I was simply promoting.

We returned to camp to find a little surprise from Pemba awaiting us. The two yak drivers had returned with eight yaks but only one yak-load of supplies. There was also a letter ordering us to relocate the Base Camp, which was too high. Doug and Alex went down with Wu to the hut by the moraine where Pemba had set up his own base. They accosted him in the middle of the night with the news that they were not going to comply with any new regulations he invented for his own convenience. After a two-hour pitched battle, Pemba agreed to allow Wu to stay with us in Base Camp in his place, as he was unable to make the journey because of his arthritic knees. Doug grinned as he recounted the story.

'I told him to stop eating meat! He thinks we're the worst expedition ever to come to China.' He shook his head. 'It was awful. I'm never going to get angry again.'

The Pemba diversion finally finished off our acclimatisation schedule. By evening Alex had worked out a new timetable, missing out the first climb and starting instead with a fairly rapid ascent of Nyenang Ri, marked on the map as 7,071 metres (23,250 feet), to the east of Shishapangma's main summit.

In fickle morning sunshine the six of us set off from Advance Base towards the slopes of Nyenang Ri. From the outset it was obvious that Nick was feeling the effects of altitude. He was now higher than he had ever been before, and was pale and vomiting violently. Within half an hour he was trailing well behind the others as he staggered painfully across the boulderfield. I could not understand why he was still trying to continue when he was so weak. Alex was sitting on a rock, waiting. He was feeling the pressure of his own schedule.

'Nick, you're being stupid. You've had it, you might as well go down now as in twenty minutes.'

'It's my stomach. All I need is another day to rest.'

'You're clutching at straws. You don't have the years of slog necessary. I'm sorry, but charity ends at five thousand metres. What do you think, Roger?'

'Well, I agree, but Nick's got to reach his own decision.'

'Bloody hell, Roger! Don't be so bloody amateur. These are mountains you know. They kill people.'

I left the five of them in heated debate and trudged on up the moraine. What in hell was I doing here in the middle of all this? The mountains were silent – dazzlingly, mockingly beautiful in the morning sunshine. The cold space around me was so vast, so empty, a place of purity and savage desolation. I was drawn back to the mountains because they never failed to remind me that there was also a clear space within, a space which so easily became crowded with the all-consuming business of everyday living. To leave the noise and bustle of the world behind was to be aware once more of that elusive inner peace. What was the point of slogging all the way up here if only to bring the clutter and petty bickering along too?

Recognising the kind of climb this was going to be made me once more sharply aware of the dangers involved. Why was I afraid of *this* mountain, where before I had suffered no more fear than was necessary for survival? All I knew before was that I needed to climb, and the urge was compelling enough to make the risks acceptable. This time the lure was Tibet. There was something here I wanted to discover, something no more tangible than that desire to reach the top of the mountain, and I did not want to get myself killed before the quest had properly begun. Of course, Tibet, like climbing or anything else, could offer no insights to a closed mind. This experience too could degenerate into simply clinging to a self-image. For me the great delight of climbing had been the freedom from preoccupation with self that came from the intense concentration inspired by risk.

I heard Alex yelling behind me and turned to see him heading off to the right. By the time I reached him at the edge of the glacier he was already uncoiling the rope.

'Better tie on for this one.'

The glacier was a smooth, undulating sweep of new snow flowing imperceptibly from the col above. We both knew that the snow could hide potentially lethal crevasses in the ice it covered. Until a well-trodden trail had been established across it, it would be foolish to go unroped. Alex's anger had been overlaid by an instant boyish charm. It was too sudden.

'I'll be too slow for you,' I said. 'And then you'll get cross.' I saw the grin of amusement before he managed to hide it.

'Just go at your own pace.'

I tied into the rope. Temporarily I was part of the equipment that would get him to the summit of the mountain as quickly as possible, rather than a potential obstruction to be removed. I was slow, perversely and deliberately so.

His dry sarcasm reached me from the other end of the short rope.

'Did they teach you to kick the snow off your crampons like that?'

I pointed to the steep rocky ridge above us.

'You thinking of climbing that?'

'Yes, that's the kind of Himalayan climbing we do. But you have to remember there's only a few world-class climbers who are capable of that kind of thing. Just because we talk about it as if it's easy, you shouldn't think it *is* easy.'

We untied at the far side of the glacier and Alex disappeared over the moraine without a word. I knew he was demonstrating the speed at which he could travel without my presence, so I sat and waited for the others. I was struck by the lunacy of two people like us trying to climb a mountain together: it was funny in spite of being dangerous. Alex was exercising considerable restraint on his tongue for the sake of my feelings, but I knew it couldn't last much longer.

Doug and Roger appeared, following our footprints across the glacier. Roger went after Alex; Doug sat and lit a cigarette. Nick and Paul had gone down. Paul had not been complaining about problems with his lungs, but they had become increasingly painful over the last few days. He had finally decided he would have to descend to low altitude or risk permanent damage to them. Doug was shaking his head.

'I could have wept,' he said. 'The group's falling apart and we haven't started climbing yet. There's no need for such pushiness at this early stage. Paul will probably go straight home. I hope he's still in Base Camp when we get back.'

We caught up with Alex and Roger at the crest of the ridge. I looked over the edge.

'Ooh, that's a surprise.'

They laughed. The other side of the ridge dropped sheer to the main glacier a few hundred feet below. We followed the crest up for several hundred feet. The sloping side of the ridge was covered with snow and bluish-white ice which lay thicker as we went higher. Soon the only bare rocks to be seen lay on the crest of the ridge itself, and this pathway became gradually narrower as the ice encroached. Aware of the drop below us, I was keeping as far from the edge as possible without skating down the ice slope below. Some of the rocks sticking out of the crest sounded hollow under my feet. Roger, with his guide's instinct, had fallen into step just behind me. He was chuckling at my obvious caution.

'Climbing isn't for those who don't like big drops.'

'Climbing isn't for lazy cowards.' I grinned ruefully as I

stopped for a breather at the first solid-looking rock.

A little further up, the rocky spine disappeared into the ice for the last time at a small snowy col. Doug was busily digging a bivouac ledge and Alex was complaining that he didn't like the place. Roger and I started to melt snow for tea. My fingers were cold and clumsy, and I almost dropped a water-bottle as I tried to pick it up. I felt a momentary clutch of vertigo as I watched its imagined trajectory, skittering away down the steep ice above which we perched, cramped on the small ledge. Alex started to dig his own ledge.

The afternoon weather was well on us now. Sharp gusts of wind hit the ridge, bringing flurries of snow. Bivouacking was an even more uncomfortable process than usual, as the wind-blown snow found its way into everything, to melt in the creases of sleeping bag and down jacket. In the gathering dusk there seemed to be far too much equipment and far too little space in which to stash it. During the night the wind rose to savage gusts which felt as if they would rip the flimsy bivouac tent from its moorings. I awoke several times as freezing condensation splattered on to my face, only to drift back into an uneasy sleep. I dreamed my boots disappeared out of a rip in the end of the tent and slithered off down the icy slope, with me scampering after them in my red woolly socks.

Next morning I had no headache, but my body was telling me it had just spent a night at 19,000 feet. Doug helped me to pack. A foot of snow had fallen in the night, swathing the valley below us in a blanket of white. I tightened crampon straps with freezing fingers, scanning the icy ridge above. Despite Alex's comments, I knew they would not, in fact, attempt to climb the steep rock wall directly above us, to which this ridge was leading. The only alternative would be a rising traverse to the left across steep blue ice, with sheer rock below it and crazily angled séracs above. It would have looked unattractive even if my limbs had not felt so sluggish, as in those childhood dreams where you are pursued by monsters. I had been higher than this before but had not gained altitude as quickly as we had this time.

I knew as I set out that I would not reach the ice traverse, and yet, irrationally, I would not turn back until I was forced to do so. The ice on the ridge ahead rose in a series of small steps, not technically difficult, but poised directly above the vertical drop to the glacier, now 1,500 feet below. The others were loping ahead, unroped, moving easily over the hard ice. I paused at the first small step, looking first up at the shiny ice, then down the dizzying drop to the boulders far below. What kind of controlled insanity was driving me to push myself to the limit? It wasn't difficult, but I was feeling the altitude, and a fall here would be my last. I was on the edge, between the limits of endurance and the invitation to disaster. I felt sure the others were at least partly motivated by this pushing of limits, although they rarely spoke of it, and anyway their skill and experience put their testing-ground higher and steeper than here. For each individual comes his or her own particular time and place.

I reached the top of the ice bulge and let out the tension in a long, slow breath. There was a bigger step up ahead, and I could see Doug waiting at the top of it. After that would be another, and then another. Where would I make the decision to turn back? Would I fail to reach the traverse because I turned back or because I fell off? I remembered the cryptic reports I had read of mountaineering accidents, and wondered how many of them had begun just like this.

Even from this distance, I could see the slump in Doug's shoulders as he smoked. I knew he felt caught between conflicting loyalties and ambitions, and I was all that was left of one half of the conflict. We had talked for a long time the previous evening, about our past climbing trips, and how we felt about our involvement with the sport. I had become aware that many of his ideas and experiences were close to my own, although his strength and mountaineering skill were far beyond mine. Part of him was content to trim his style to fit my abilities. He was carrying more than half the weight for the two of us. His original plan for a first climb had been to tackle an easier peak at a slower pace, but we both knew that his ambition to succeed on the big mountains was a more powerful drive than esoteric diversions in other directions. I felt great empathy for a fellow-Geminian trying to reconcile conflicting aspects of his personality. He wanted to make a space for people like Nick and myself on an ambitious expedition in a remote area, not realising that it was unrealistic to expect young adventurers like Alex and Roger to prejudice not only their chances of success but also their margin of safety. It was even more ridiculous to expect someone like me to climb as they did – swiftly and unroped on an exposed ridge – and to survive.

I struggled to the top of the second step, cursing the pride that would not allow me to ask for a rope. I could hear Alex's angry voice from somewhere above.

'If you can't stand up on that stuff, you've got no business being here.'

Dead right, I thought, glancing briefly at the gut-wrenching drop below, digging both axes deep into the ice as my pack seemed to increase in weight with every step. Why was it so hard to make that decision to give up, even when it was obvious that to continue was reckless, not to say suicidal? Doug was avoiding my eyes.

'What are you going to do?' The outer conflict had met the inner. Doug was waiting for me to ask him to rope me across the glacier we had traversed yesterday. It would be as much of an unknown entity as when Alex and I had first crossed, for the night's snow had obliterated our tracks. I knew Doug felt responsible for having encouraged me to come this far, and I could see him struggling to overcome his own ambition. If he were to see me safely down now he would not be able to return and catch up with Alex and Roger. That would put him out of the acclimatisation climb and set him back seriously when it came to tackling the Face. I thought, he ought to come with me: he got me into this. Then I thought, you got yourself into this: you didn't have to listen. I had known when I crossed yesterday that I would have to re-cross alone.

I asked him to come as far as the bivouac site, and we descended the ridge together.

5

Letting Go

We reached the first rocks sticking out of the crest of the ridge and stopped. Doug handed me my rucksack.

'You gave it a good try. This speed of ascent is fast in anyone's books. The same thing happened last year ... Oh well. Three down, three to go. Maybe one day I'll have a Himalayan trip that works out.'

He looked very lonely as he plodded back up the ridge.

Thirty minutes later, I was standing at the edge of the ice, watching three tiny figures moving slowly into the mist above.

I turned my attention reluctantly to the smooth sweep of the glacier before me. There was no trace of yesterday's footprints. I knew many climbers who would cross unroped and laugh at the cautious. I also knew a few who had died doing just that. I had never crossed a glacier alone; it seemed a pointless and lonely way to die. I found myself wondering if my Sherpa friends, who climbed for a livelihood rather than a commitment to mountaineering, felt this same cold fear when confronted with a dangerous crossing. Then, without really being aware that I had made a decision, I started walking, testing the snow with my axe, looking for cracks and listening for the tell-tale groaning of moving snow.

Slowly, fear built up like a rock in my chest until I couldn't move. I stopped, gasping. As the pounding of my heart slowed, I gradually became aware of the calm voice I had heard before, telling me to relax, that it was easy to get across. As my mind became calm, it slowly emptied of everything except the endless whiteness of the snow, and I walked out into it. Then, into the emptiness, like an electric shock, came a slump in the crust which echoed hollowly beneath my feet. I jumped back, staring at the dip in front of me. As I tried frantically to reason out what to do, my fear produced crevasses all around me, barring the path forward and also my retreat. Once again I was unable to move except for the trembling of my knees. It took a slow and conscious effort to control the rising panic. Reluctantly, it seemed this time, the voice returned.

'For goodness' sake, pull yourself together. Do you want to stand here all day with a heavy pack on your back?'

I made a large detour around the dip and reached the rocks on the other side.

As I wandered slowly back to Base Camp the sun was shining, and green shoots were poking through the patches of bare earth among the snow. It seemed as if, at last, spring was coming.

Paul emerged from the cooktent and grinned.

'Brew's on. What happened?'

I told him. 'How're your lungs?'

'They're okay. I'll give it another go in a few days.' He grinned again. 'He'll burn himself out soon and then we can all go back to normal. It's just that he's done nothing big for two years and he's desperate for a good route.'

Wu brought out cups of tea. I could tell that Paul's breezy manner masked his concern: the lungs would not heal in time at this altitude. I sipped the tea and wondered how the others were getting on underneath those nasty-looking séracs. Wu put supper on to boil. I was sure he was putting on weight. At these altitudes most people get thinner. It was extraordinary how this frail young man from southern China seemed to have gone from strength to strength as we got higher, quietly reading his books, peeling a few vegetables, sometimes going for walks. He seemed content with his lot now he no longer had to interpret between the expedition and its unloved Liaison Officer. Pemba, it seemed, was still in residence in the hut below the moraine.

It was a delight to get washed and find some almost clean clothes. I sorted out my gear, packing away the climbing equipment and setting aside the warm clothes, books, film and food I would need for exploring Tibet. The next couple of days passed immersed in the complexities of Tibetan grammar.

Muffled voices in the afternoon snowstorm announced the return of the climbers. Tea was first priority, swapping news came next. Alex seemed more cheerful after some exercise and was chatting to Nick. I found Doug and Roger in Paul's tent, catching up with events. They had traversed the ice but not reached the summit of Nyenang Ri. Then they had descended a snow chute and returned. They had made two more bivouacs, enough for this stage of acclimatisation.

Paul said, 'How was Alex?'

Doug mumbled something unintelligible, and I knew there had been a fight. He did not talk about it until later, and I could tell something was worrying him, something deeper than the straightforward clash of personalities he was describing.

'It's climbing without heart. Ticking off all the prestige routes like a mechanical man, and bringing city values into the mountains. He just uses people. He wouldn't hesitate to get rid of me if I was getting in his way.'

There was silence for a moment before I said quietly, 'Having people like me and Nick along is bound to aggravate someone like Alex. Wouldn't it be better to keep "hard" trips hard, and do the more diverse ones separately?'

Doug was quiet for a while, but I could tell he was considering more than he said.

Each day it snowed more than the last. To our bewilderment, spring disappeared under two feet of white powder. Paul had decided to go home after all, and was lucky to have departed before it got too deep. I found, once again, I was unable to leave. The others were now insisting that I did not travel round Tibet without first officially changing my visa status from climber to tourist. Wu was sympathetic but not optimistic. He had sent a request to Lhasa and Peking via Paul. There had been a brief conspiracy in the cooktent just before Paul left. I was touched that he was trying to see beyond his own disappointment and help me with my plans.

'Look, if I get a reply to this telegram before I get a truck out of Nyalam, I'll send a message back with Wu, so you can plan the best way to approach the Chinese about travelling around.' His face crinkled into its familiar grin. 'Can't think what you want to go gallivantin' off round this place for anyway. You'll just end up sitting in mud 'uts with a bunch of poons! It's about time you found yourself a rich husband and settled down.'

I watched Paul and Wu ploughing down the hill in the deepening snow. There seemed little hope that my status could be changed. I felt disappointed and betrayed. Where were the promises that had brought me here? They were still discussing the possibility of 'fitting me in' with their plans to climb an easy route somewhere. It was just another trick to delay my departure a little longer. When they had originally objected to my leaving on the grounds that any brush with the authorities on my part might result in the expedition being called off, I had thought their argument rather weak but had gone along with it. After all, none of us knew much about the system we were dealing with, and even such a remote possibility had to be considered. Now that they were about to leave for the South West Face itself it seemed to me absurd for them to continue believing that a posse of troops could be dispatched from Nyalam to haul them off! But, faced with an overwhelming majority of four to one, it was easy to doubt my own reasoning.

I wandered off for a walk in the moonlight, catching a fragment of conversation as I passed the cooktent.

'... there I was, pissed as a rat, and there was this bird looking for her handbag... '

The peaks shone cold in the pale moonlight. The air seemed brittle in its stillness. A bank of black cloud down the valley announced more snow to come. I longed to wander off into the mountains and become part of the stillness, to renew my strength. The loneliness of living with six strangers, each walled into his own world, was eating into my spirit. I was used to travelling solo or with a close friend.

Paul had been asking after my friend Judy, whom he knew. I told him she was in love, and that was why I was here.

Judy was Californian, dark and slim, a personality larger than life. We had climbed together in Canada and Peru, relying only on ourselves and each other. Those had been happy trips. A few months after Peru she had met a British archaeologist, and the tiny flat had become crowded. I was happy for her, but I moved out, struggling to overcome a sense of loss. I found myself swept up in a frenetic series of adventures – joining groups of strangers to travel across Europe, America, Alaska, Nepal – to discover that attachment to a person can throw one out of balance as much as attachment to ambition or even materialism.

The next morning I made the decision that as soon as it stopped snowing for more than a couple of hours I would leave, whether I had news from Paul or not. I told Doug I would go down and ask Pemba for transport back to Lhasa as I was not acclimatising. Maybe I would see something on the way. I was not at all sure I cared any more, but at least I had a definite plan to follow. Suddenly I felt much more tolerant of my companions' machinations. Their intense concentration on their own goals was bound to foster a certain insensitivity to anyone else's. Only after I had virtually given up was I able to see this, and realised that if I fixed my ideas too rigidly on my new plan I would develop that same intolerance.

Roger was in the cooktent, listening to his cassettes of Kipling stories.

I am the cat who walks by himself, and all places are alike to me.

Roger looked up, and turned off the machine.

'Oh, turn it back on, I like that one.'

Roger obliged, looking at me, half-smiling.

'Well, of course, you would like that one, wouldn't you?'

Perhaps only Roger, of them all, really understood why I spent so much time on my own. His appearances in the cooktent as often as not were out of synchronisation with the others'. A missed meal would usually produce a degree of grumpiness, yet Roger seemed to be able to avoid identifying too closely with his own bad moods. Perhaps it was his interest in the 'Inner Game' approach to his sport which gave him a sharper sense of self-awareness. I knew he felt disappointment with the increasingly tight timetabling, so that the spontaneous approach to Alpine-style climbing had been lost. He said later he felt that Chinese bureaucracy had taken control of our expedition after all; in resisting the system we had come to share it. My own diary records, 'But the dream had become a military exercise with no room for dreamers ... '

Alex was recovering from food-poisoning inflicted by over-rapid consumption of bean stew. I wondered if he would ever go climbing with a vegetarian again. Nick was pottering about the kitchen. His communications system was sufficiently eccentric to make it impossible for anyone else to work with him, but left to himself he could produce pancakes without equal.

During the last four days, Doug had remained ensconced in his tent with his books and a plentiful supply of munchies. As the snow piled up outside, a small rodent moved in under his flysheet and lived happily on toffee-covered nuts and sugar biscuits. His brief conversations at mealtimes mainly concerned his attempts to ambush the creature with a camera.

I arrived at Doug's tent bearing tea. He unplugged Dylan from the cassette player, and scooped out a place for me to sit among the biscuit packets, books and tapes which littered the floor.

'I suppose you're wondering why I'm so grumpy?'

'Oh, not really,' I said smoothly. 'It's obvious you're just off in one of your *moods* again.'

For a minute he thought I was serious, then his face relaxed.

'I'm retiring. Alex and Roger are better off climbing the Face in their own style. I'm going to use the rest of the time to see Tibet. It's probably the only chance I'll get.'

My first reaction to this bombshell was to feel reassured that the aggressive atmosphere was not just the result of my own neurotic imaginings, as Doug had tried to convince me. When the 'lighthearted banter' was directed his way it affected him far more profoundly, and he was now planning to abandon the climb altogether. This sense of gratification was not satisfying for very long, however. The team was falling apart. While I knew I could do little to help Doug and Alex face up to their differences and work them out, I did feel partly responsible for fostering Doug's other interests. It was clear that the rapport between Alex and Roger was making him feel left out now that just the three of them were fit to tackle the Face. More than anything, Doug needed the reassurance of being the central figure in the group of diverse individuals he had brought together. I spoke cautiously, unsure of what would or would not offend him.

'Are you sure that the middle of a trip is the right time to change plans and retire? It would almost certainly mean retiring from your next trip as well, the one to K2.'

Doug began to talk a little about his ideas for K2, how he was hoping to go there with a group of friends with mixed interests and abilities who could each find something satisfying to do. Behind his words I could see a restlessness which went deeper than his dissatisfaction with the way this trip was working out. Besides trying to become less attached to his ambitions, he had begun to question the value of the ambitions themselves.

'What did the others say?'

'That it's my decision. They wanted me along but could do it without me if necessary.'

'Have you ever had someone on an expedition who had definite interests in other directions?'

'No.'

'Perhaps it's better not to have distractions on climbing trips. You either have to close your mind, as Alex has, and thrash all the distractions out of the way, or else you allow them in and end up not climbing. I'm sure you'll feel you've failed if you give up halfway through. Promise yourself another trip some time especially for distractions!'

There was a long silence while Doug turned the situation over in his mind. I considered the possibilities. Alex had been so weak and exhausted from sickness and diarrhoea that morning that he could hardly stand. Suddenly I felt a great fear for Alex, an irrational kind of certainty that if he went climbing without Doug he would be killed on the mountain. All the angry things I had said about him faded into proportion when balanced against the stark reality of the risk. Perhaps this was why some of us needed to climb, to remind ourselves that human relationships go deeper than petty squabbles. I interrupted Doug's ponderings.

'Think how you'd feel if anything happened to Alex or Roger. Alex is still very weak, and you know what he's like – he's ambitious enough to push himself too hard and get sick again. Then Roger would have to get him out on his own.'

There was a long pause. Footsteps crunched through the snow outside, and the zip on the tent door rasped open. Alex's unkempt mop of hair and pale face were thrust through the gap.

'I've come to tell you you've *got* to come climbing. You're a climber, not a tourist!'

'It's okay, youth, I've already decided that.'

Alex looked from Doug to me, and back again in surprise. Clearly he had not reckoned on the two of us coming up with that answer.

One by one we drifted back to the dubious comforts of the cookshelter. Nick was in residence, making pancakes. Delicious though they were, their manufacture had been dominating the use of every stove and utensil for the past two hours, and Roger and I found that our attempts to start a meal and brew for five people were floundering under a welter of sticky pots and spoons. Roger's impatience erupted into something between a howl and a snarl.

'Hungry climbers have been known to *kill*, you know!'

Nick scuttled out of the kitchen and retreated to his tent.

Chuckling to himself, Roger settled into a session of pot-washing.

Alex had been listening to the latest events in the Falklands crisis on the crackly reception of his powerful long-wave radio. He turned off the wheezing static and reached over for some vegetables to peel. Looking across the clutter of pots and pans at me, half puzzled, half amused, he said, 'I don't understand you. You're so serious about everything. I mean, girls I know can really get into things and enjoy themselves. Some of them went down to the Costa Brava last year – they were on the beach all day, then out for drinks and discos in the evening, picking up blokes, getting laid when they felt like it. They knew how to have a *good time*.'

I grinned. 'I'd find that as boring as you'd probably find learning Tibetan.'

Alex shook his head. 'We're just different. I don't understand you.'

I wondered why he had even stopped to consider it when his single-minded concentration on the summit of Shishapangma seemed to have erased all else from his thoughts. And yet, for all Alex's bluster, there was a more sensitive side to his personality – a side he was trying to push away before it blunted the driving edge of his ambition. It was not me he found disturbing, but the reflection he saw in me of that part of himself he was afraid might slow him down. His harsh words on the slopes of Nyenang Ri had not quite succeeded in concealing his genuine concern for Nick's safety on the mountain. It was this concern that had prompted him to wait for me on the moraine slope when I was ill with dehydration – while Doug, overtly the most sensitive member of the group, had managed to go on convincing himself I was just being moody. Alex's pragmatism made him fully aware of the responsibilities involved in bringing less able climbers into extreme situations. His impatience with Doug's attitudes stemmed partly from the fact that, while Doug's open generosity prompted him to invite people along, he did not share Alex's sense of responsibility in making sure they were not courting disaster for themselves or others once they were there. I was glad they would be climbing together, now these complications were out of the way.

The persistent snow seemed to be easing and plans were under way to leave Base Camp the following morning; they would go to Advance Base with Nick ferrying loads, and I would descend to Nyalam. About mid-afternoon I wandered back into the cookshelter to find Alex and Roger peeling potatoes to take to Advance Base. They were conversing in falsetto voices and giggling. This seemed a little odd until I noticed the almost-empty vodka bottle on the table.

'Come in, dearie,' squeaked Roger. 'We've cooked you a nice chapati!'

A rubbery chapati flew, frisbee-like, in my direction. I fled.

Doug found me later in my tent. 'They're pissed!' I don't know why he should sound so surprised.

'I know. I can't cope, that's why I'm here!'

That evening the chapati was being referred to as 'Alex's brain' and was being passed around for re-programming.

The weather played its usual fickle tricks on us by producing a violent thunderstorm, orchestrated with wind and avalanches. Spindrift filled the kitchen and lurid flashes of lightning illumined the shambles of our camp.

And then, towards midnight, everything calmed and the new snow settled in the stillness. The clouds melted away and a clear, cold light etched the blue-black mountains around us sharp against a pale sky.

Morning brought a flurry of activity as everyone crammed essentials and non-essentials into rucksacks. Mine was heavier than I had intended, mainly because of the heavy tomes of Tibetan grammar – all crammed in with socks, tsampa and canisters of film. Goodbyes were hurried as a cold wind brought fresh flurries of snow and precluded lingering conversations. The four climbers set off up the moraine slope, Roger leaving a linear trail with his skis.

I grabbed a last brew in the deserted cooktent, then covered the stoves and food. A raven settled on the rubbish heap, ignoring me.

Plunging into the untracked powder snow I set off downhill. I skirted the frozen lake, then turned and looked back for the last time, scanning the ridge above. A tiny figure on the skyline stopped and waved, then was gone.

PART TWO

The Desert

Whatever you can do, or dream you can, begin it . . .

Goethe

6

Into Exile

I stood on the crest of the lower moraine, looking down into the empty valley. Black, snow-veined rock rose out of the tumbled scree slopes, to be swallowed up in swirling grey cloud. The memory of the shimmering gold plateau beyond the mountains seemed a mocking illusion out here in this vast cold cauldron of snow and shattered rock, echoing to the heavy rumble of thunder which heralded more snow to come. It occurred to me that no one else had made this journey alone. Even Paul had gone down accompanied by Wu. This thought seemed to make the mountains grow in size all around me, until I was no more than an insignificant speck floundering through the soft powder snow that blanketed the great empty arena. Yet even this perception brought only a momentary stab of fear, which was immediately replaced by an even greater surge of exhilaration and excitement. I had been confined in Base Camp too long, mentally pacing the intangible restraints which had kept me there. Now I was free, and for the moment, at least, no environment could seem too hostile.

The crest of the lateral moraine was far more undulating than I remembered. The lee side of the dips had drifted deeply in the up-valley wind, forcing me to struggle thigh-deep on each uphill section. The downhill parts were easy, being almost blown clear of snow, but there seemed precious few of them for a downhill journey.

I stopped to rest before the last long descent to the river. The heavy snow had changed the landscape dramatically since our journey here, and I could not be sure I was following the route we had used previously. I was simply relying on a general sense of direction, and picking my way between the rocks and cliffs on the hillside. As I stared absently down the slope, my eyes suddenly strained to focus on the boulder-strewn expanse of whiteness. I could have sworn one of the rocks was blue. Couldn't be. Then it moved.

'Wu!' I yelled into the cold air.

It moved again, and the boulder next to it came to life and stood up. I slithered down the slope, aching legs and heavy rucksack temporarily forgotten. Wu looked exhausted. He had spent the night at Pemba's hut, and then asked Nyima, who had been staying there to cook for Pemba, to carry his pack. Nyima bounded over, looking like a demented rabbit, woolly ear-flaps of his hat tucked up at an erratic angle. Wu handed me a note from Paul.

> Elaine
> I'm leaving on a truck for Lhasa today. Replies from telegrams don't look too promising, I'm afraid. Authorities in Lhasa said no problem, go where you like at local rates, and then the reply came from Peking – members must only travel as they did with the expedition. So much for the autonomy of the Autonomous Region! I'm off back to Delph as fast as I can. Good luck with your travels, and don't forget what I said about finding a rich husband and settling down. Still, I suppose you'll end up living in a mud hut with a poon!
>
> All the best
> Paul

I grinned as I stuffed the letter in my pocket. It was good to see Paul's sense of humour surviving the disappointment of having to quit. Wu was looking concerned.

'It will be difficult for you to explain your situation in Nyalam

One of many meetings – Doug, Jigme, Nick, Wu and Pemba.

Ruins of the old village of Nyalam.

Dawa and Pema outside their house.

Chozom carding wool.

without an interpreter. I have to take these letters to Base Camp so I cannot accompany you.'

I suggested he write a letter in Chinese explaining that I had to return to Lhasa because I was not acclimatising, and sat on a rock for a while watching him, a tiny figure hunched over his writing, alone in an expanse of whiteness and black boulders. It was somehow incongruous, as if his picture had been superimposed on the background as an afterthought. He handed me the letter, shook my hand, and turned and plodded up the hill after Nyima.

By the time I reached the river I knew Pemba had seen me. He was waiting by the battered door of the hut as I approached, and handed me a tin can of salt tea as he waved me inside his temporary home. The sooty interior was full of smoke. As my eyes adjusted to the gloom, I began to notice the hoard of aluminium bowls, crates of eggs, cans of meat and numerous other commodities which had failed to reach Base Camp. Pemba read Wu's letter with difficulty, then countersigned it. I put it carefully in my pocket, as this was all I had by way of travel authorisation while in Tibet.

'You should stay here for the night. Nyalam is too far.'

'I'll be fine, thank you.'

I had no desire to spend any more time than necessary in this squalid hovel. I ducked outside the low door and heaved my rucksack on to my back. Its weight seemed to increase with my tiredness. A hundred yards past the hut I paused by the bridge across the river. It comprised only a single log between the boulders either side of the water, angled downwards as the boulder on the far bank was somewhat lower. The river spread out in wide shallows above the bridge, and it looked possible to wade across even though the waters had been swollen by the recent snow. The sloping log looked wet and slippery, and the river swirled in a deep green pool beneath it. Still, it seemed foolish to get soaked wading across when there was a bridge to use. Having made what was possibly one of the worst decisions of my life, I set off cautiously across the log. I was almost across when my foot slipped. My pack pulled me backwards, but I almost managed to recover my balance by sitting down quickly, partly on the end of the log and partly on the boulder at the far side. I was about to congratulate myself on my quick reactions, thinking I had got away with the mistake, when I suddenly realised that my pack was still off balance and was slowly tipping over, pulling me head first into the river. Even as I gripped the log with desperately aching fingers I was vaguely aware that, again, my reaction was the wrong one. I should have released the waistband of the pack and wriggled out of it. Yet if I let go of the log I would fall immediately and not have time to get out of the pack. The thought grew in my mind of how unbelievably heavy the pack had become once it had gone off-balance – and then there was nothing but icy water and confusion.

Swimming-pool experience had taught me that when you fall into deep water you have only to wait and your head will break the surface. Then you know which way up you are and can begin to rescue yourself. The more I waited the more this did not happen, and my lungs were screaming that I had held my breath too long. Into the panic and confusion came a quiet voice telling me to stop struggling and *think*. In the stillness that followed I became aware that I was lying face-down – and that my pack had shunted forward and was holding my head under the water. Even with this knowledge my efforts were not enough to shift it. The pack was just too heavy. I found it required too much concentration at this stage to work at unfastening the waistbelt while I was consciously reminding myself not to breathe. Eventually I managed to roll over on to my back, with the pack underneath, and breathe again. This first priority over, it then became possible to scramble out. I had been close to drowning within three feet of the bank.

I sat down in a snowdrift, oblivious of the falling snow, and tried to force my mind to assess the situation. Although various bits of equipment which had been slung over the pack or my shoulder had disappeared in the river, the camera Doug lent me to complement my own was still intact, but, of course, soaking wet. For some reason my mind became focused on a deep concern for the camera, and the fact that new batteries were unavailable in Tibet. I carefully unscrewed the battery compartment and began to wipe the batteries with a piece of wet tissue from my pocket. I was interrupted in my concentration by a strange rattling around my ears. It took me a few minutes to realise that my wet hair had frozen in the blizzard and that lumps of ice were clattering together in the wind. Gradually it dawned on my dazed mind that perhaps I had got my priorities wrong, and that a functional camera might not be of much use to someone who has just died of hypothermia. Dry clothes might be a good idea. There were unlikely to be any in my pack. Maybe I should head straight for Nyalam. I stood up and started walking.

After a few paces I stopped. Something was wrong. The river seemed to be flowing uphill. Suddenly the internal warning signals started flashing, and with a sense of almost physical shock I realised just how stunned and disorientated my body and mind were from the fall, the water and the numbing cold. The only way to survive in this twilight valley of snowdrifts and blizzard would be to spend the night at Pemba's hut, however unsavoury it might be. I headed back across the tundra.

Pemba didn't look particularly surprised to see me.

'Told you it was snowing. Soup's on.'

Nyima had returned from Base Camp and was tending a pot of noodle soup over a smoky fire. His efforts at cooking were not much more impressive than his yak-handling, but the hot soup he handed to me in a jagged tin can was the best thing I had seen all day.

Pemba seemed glad of the company, and was unusually cheerful and talkative. Perhaps even he was beginning to find his solitary vigil rather boring. Between noisy gulpings of soup, he gave an elaborate account of his part in the Chinese ascent of Everest in 1975. Most of the details were lost on me, but it seemed that (in Pemba's opinion at least) he was one of the stronger members of the team, and had reached 8,000 metres on the mountain.

I found my attention drifting away, musing on side issues such as the speed with which Pemba's arthritis must have got worse since 1975 if he could now walk no farther than two hours out of Nyalam along a flat valley bottom. He had become involved with climbing and the CMA after helping to transport loads for the 1960 Everest expedition, and I wondered if he was aware of the controversy and scepticism with which the news of that ascent had been received in the West. None of their descriptions of the mountainside had been consistent, either with each other or with the descriptions of previous parties. The official report (under the name of Shi Zanchun, our host at the CMA) had been taken up mainly with the heroics of the climbers and the power of Chairman Mao's homilies to move them up the mountain – and, of course, the political significance of this unimpeachable and spectacular feat. It was not until the 1975 photographs appeared in Western journals that it became clear that there was in fact a correlation with the earlier account. What emerged was that a genuinely remarkable ascent had been cast into doubt by the propagandists who re-wrote Shi Zanchun's original report. The crux of the problem appeared to be that the climbers had placed a plaster bust of Chairman Mao and the Chinese national flag somewhat below the summit and covered them with stones before continuing to the summit proper. Presumably not wishing their national emblems to be anywhere less than the summit, the propaganda writers had transferred this event to the summit itself – an unconvincing statement, as the summit of Everest is a perpetual glacial cap, without a rock in sight! It seemed ironic that they had not allowed their true achievement to speak for itself.

Pemba was still talking. Between spells as Liaison Officer, his job was to instruct other climbers. He also had a farm near Shigatze, where his wife and two children lived. He had money in the bank and a radio, and thought he was much better off than his parents who, he said, had not been free to leave their farm, and had to give half their crop to the landlord. His father had owned some yaks which had eaten the landlord's barley crop, whereupon the irate owner beat him so severely that he died of his injuries. Things were very bad after that, and Pemba repeated that he considered himself to be better off now he was working with the Chinese.

I looked around the squalor of the hut, barely visible in the flickering light of the smoky fire, and then at the piles of food and equipment stashed against the walls. It was clear that Pemba was planning to make himself quite a profit at the end of the expedition. What amazed me was that he seemed content to live in such appalling conditions in order to do so. Base Camp had been primitive, but it was pristine compared to this place. I smiled as I remembered the team's complaints about the stink of the yak drivers. No one would use the tent they had slept in because the smell clung to the canvas. I have never found the odour of soot and animals particularly offensive and spent hours practising Tibetan with the patient Namgyal, oblivious of the others' derogatory comments. This place reeked of things far worse. It seemed best to try to sleep through it.

It was a cold and unhappy night. My books and film had stayed dry, packed tightly in the middle of the clothes in my pack. Everything else was wet, including my sleeping bag. It was said of Milarepa that the power of his meditation was so strong that he was able to sit all night by the side of a frozen lake and dry out successive wet shirts by his own body heat. I wondered grumpily how he would have got on with a wet pile suit, long underwear, wool sweater and sleeping bag. Certainly it was beyond my capabilities, and I awoke next morning stiff and cold, my damp clothes clinging to my aching body. Slowly, I began to shuffle around and pack. Pemba watched me with curiosity.

'You got really wet in that snowstorm, eh?'

I didn't tell him about the river. It would only mean another lecture on not wandering around on my own. Nyima was going back to Nyalam and said he would walk with me. The bridge was now dry and not difficult, but I avoided looking down as I crossed. I paused on the far side, feeling as if my gaze was being drawn back to that swirling green pool against my will. I tried to push aside the mental picture of a bloated body lying half-submerged in the icy water. It was still too soon to be able to admit how close I had been to death.

The morning sun and the brisk pace began to dry my clothes and ease the deep, aching cold from my limbs. I even felt optimistic about my chances of seeing something of Tibet before being whisked back to Peking. Just before the Nyalam hydroelectric plant we came to the first yak-herders' huts in the valley above the village. Two girls were spreading laundry out to dry on the grass beside the hut. As we approached they dropped the clothes and jumped on the dog, which was making it quite clear that it would dearly like to tear Nyima and me limb from limb. They waved us into the hut, while the dog snarled at us from under their skirts.

Inside the smoky room, the girls' mother was stoking a brazier with dried yak-dung chips. A younger sister handed us tea in china cups. The two girls came inside and served out boiled potatoes from the pot on the brazier. It was so good to eat fresh boiled potatoes again, after weeks of dried food at Base Camp.

The family were relatives of Nyima's. They lived in Nyalam, but had recently come up with the yaks for the spring grazing. While Nyima was providing them with graphic tales of the snow higher up the valley the baby started to squall from its huddle of blankets in the corner. Nyima leaned over and stuck a piece of candy into its mouth, and it went back to sleep with the end of the toffee still protruding. I wondered if it would choke, lying flat on its back like that, but its mother seemed unconcerned.

The advent of spring had done little to change the appearance of Nyalam. In the shady corners the heaps of snow might have been a little smaller and greyer, and perhaps the mud in the streets was deeper and wetter. The commune workers went about their business as usual, all looking much alike in their uniforms of bulky blue or khaki denim, cropped hair covered by matching caps. I found the Commune Leader cleaning out the municipal drains with a bucket and a shovel, an impressive example of the equality of the proletariat. He straightened his back and gave me a toothy smile of welcome. I handed him Wu's letter, still damp and crinkly from its soaking in the river, and he smiled again and nodded enthusiastically, assuring me in sing-song Chinese that there would be a truck to Lhasa tomorrow morning. This information was translated into Tibetan by a helpful passer-by, who was then sent off to find the key to the village guest room.

It started to rain, and a woman came out of a nearby house

and invited me inside. The single whitewashed room was little different from the other rooms I had seen in Nyalam, with its small electric ring for cooking, a single bed, a wooden table and a couple of tea-chests for storage. News travelled fast, and before I was half-way through my cup of salt tea a number of people had squeezed themselves into the small room to look at the stranger.

The babble of chatter and questions fell silent as one of the village officials bustled into the room, waving a bunch of keys. He gave me a 'you-shouldn't-be-here' look and hustled me out of the door. My room was just across the street, and yet, from that moment on, a barrier had fallen between me and the village. Nobody came to see me except the two girls, Metok and De'chen, who brought my food and came back later to collect the dishes. People I met in the street would nod politely and then hurry past to go about their business. Perhaps the village officials were, after all, a little uneasy about the fact that Peking had ruled Nyalam out of bounds for foreigners. If so, the lure of making a few *yuan* on the side still proved the stronger motivation, as I was to discover the following morning.

I packed my half-dry belongings into my rucksack and wandered out into the street to look for the Leader. After twenty minutes of futile searching, I was informed that he had gone to a political meeting in Shigatze. His deputy, a tall thin Tibetan whose shapeless denims hung loosely from his bony limbs, shuffled his feet uneasily.

'Ah, there is no truck to Lhasa today. There will be one tomorrow.'

It was no good demanding to know how the Leader had gone to Shigatze if there was no transport. There were trucks rumbling up the road every few hours, but the system decreed that the local officials had to authorise transport, and therefore it was entirely their decision how long I would be kept here. Much as I wanted to see Tibet, I had already seen more than enough of this particular corner of it. I hoped they had no plans to keep me here until the others came down off the mountain.

Back in the whitewashed four walls of my room I unpacked again and finished drying my belongings over the lethally-wired electric ring which sat on the concrete floor. I felt confined and restless, constrained from wandering around the village by the fact that Nyalam was supposed to be out of bounds to foreigners. I was aware that, on their return, the expedition could be penalised for any misbehaviour on my part, and that Base Camp was still very close, with an antagonistic Liaison Officer near by. It was better to avoid making too much of a scene about demanding transport out.

De'chen arrived to collect the dishes, and delivered a lecture on the benefits of eating plenty and becoming strong and healthy. My gaze wandered from her to the untouched meal without enthusiasm. Spinach and meat, boiled for hours in soy and served in grimy bowls with a grey-brown scum around the inside, reposed greasily on the table.

'*Shim-bu mindu.*'

My expression must have lent weight to my words because she removed the offending food without further protest. The food I had eaten so far in Nyalam had inflicted a mild bout of food-poisoning which was necessitating more visits than I cared to make to the commune lavatory. The spring weather served only to increase the stink, and the place was crawling with large white maggots.

Four days later, I was still being assured that there would be a truck 'tomorrow'. Judging by appearances the food had not improved, and I felt disinclined to test it beyond visual inspection. With luck, my supply of tsampa could be eked out until I left. I was getting bored. Somehow I could not settle to any reading with the knowledge that I just might be leaving the following day. Throwing caution to the winds, I took myself for a walk round the old part of the village.

The buildings were in ruins. Here and there a room remained intact, perched on half-standing walls, surrounded by the crumbling shells of other rooms – places of security and privacy now exposed to the elements and the public gaze. People were still living among the ruins. Buckets and utensils stood outside doorways whose empty gape was covered by pieces of ragged blanket. The whole place was being systematically demolished, and the stones were being used to build a new village a little to the south of the old one. The village gompa had been cut in half, and the surviving portion, which was about the size of two houses, was being used as a wood store. I followed the sound of hammering up on to the half-finished roof of one of the new houses. A group of carpenters perched on the wooden slats, hammering the joists into place. They looked up and greeted me in Nepali. Surprised, I asked them where they were from, and learned that their homes were in Barabise, about forty kilometres over the border. They were brought in by bus, and would stay for three weeks of carpentry and roofing before being transported back again. The Tibetan foreman explained proudly that they were rebuilding the village with wide streets so that large trucks could drive between the houses. No, he said, they were not going to rebuild the gompa. When they had no more use for it as a wood store they would pull it down and use the materials.

I looked at the new street that was emerging from the rubble. The houses had Tibetan architectural features, such as the shape of the windows and doors, but the basic concept was that of Chinese commune buildings, with single-room units opening on to a common street. The traditional Tibetan houses were an extended-family complex of rooms and interconnecting courtyards surrounded by a high wall. I scrambled down from the roof and picked my way through the rubble in the new street. An old woman was walking back to her house, carrying a brightly painted Chinese vacuum flask. She looked me up and down with curiosity, glanced over her shoulder, then invited me in for tea.

The ground floor of the house would have been a stable in a traditional home, but there were no animals in this one, just neatly stacked rows of dried yak-dung for fuel. The steep, ladder-like stairs led to the single first-floor living room. The walls were papered with Chinese newspapers and brightly coloured 'Progress of the People's Republic' posters. Tibetan houses I had visited in Nepal all contained an elaborate household altar and several pictures of the Dalai Lama and other senior lamas, each draped with a white katak (a sort of ceremonial scarf made of silk or cotton). I could see nothing like that in this room. Then, in a dark corner, I noticed a small framed picture of Chairman Mao. It was draped in a white katak.

I wondered if I would ever get used to the spontaneous hospitality of the Tibetans – even those obviously a little cautious about official disapproval. Presumably everyone was as curious about me as I was about them and their changing lifestyles. We talked families and houses for a while, then I asked my hostess if she knew anything about Dopa-puhk, Milarepa's cave. She had heard of neither, she said, and seemed no more interested in them than had Metok and De'chen when I had asked them the same question yesterday. This village was erasing its past, stone by stone, and mind by mind.

I was careful to avoid political discussions with anyone, as refugees I had spoken to in India and Nepal had been emphatic that it would be either meaningless or dangerous. They had described the indoctrination process which the Chinese used to win the Tibetans over to their point of view. Each member of a community had to attend regular political meetings, where they stood up in turn and made a speech about how cruelly the old system had treated them and how wonderful it was to have been liberated by the Red Army. Those not expressing enough vehemence were accused of being reactionaries and were subjected to *thamzing*, or 'struggle meeting'. Basically, this entailed being handcuffed and beaten up by their family and friends, who had to display great enthusiasm for this task on pain of being denounced in turn and subjected to the same treatment. All I could expect to hear from Tibetans was great praise for the Communist system and the Chinese liberators. Anyone expressing criticism would run the risk of being overheard and reported to the authorities. I was suspicious that the exiles' stories were exaggerated, or perhaps out of date, but at the same time it seemed unfair to risk other people's safety for the sake of political conversations.

I found myself hoping that the blasts of loudspeaker songs

and speeches were now the only methods of persuasion. At first I was surprised that no one seemed to object to this strident assault on their ears. But then, people tend to get used to anything that happens regularly over a long period. I perceived Chinese propaganda as crude only because I was unused to it. That of my own country was tuned to the habits and senses of the population at which it was aimed, and I had become as oblivious of its presence as the Tibetans appeared to be of theirs.

It was hard to tell if it was my repeated requests or my excursion round the village which prompted official action. That evening the deputy Leader knocked politely on my door. In order to reassure me about the morning's transport, he would take me down and show me this very evening. A truck and a bus were parked on a dusty patch of ground by the roadside, next to the barrels of gasolene stored for refuelling. Both were going to Lhasa the following morning at ten o'clock. The bus was carrying returning Khampa exiles on a visit to their families in eastern Tibet. A few of the visitors were hanging around by the bus, hands in their pockets and shoulders hunched against the chill evening breeze. One of them sauntered over to where we were standing.

'Hello. Where are you going?' There was hardly a trace of true Tibetan accent in his flawless English.

'I'm trying to get to Lhasa but there seems to be a shortage of transport,' I replied drily, for the benefit of the deputy Leader.

'Our bus is going to Shigatze and Lhasa before heading out east to Kham. You are most welcome to travel with us as far as Lhasa.'

My escort may have spoken no English, but the young Khampa's expansive wave of the hand towards the bus left little to the imagination. He interrupted hastily.

'Oh, that won't be necessary. We have already made arrangements for you to travel in the truck. It will be more comfortable for you. Now come.'

He turned and headed back towards the village, motioning me to follow him. I smiled wryly at how the official concern for tourists' comfort switched from trucks to buses and back again, depending on what happened to suit their current policy. Back in the village I turned down a side street, then doubled back to where the vehicles were parked. Gyatso, the young Khampa, was still lounging by the bus. He grinned as I approached.

'I'm surprised they let you out with undesirables like us hanging around.'

'They really don't seem to want tourists fraternising with visiting refugees.'

'They basically don't want anybody fraternising with anyone else. I went round the village just now, to try to buy some meat for supper. I went into a house and started talking to the old lady who lived there – and she was quite frightened. She said, "You shouldn't be here! We'll both get into trouble, so you should leave now." So I left. And I had to come back here with no meat.' He made a wry face. 'We had to wait twelve days at the border for a Chinese bus to take us to Lhasa. The food they gave us was terrible, so we were hoping to cook our own now we are here. I don't suppose the prepared food is any better in Nyalam.'

I laughed. 'It's not very good. Everything that's been shipped in from China seems to be so stale. Perhaps you just can't make Chinese food with what's available here.'

'The Chinese won't eat much of what's locally available anyway, such as yak produce or barley. But I think the food preparation is bad because nobody cares. You get paid the same however much or little you work, and if you try hard you'll achieve nothing if someone else on the team is slacking. I don't really remember Tibet because I was only a small child when my parents carried me across the Himalaya to India, but my parents' stories gave me the impression that people were much better off before the Chinese came than what I've been seeing here so far. Maybe homesickness glamorises their memory, but I'm sure if things had been fine they wouldn't have gone to all the trouble and hardship of trying to escape.'

I thought of Pemba's story.

'Our Liaison Officer reckons he's much better off now he's working with the Chinese. He also said he didn't understand why so many Tibetans ran away, because the Chinese didn't do all the dreadful things that were expected of them.'

'I'm sure he'd like to believe that now he's working for them. As a child I listened to so many stories from my family and friends of the torturing and killing they had witnessed in Tibet before they fled. Why make up grisly details of your uncle being flayed alive if it wasn't true? Why risk dying from cold or starvation in the mountains if there wasn't something worse behind you? Many of my friends in India had received "re-education" in Peking and returned as cadres in the commune system. But even they lived with the fear that if they did not constantly spy on and accuse their fellow-Tibetans, they in turn would be denounced for harbouring "attitudes against the Motherland". Then we hear broadcasts from Lhasa, "Refugees come back, all is forgiven." How can we trust that?'

I said, 'Maybe it is changing, though. The official line seems to be that all that was due to the mistakes of the Gang of Four. They say they are allowing religious freedom again, and after all, here you are, back on a visit to your relatives.'

He shrugged. 'Maybe I'm being unreasonably suspicious. But it only needs a change in the government and all those who have aired their views or practised religion could be rounded up and imprisoned or shot. It's just a change of policy to them, but it's life or death for us. I'm inclined to stay in India and see how things develop. If the Dalai Lama thinks it's safe to go back, then a lot of Tibetans would follow his example.'

I had the feeling that he had been through this conversation before, no doubt with Western visitors to India. I asked the inevitable question.

'Is Buddhism still important to the Tibetans who now live abroad?'

'In many ways even more so than it was before. For most refugees, it was all they had. They had lost all their land and possessions, and many had lost their families as well. The only way they could come to terms with it was to recognise that this freedom from material and human attachments gave them a better opportunity to practise the spiritual path. Spiritual happiness has always been the ideal for Tibetans, but people being what they are, it's so easy to get distracted! I've had a good education, a Western education – but I don't find any contraditions. I feel that everything I've learned confirms what Buddhism taught me. Personally, I feel that gives me a stronger conviction than if I had grown up in Old Tibet, where people tended to accept blindly what the lama told them. I'd like to talk to the commune workers here at length, and find out what they really think, but I'm afraid of getting myself into trouble. I'm sure they'd be in trouble too if they said anything controversial.'

It was getting dark, and I turned to go.

'Don't forget, there's room on the bus if the truck doesn't work out.'

'Thanks. Have a good journey.'

The following morning I packed my rucksack for the fourth time and was out in the street before nine o'clock. The deputy Leader was talking to a group of khaki-clad workers outside the commune offices. An uncomfortable silence fell as I approached. The deputy began to walk back towards the offices, but I headed him off.

'There is no truck today. Tomorrow.'

I looked down towards the road. The dusty refuelling area was empty.

'But you said. . . '

He gave a gesture of impatience. 'Tomorrow.'

'No!' I wailed. 'It's too much. Your food is making me sick, and all you do is tell lies. . . '

People were drifting over to see what all the commotion was about. There was much head-shaking and clucking of tongues. I looked around from one blank face to another.

Then I walked out.

7

Yak Herders

The road looped around a rocky bluff. I turned and took a last look at the village. The dark figures were still standing watching me. Then I was round the corner and the village was out of sight.

The arid hillsides shimmered with colour against the flawless blue sky. A lammergeier soared on the updraught, and my spirit went with it, until in my mind I could see the horizon stretching away to the dust haze of the distant plateau.

Freedom . . . I had been in my 'cell' for only five days and had even been able to go out a little . . . what must it be like to be roaming the hills after months or even years in prison? My thoughts went back to Heinrich Harrer, and I understood why he had undergone such hardships to escape the internment camp and cross the Himalaya into Tibet. Then the magic of the people and the mountains caught him, and his wanderings continued for a different reason.

Some nomads were approaching me, driving their yaks before them with calls and whistles. The yaks ambled down the road, their hoofs stirring up a great cloud of ochre dust which settled in their shaggy hair. A man walked over and greeted me.

'Where are you going?'

'Pankyeling. How far is it?'

He frowned, then held up two fingers.

'Two hours, maybe three. Stop and have some food with us.'

I saw two women setting up rocks for a kitchen, with a battered, sooty pot perched on top of them. Two children were scurrying around in the scrub collecting firewood. It was tempting: good food and good company were things I had sadly missed these last few days. But my desire to reach Pankyeling before pursuit from Nyalam reached me was even greater. Regretfully, I declined and walked on.

The road was quite steep, twisting its way up the narrow valley, perched a hundred feet above the boulder-strewn river. I walked easily, with the euphoria of freedom and the light-headedness of starvation. Groups of peasants working in fields perched among the craggy outfalls of the mountains would call and wave, then bend again to their labours.

Then, at a bend in the road, I reached the tiny village of Pankyeling. I stopped, and looked around for signs of the gompa. There was nothing, not even a broken wall. The village was so small, and the rocky area around it so open, there was no place any ruins could be concealed. I scanned the rubble-strewn crags above, but if there was a cave there it would take weeks of searching among the broken rocks to find it. In any case, what would identify it now? A long-disused hole in the mountain, half-filled with dirt and rubble, probably forgotten by the people who lived here. I turned away, disappointed. Milarepa belonged to another world which had vanished for ever.

I walked on, my footsteps muffled by the heavy dust. Half an hour later I was looking across the valley to a village which I supposed might be Tashigong and, behind it, to the high pass through the mountains which led to Chuwar, the place of pilgrimage. This way would be too steep and ice-bound for me to attempt it alone. Or were my vision and judgment being affected by the growing conviction that there would be nothing to find when I arrived? Why was I going there anyway? Could it be that I was searching, not for the stupa, but for the intangible something that the pilgrims could see and I could not?

This was no time to sit in reflection and self-searching. I was convinced that sooner or later the authorities would be driving out of Nyalam to look for me. Retribution must surely come to officials who lose valuable tourists. I had tasted freedom, and decided it was too good to give up. I found myself scanning the crags and boulders that towered above the road, looking for a place to hide if I spied the tell-tale dust cloud of pursuit far back down the valley. I tried to convince myself I was being childish and melodramatic. Whatever it was inside me that had prompted my sudden and irrational departure from the village had also decided it was not going back. No matter that the very idea of walking all the way to Shigatze was as ridiculous as it was impractical. Something would turn up.

Meanwhile the effects of walking almost twenty miles after five days on starvation rations were beginning to make themselves felt. To my left a valley wound into the mountains, to lose itself in the snowfields of the Shishapangma massif. In this valley, about half a mile from the road, was a tiny village. The possibility of food and shelter away from the highway was inducement enough. I turned away from the road and stumbled across the rocks and tussocks towards the houses.

Some peasants were working in the fields, chipping away at the dusty soil with crude hoes. Their greeting was encouraging, and I walked on, falling into step with a plump girl returning home after her day's work, her hoe and spade hoisted over her shoulder.

'*Tashideleg*.'

'Ooh ... ' She ducked her head, giggling from shyness, and skipped to the far side of the village street to continue her walk.

The walls of the courtyards and houses were built of the alluvial rocks brought down by the glacier-fed river that swept down this valley from Shishapangma. My friends were up there, somewhere in the snow and cloud. What were they doing? Were they still alive? I lacked the energy for such large speculation, and followed the plump girl into the courtyard of one of the houses, where the stone walls were plastered with round yak-dung pancakes drying in the sun.

'Ooh ... ' She just stood and stared at me, and a young man came out of the dark doorway and stared also.

'*Cha du*'?' I asked hopefully. It was very evident I was still in the region which had previously been closed to all Westerners, because they both continued to stare in amazed silence at the strange yellow-haired monster that was sitting in their front yard demanding tea.

Then the spell was broken; the young man regained his composure with a visible effort as the tradition of hospitality took over.

'*Cha du*', *cha du*',' he insisted, nodding his head energetically and seizing my pack as he led me into the house. The sunlight was blotted out as the plump girl followed me through the doorway and I stopped, blind, in the darkness. She collided with me from behind, then with a shy giggle took my hand and led me through another doorway to an inner room lit by a tiny glassless window in one wall.

As my eyes adjusted to the gloom, I began to make out the rug-covered benches lining the walls, and the iron brazier standing beneath the smoke hole in the soot-festooned ceiling. There was no fire burning, and the room was chill. An old woman came in with an armful of dried yak chips which she began to poke into the brazier to prepare the evening fire. She nodded and smiled showing some surprise but not letting it interfere with her chores, and then motioned to me to sit on one of the benches, where my pack was placed carefully beside me. Then, while she lit the fire, the girl took a Chinese vacuum flask from one of the shelves lining the back wall and poured some salt tea for me.

'*Tsampa*?' she enquired, spooning it out of a cloth bag without waiting for an answer. The warm drink and the meal were welcome and I smiled my gratitude.

Another young man came in and joined us, smiling shyly and watching me. It was as if everyone was waiting for a full and detailed explanation of myself, which my exhaustion and limited Tibetan would not allow.

I told them my name, which they could not pronounce, and that I had come from Shishapangma via Nyalam, which they could not believe. Then they introduced themselves.

The old lady, *ama* (mother), was called Namgyal, the same

name as our yak driver. Tibetan names all have meanings and are good for either sex. Her two sons Pema and Dawa were the young men who were still surveying me with great curiosity; and the plump girl, Phurbu, was their *nama* (wife). *Nama* means literally 'daughter-in-law'; Tibetan tradition among farming families was to keep all the sons at home to work the land, and a girl from another family would come as *nama* and be married to all the brothers. It was a mark of status to win a girl from a socially superior family as the household's *nama*. She would use her higher status to keep the boys in order: the success or failure of the husbands as farmers and members of the community would be attributed to her influence. In larger families she would also seduce the younger brothers into the marital group as they reached puberty. There were alternatives for younger brothers – they could join a monastery or become traders. They could also marry a wife of their own, but to do this they must leave the household. Most Tibetans regarded the multiple marriage as the ideal situation. It was practical in that it kept the labour force together, avoided the division and impoverishment of the farms, kept the population stable, and embodied the Buddhist ideal of sharing.

Pema and Dawa were both considered to be fathers to Phurbu's child, a little imp called Tashi. He chose that moment to come running into the room at full speed and slither to a halt upon seeing me, before ducking behind his mother's skirts to view the stranger from a point of safety. Phurbu shooed him out from under her feet.

I wooed his friendship with peppermints from my pack. Cautious at first, he soon responded to my heavy bribery and was romping all over me, trying to peek into my pack for more goodies, examining my clothes and trying to steal my bootlaces. The atmosphere relaxed amid his uninhibited onslaught, and Phurbu clucked her tongue in disapproval while at the same time laughing at his antics.

'How old is he?'

'Eight.'

I had guessed five. The altitude and harsh climate stunts growth and ensures that only the toughest survive.

Pema and Dawa were admiring my boots. Sensing an opportunity to do some trading, I wriggled my feet out and passed the boots over for them to try on. Pema squeezed them eagerly on to his broad feet and strode about the room, rocking on his heels to admire them.

'Let me try yours,' I said, pointing to his discarded felt boots lying by the bench. He pushed them aside with an expression of horror.

'Oh no, they're much too smelly!'

Phurbu disappeared for a few moments and came back with a pair of unused boots of black and red felt.

'I made these,' she said, a little coyly.

I tried them on. Phurbu took the tapes binding her own boots, and bound the tops of my new boots around my calves. I joined Pema walking around the room to admire my new acquisition. They fitted, they looked good, I was going to keep them. Pema found it difficult to believe I really wanted to trade, and offered my boots back. Eventually he became convinced, with an expression of sympathy for my madness. Evidently he considered European boots to be far more valuable than the beautiful handmade felt *sompa* they had given me.

Then they wanted to see the rest of my things. I pulled out my down sleeping bag and fluffed it up.

'For sleeping on the mountain, in a tent.'

Dawa picked it up, weighing it in his hands, obviously impressed.

'He herds yaks up on Shishapangma,' said Purbu.

'I live in a tent a lot of the time,' added Dawa. 'I sleep in these.' He showed me the heavy woollen blankets he used against the frosty night air. Heavy, but with yaks to carry them they were a warmer and more reliable asset to a herder's life than fickle down, which is lethally useless when wet. Dawa either knew this or sensed it, for while he was curious and interested in the down bag, he made no offer to trade it for his trusty blankets.

Then came my few spare clothes. Tashi snatched my orange T-shirt and struggled into it, pulling it down over his one-piece suit of black homespun. When his head emerged he spied my green woollen hat, crammed it over his matted hair and went prancing about the room like a miniature clown, as irrepressibly naughty as all Tiblets seem to be. But curiosity got the better of him, and when he came back to see what else would appear he was caught and held struggling between my knees while I stripped him of his new-found finery. Shrieking with delight, he plunged his hands into the pack and dragged out a tangle of socks, gloves and underwear. Phurbu pounced before he could whisk it away.

She held up a pair of pink-flowered knickers, turning them over in her hands in obvious puzzlement.

How could I explain the use of an item so patently useless in this country? I held them against my hips and shrugged. She obviously considered them odd, but decorative. Socks and gloves had a function easily appreciated, less so the toothbrush, toothpaste, facecloth and soap, but she liked the smell. Then she found the Tampax, and I began mentally sifting through the Tibetan words I knew to explain that one, without making it appear to be some strange Western fertility rite, but was saved the trouble. A second pair of finger gloves had surfaced, and Phurbu was carefully trying them on, turning her hands this way and that to admire them, murmuring, 'You don't really need two pairs, do you?' So I gave them to her, confirming everyone's opinion that after already having given away my valuable boots, I did not value my valuable goods.

I began to stuff the assortment of clothing back into my pack. I happened to look across at Dawa and noticed that he was holding a pair of long socks and looking across at me wistfully. He was the only one without a present, so I told him to keep them, hoping I was not creating a legend in the region that all Westerners had so much wealth that they gave it all away at the first opportunity.

Phurbu straightened her hair, which had become untidied in the romp with Tashi. It was black and glossy, hanging in two long braids which she wound about her head. Braided into the hair, from crown to nape, was a string of turquoise and coral. This signifies that a girl is married, although it does not have great monetary value. The valuable jewellery is a necklace, or *gul-gyan*, which is given to a girl by her family when she marries and these days is usually worn inside her dress, out of sight.

'You are *nama*,' I said, touching the stones in her hair.

'Aren't you married? There is nothing in your hair.'

I took off the turquoise bracelet I had been wearing and handed it to her. Laughing, she braided it into my hair.

'Now you are *nama*, but you have no *magpa*. You could borrow Dawa. Or even Pema!'

The husbands were laughing too, and I joined in, noticing that Tibetan women seemed to have as ribald a sense of humour as their men. I wandered over to admire the weaving that was stretched on Phurbu's loom by the tiny window.

The hand-spun wool had been dyed with colours from plants collected from the mountainside. Then it had been woven into narrow stripes. The band of woollen material was about ten inches wide; Tibetan aprons are made from pieces of this striped material sewn together. Other clothes, such as tonga, the wrap-around dresses of the women, are sewn in a similar way from pieces of plain black homespun.

Pema had disappeared, and I wondered vaguely if he would be spreading the news of the foreign visitor. As I was not in a position to change my present situation in any way, I dismissed the thought as soon as it arrived.

Dawa was interested in England. He had never heard of it, but was determined to find out more about the country while I was here. I admired his ingenuity at forming questions; he was groping with a subject about which he had no background on which to base a line of inquiry. He was also very quickly learning to speak to me using the limited Tibetan vocabulary I knew.

'Where is England? Is it near India?'

'Further than India. Two days by plane.'

He still looked puzzled.

'One year walking.' This produced a response.

'That *is* a very long way!'

'I didn't walk. I came by plane.'

'Are there very many people in England?'

'Yes, many more than in Tibet.'

'Many cars and trucks?'

'Yes, almost everybody owns one car.'

'What are the houses like?'

'Ah, well, they're bigger than this, and there's a lot of *things* in them ... ' I found myself mentally preferring the friendly warmth of Dawa's house, and did not want him to feel I was saying that English houses were superior just because they were materially superior. '... England can be quite crowded and noisy sometimes.'

Dawa lapsed into silence to ponder the new information. I wondered what mental picture he was creating of a country he had never seen. From time to time I could hear him murmuring to himself, 'Eng-a-land ... Eng-a-land ... mmm ... ' He wandered outside and I could hear the clopping of hoofs and the soft snorts as he brought his horse into the outer room for the night.

Phurbu touched my arm to attract my attention.

'*Ching-pa*?' she asked.

That one was not in my Tibetan grammar book, so I shook my head and looked suitably puzzled. She appeared baffled that anyone could fail to understand such a simple question and looked across to Namgyal for help, but Namgyal's careful enunciation of the word produced no more understanding from their strange visitor. Now they were both giggling as they conferred as to the best way to explain. Finally, Namgyal hoiked up her skirts and squatted, making explicitly clear pissing noises, as both of them dissolved in uproarious laughter. I joined the merriment: well, it was a pretty basic question and Tibetan grammar books do not hold all the answers.

'Yes, okay, *ching*,' I agreed, when we had stopped giggling.

'I'll take you,' said Phurbu. 'There's a horse to go round now, and it's dark outside.'

She took my hand and guided me through the low doorways, past the horse and across the uneven cobbles. At the end of the little street was a small field.

'Here,' she announced, and I followed her example.

The stars were brilliant in the night sky, and on the way back to the house I caught sight of the dark shape of a ruined wall, black against the rocky skyline behind the village.

'Is that a gompa?'

'*Gompa mindu*',' she said, and walked back to the house. I could not tell from the inflection if she meant 'It never was a gompa', 'It isn't a gompa now', 'I don't know' or 'I don't want to talk about it'. So I changed the conversation to household matters.

'Did you make this tsampa?' I was finishing off the last of the tsampa they had given me.

'Yes, we grow it ourselves in the fields, then we grind it into tsampa.'

The ripe barley grains are roasted on hot sand until they burst before being ground into flour. Because it is already roasted, tsampa can be mixed with warm tea and eaten immediately. It is a tasty and practical food, and a staple of Tibetan diet.

Barley is a hardy enough grain to grow well at these altitudes. When the Chinese arrived in the early Fifties, they tried to replace the barley with wheat, which they preferred. The crops withered in the harsh climate, adding to the famines which had followed the wholesale export of grain to mainland China, to assuage the food shortages there. All across Tibet there was a massive mobilisation of labour to build irrigation schemes, and to utilise waste land and fallow fields. Chinese statistics showed that production quotas had actually risen, but because of exports, and the quantity required to feed the army of occupation, there was not enough left to feed the Tibetans themselves, and thousands starved. Listening to the stories of Tibetans in Nepal, it seemed that shortage of food had been as much the cause of their flight into exile as the purges of the Cultural Revolution. Seen in this light, the enthusiasm the Nyalam commune workers showed for the food on offer seemed far more understandable. Any food is better than no food. My refusal to eat it appeared by contrast as the mere fastidiousness of a spoiled Westerner.

Namgyal was adding more dried yak-dung to the brazier.

'Would you like to eat supper?' she asked.

Encouraged by my enthusiasm, she produced rice and chillies, and some potatoes. Dawa brought in a piece of dried goat meat and cut it up for the stew. With three of them to prepare the food, supper was soon boiling on the brazier. Tashi must have been hungry too, for he ceased his mischief and retreated to a quiet corner to let the adults get on with their work.

'What food do you eat in England?' asked Dawa.

'We have all these things; rice, potatoes and meat.'

'You mean the food is the *same*?'

'Some is the same, like these things. There are some other things too.' Not only the words, but also the concepts were lacking.

'We don't drink tea with salt and butter, we drink it with milk and sugar. And we don't have tsampa.'

'Eng-a-land ... mmm ...'

Dimly, I became aware of an increasing disturbance at the back of the room. The doorway was spawning a crowd of people surrounding a tall blue-clad Tibetan.

The authorities had arrived from Nyalam.

A plump young Tibetan emerged from the shadows into the firelight, distinguished from his companions by his build and well-fitting Western clothes. The Nyalam dignitaries and their driver hovered in the background, while the newcomer explained his presence. He was part of a second bus-load of visiting exiles, and on arriving in Nyalam had been requisitioned by the officials to act as interpreter.

'They are most worried, because you do not understand Tibetan very well, so you could not understand that you only needed to wait a few days and a truck would take you to Lhasa. It was quite unnecessary for you to leave on your own, and we have come to take you back to Nyalam.'

'No chance.'

'Beg pardon?'

'What they didn't tell you was that I've already been watching trucks go through that village for five days. There's no way they are going to let me get on one of those trucks if they can make a profit by keeping me in Nyalam. If I'm staying here, at no profit to them, you can be sure I'll be authorised on to the first vehicle out tomorrow morning.'

He paused, reassessing the situation. 'I think I am beginning to understand your problem. But I cannot very well express this opinion to the authorities.'

'You could suggest that it would be very embarrassing for them to have to explain why a visiting tourist came down with severe food poisoning.'

I noticed his hastily concealed smile of amusement. He must have tried the food as well. He paused again, mentally constructing the rephrasing required by translation and diplomacy. After a long discussion with his companions, he turned back to me.

'It may not be permitted for you to stay here. They would have to make special arrangements, not only with the authorities in Nyalam, but in this village as well. Otherwise the family may be punished.'

The bottom line. Why had I ever thought I could bargain with people who wielded this kind of power? I recalled the gruesome tales I had heard of the Cultural Revolution, and wondered with a shiver what kind of punishment was meted out to a family of hill farmers who gave shelter to a stranger. The debate resumed in the smoky shadows, and I tried to resign myself to being detained in Nyalam until the rest of the expedition returned from the mountain. Then, to my surprise, my interpreter turned to me again, with the news that the officials had agreed to arrange permission for me to stay where I was, and be picked up by truck the following morning.

'Are you sure the family will be all right?' I said.

'Don't worry,' he replied. 'I'll make sure they make all the necessary arrangements.' Then, more clearly, 'The truck will collect you here at seven tomorrow morning. The family will be responsible for making sure you get on it.'

The visitors got up and left, with scarcely a nod in my direction, and the room was quiet except for the crackle of the fire. The family busied themselves with preparing supper as if nothing had happened, while I struggled to find some kind of logic or pattern to the system in which I found myself. It seemed to me that everything was largely a battle of nerves: while the local authorities had almost total power in their own areas, they were still subordinate to the regional and national governments, and had little or no powers of coercion over me directly. This put them in a position to do as well as they could out of my presence, but they would back down rather than face a confrontation with a higher authority by which they might be found to be in the wrong. Therefore, I figured, they would be unlikely to punish the family if it might draw attention to their failure to provide transport requested by a Liaison Officer – a representative of the government in Peking. I hoped my logic was correct, for it was a heavy responsibility to know that my very presence could bring trouble to anyone who helped me.

I slept fitfully. Fear of missing the truck and bringing recriminations on my hosts tied a nervous knot in my stomach. We breakfasted before it was light. Pema kept watch outside for the arrival of the truck. Nine o'clock came and went, and I began to convince myself that I had been overlooked. Perhaps I could spend the day hiking up into the mountains with Dawa and the yaks. Then there was a grinding of gears on the road below, and Pema arrived, breathless, to grab my pack and hurry down ahead of me.

The driver, a smart young man sporting a leather jacket over his khaki drabs, was clearly annoyed.

'You're two hours late,' he snapped, looking ostentatiously at his watch.

The fact that he himself had only just arrived offended my sense of justice, but I managed to bite back my retort. Increasing his antagonism would not make my life any easier. The family and half the village stood and waved at the roadside as the truck lumbered off in a smother of dust and a belch of diesel fumes.

The dirt road climbed steeply, twisting and doubling back on itself to reach the summit of the 18,000-foot Thong La Pass. More and more barren hills came into view with each switchback, until it seemed that eventually all Tibet lay spread out below, with the Himalaya beyond forming a jagged, impregnable barrier of snow and ice. The account of this journey in

Milarepa's life-story had given no impression of the vastness of the distances involved. After his exploits as a black magician, he was forced to flee the wrath of the injured villagers.

> ... I fled quickly and ran to Nyenang [Nyalam]. Having been bitten in the leg by a dog I could not arrive on time at the meeting place. My companion reached Tingri ahead of me. He asked the keeper of the caravanserai if someone resembling a yogin had arrived. The keeper answered, 'He has not come. But all you so-called yogins are very fond of drinking. In the next village there is a beer banquet.' My companion went into the banquet hall and sat down beside me. He said, 'Why were you not at the meeting place yesterday?'
>
> 'Yesterday I went to beg. A dog bit my leg and I could not walk very fast ...'

The journey from Nyalam to Tingri would take the best part of a day by truck: to cover the forty miles in a day on foot might just be possible, but would be impressive by any standards. It was not until later in his life, as a by-product of intensive meditation, that Milarepa acquired *lung-gom*, the ability to cover several weeks' journey in a single day.

West from the pass, beyond the snow slopes of Shishapangma and the blue water of Peykhu Tso, lay the village of Kya Ngatsa in Gunthang, Milarepa's birthplace, and the beginning of his extraordinary story.

Milarepa came from a wealthy family, but his father died when he was seven, having entrusted the estate to his brother until his only son's majority at fifteen. The uncle and aunt abused the responsibility and seized the property for themselves, making Milarepa, his mother and his sister work for them as servants. They bore the hardship until Milarepa was fifteen, when they requested that the property be returned, according to the will. The uncle and aunt, becoming completely consumed by greed, denied the existence of any will and refused to part with anything. They continued to treat the family with immense cruelty. 'For clothes some strips of rags were thrown over our shoulders ... working without rest, our limbs became raw and sore. Due to bad food and poor clothing we grew pale and emaciated.'

Milarepa's mother became obsessed with hatred and a desire for revenge on their oppressors. Using her last secret hoard of money, she sent young Milarepa away to learn black magic so as to destroy the uncle and aunt and their family. Even at this tender age, it seemed that Milarepa was possessed of a single-minded determination to persevere at a given task until he succeeded. He studied for over a year until he had mastered the techniques he needed. On the day of the wedding feast of the uncle's eldest son, one of the servants 'did not see the many horses tied up in the stable, but instead she saw scorpions, spiders, snakes, toads and tadpoles. She saw a scorpion as big as a yak which grasped the pillars between its claws and tore them out. At this sight she fled, terrified.' The great house collapsed, killing thirty-five of the uncle's family who were inside. The uncle and aunt survived as they were out at the time, discussing the banquet and the speeches.

The villagers, perhaps not surprisingly, did not take kindly to this kind of magical violence, and threatened to kill Milarepa and his mother. In order to frighten them into keeping their distance, Milarepa called down hailstorms and destroyed the ripe harvest. It was at this point that he was forced to flee from their anger, first to Nyalam, and thence to Tingri.

The truck laboured and spluttered in the thin air of the pass, wheels mushing into the mud formed by the melting heaps of winter snow piled on either side of the road. Below and beyond us now, the brown hills levelled and flattened themselves into the high, cold Tibetan plateau, with the flat plain of Tingri Maiden spreading south and east towards the Everest massif. To our right lay the ruins of Lang-Kor, the site of the ancient centre of teaching founded by Pha-dampa Sangye, an Indian yogin who was a contemporary of Milarepa's – and, incidentally, the indirect reason that Tingri got its name. The story goes that the Buddha told Pha-dampa he should go and teach in the country where the small stone he was holding would land. He then threw the stone right over the Himalaya, where it landed with a resounding 'ting' on the top of a small hill.

Pha-dampa searched diligently for many years, eventually found the stone, and began teaching in the area. In Tibetan, *ri* means 'hill', and so this area became known as 'Ting-ri'.

Pha-dampa's last, and some of his finest, teachings to the people of Tingri include these verses:

> Ever transient is this world of ours; all things change and pass away;
> For a distant journey even now prepare, O Tingri folk.
>
> Likes and dislikes leave no traces, like the flight of birds through air;
> Cling not to experiences; ever changing are they, Tingri folk.
>
> The seeing of reality,* like a dream by one that's dumb,
> Cannot be described in language to another, Tingri folk.
>
> All creation, within and without, is contained in one's own mind,
> Like the water in the ice; seek to know this truly, Tingri folk.

There are many versions of the famous meeting between Pha-dampa and Milarepa, after the latter became a great meditator. According to one story, Milarepa went to meet the Indian saint at Thong La. He then transformed himself into a flower at the side of the road. As Pha-dampa walked past him he thought to himself, 'He does not know who I am, so perhaps he does not have clairvoyance after all.' Pha-dampa turned round, walked back, kicked the flower and said, 'Hey, you, Milarepa, get up!' Whereupon Milarepa resumed his own form, and shook Pha-dampa's hand, saying, 'Welcome to Tibet.' Had the meeting taken place during the winter months, Milarepa would certainly have been the only flower on the Thong La! The two adepts subsequently engaged in numerous contests of each other's mystic powers. Buddhism forbids the display of such powers

* Reality, or Ultimate Truth: the actual way in which all things exist; emptiness.

for selfish motives, stressing that they are merely by-products of meditation towards the supreme goal of enlightenment, and not goals in themselves. Milarepa and Pha-dampa took the opportunity to teach the true path to those who had come along to spectate.

What changed Milarepa from a murdering black magician to a religious devotee and practitioner of meditation? The key seems to be in the conversation with the teacher who instructed him in the art of black magic. One day the teacher returned from the house of his wealthy benefactor, silent and downcast.

> I asked him, 'O Master, why this silence and sad face?' He replied, 'All composite things are impermanent. Yesterday my very kind benefactor died. That is why the cycle of birth and death troubles my heart. But above all I am old. And from the white teeth of my youth to the white hairs of my old age, I have done harm to many beings by evil spells, magic and hailstorms. You also, though young, have accumulated crimes of magic and hailstorms. These crimes, too, will be on my head.'

These thoughts echoed all too clearly the feelings of remorse Milarepa was already beginning to experience for what he had done. How long before he, too, would be faced with the prospect of imminent death and subsequent rebirth into a realm of suffering? He became consumed with fear that his actions would hurl him into countless future lives of violence and counter-violence. His only chance of escape lay in finding a practice which would free his mind completely from the self-created seeds of his own downfall. He found himself restless and unable to sleep, obsessed with the thought of finding a lama who could show him the true teaching.

As his master was also intent on seeking the true path, Milarepa set out on his search, '... with a yak and a load of woollen cloth'.

8

Embracing Tingri

The truck driver lit up his twentieth cigarette of the morning, a cheap Chinese brand which filled the cab with acrid smoke. Without exception, every male I had seen in Tibet who had donned the khaki uniform and taken on jobs within the Chinese system had also immediately begun to support Chinese cigarette exports. The change was the more noticeable as the habit was virtually unknown in Tibet in previous years. We were passing the village of Tingri, and my desire to get out and explore was heightened by the nausea brought on by the jolting truck and heavy tobacco smoke. Enough was enough, I thought.

'Stop.'

'Huh?'

My gesticulations and the greenish tinge to my complexion must have left little to the imagination. The driver slammed on the brakes and turned the truck into the dusty commune compound of Tingri. Within minutes of getting out of the truck I was surrounded by a blue and khaki crowd, all discussing my presence with interest, but making little attempt to communicate with me.

The driver was getting agitated, and glanced more and more frequently at his watch, anxious to get me off his hands so that he could make it to Shigatze on schedule. It seemed there were

Tashi and Sonam at home in Tingri.

Tingri village, with the Himalaya range behind.

Tashi churning butter in the outer room of her house.

no officials around, but the place was being prepared for a large political meeting that evening, so everyone in the compound was of the opinion that there would be nowhere for me to stay for the next few days. I tried to reassure them that I had a tent, and would be quite happy to camp. This idea produced more alarm than reassurance, and a large lady with gold teeth and a denim cap ushered me into a small concrete room opening on to the compound.

'You can rest here for a while and then you will have to go.'

The clean bedcovers were taken out, and dirty ones brought in and thrown on the bed.

'Sleep!' exhorted the woman.

To do so was not easy with about thirty people crammed into the room, jostling each other for a better look and babbling excitedly. I could hear the much-abused gearbox of the truck groaning into action as the driver took the opportunity to safeguard his schedule in Shigatze. It occurred to me that the only way to disperse this rather noisy crowd of spectators would be to present them with a spectacle which was undeniably boring. I lay down and pretended to sleep. Gradually everyone drifted away. The last few die-hards, a group of soldiers, tried shouting and stamping to get some reaction, but eventually they, too, gave up and left. As soon as it was quiet I decided to comply with the rest of the gold-toothed woman's orders and leave, before I caused any further inconvenience either to them or to myself. Although I did not, in fact, have a tent I figured I should be able to sleep in the open quite comfortably in my sleeping bag in this rainless climate. I headed for the old village hoping to find a yak-free bivouac site.

Without really being aware that I had been drifting in any particular direction, I found that the twisting streets had directed my steps up to the summit of the little hill on which Tingri was built. The area was flat and had recently been bull-dozed, shattered rocks and fresh gravel showing light against the dark backdrop of stormclouds that overhung the Himalaya. I had seen a picture of old Tingri in one of my books, with the village gompa perched on this hilltop above the village. Not a trace of it remained.

Beyond the village the brown sweep of Tingri Maiden stretched away to the mountains, with only a range of low hills between. Everest, called by the Tibetans Chomolongma, lay on the left of the horizon, half hidden in the looming clouds. Chris Bonington's expedition would have passed through Tingri on their way to Everest. I wondered how far up the mountain they were. Cho Oyu was directly south from here, and to the right of it I could see the gash of the Nangpa La Pass, which led to Solu-Khumbu in Nepal. I had listened avidly to so many stories of my Sherpa friends' trading adventures in Tibet, it seemed almost impossible that I should now be here, looking back on the pass from the other side. Since the reopening of the border, the Sherpas load up their yaks with buffalo leather and take them over the 18,000-foot pass – a four-day journey from Namche Bazar to Tingri. In Tingri they would trade the leather for wool, both raw and woven, salt and, more recently, Chinese shoes. The Sherpas themselves had migrated from Tibet via the Nangpa La five centuries ago, and had maintained cultural as well as trading ties with their homeland. With the help of the lama of Dza-Rong monastery, they established monasteries of their own in Solu-Khumbu. Now Dza-Rong itself was in ruins, destroyed when the Red Guards reached the northern slopes of Everest in the mid-sixties. The lama fled across the Nangpa La, and took up residence in one of his own fledgling monasteries in Solu.

Beyond the village, on the edge of the plain, dozens of people were working, standing up to their knees in pools of muddy water to dig away at the ground with picks and shovels. The mud was being loaded on to horse-drawn carts, and hauled away to where other groups were pushing it into moulds to make adobe bricks. Beyond this small area buzzing with activity, the dry plain stretched away, quiet and empty, to the darkening mountains.

It was time to find a sheltered spot for the night. I turned to go, then stopped. On the grey face of a newly shattered boulder someone had carved the mantra of Chenrezig, the Bodhisattva of compassion, 'OM MANI PADME HUM', in Tibetan letters a foot high, picked out in coloured chalk. I looked further, and saw another, and another, colours glowing softly among the bare rocks and gravel. The workmanship was crude and hasty, but for me the carving had changed the feel of that hilltop, beyond merely adding some decoration. In my mind I could see the group of villagers, working quickly and quietly, perhaps at night, to put back a little of what that place meant to them. It made me realise that a monastery is only the tangible expression of the faith of those who build and use it. The destruction of the bricks and mortar may be mourned by some for the loss of priceless antiques and art treasures, but so long as some small part of the faith which created it remains, the tangible expression will always manifest itself again.

A vicious wind was cutting down from the mountains, flinging sand and dust into my eyes. I made my way back through the twisting streets. My food was almost finished and I had nowhere to stay, yet somehow I felt inexpressibly happy.

The high, sun-bleached walls on either side of me enclosed courtyards leading to single-storey houses and stables. Around the edges of the flat roofs were stored layers of neatly stacked yak-dung pancakes, drying in the sun to be used as fuel. These in turn were edged with a layer of juniper twigs to be used as kindling. This fuel marked the white-walled adobe houses with a darker band, creating geometric patterns as the village rose up, tier upon tier, around the base of the hill.

The maze of streets ended abruptly at the edge of the open plain. A group of women were preparing bundles of firewood near by, laughing and gossiping as they worked. They waved, so I waved back.

'*Tashideleg*'

'*Tashideleg*.' Then they caught sight of my boots and exploded with hoots of laughter, pointing, nudging each other.

'Hey! Those are good! Where did you get them?'

'From some farmers on Shishapangma. Do you like them?'

'Better than mine!' cackled an old woman, lifting her foot to display the battered felt boot that adorned it. They continued to giggle and chatter, looking like a flock of brightly coloured birds against the drabness of the dusty plain, with their striped woollen aprons, heavy earrings and hair braided with red wool.

I walked over to a heap of carved 'mani' stones, some broken and defaced, all piled in a protective heap between the village and the solitude. A woman, perhaps in her fifties, her neck swollen with a large goitre, left the group and followed me.

'Chomolongma's over there,' she said helpfully. She seemed to be waiting for something, perhaps a reaction, or an explanation of my presence. Nothing coherent would form in my mind, even in English, let alone Tibetan.

'The mountains are very big . . .' I said vaguely. She was still watching me intently. She had a strong, handsome face set in a severe expression, heavy lines etched on her weatherbeaten skin. Her eyes were bright and alert, and I felt they would miss little. Then she smiled, the warmth and humour of her eyes spreading to the rest of her face. It was as if she had been weighing me up, and had reached her decision.

'*Cha*?'

I nodded my thanks to the invitation, and she turned and led the way through the twisting streets to her house. From the fragments of conversation that reached me over her shoulder, I gathered her name was Tashi, but could glean little else. She pushed open the wooden door in the high adobe wall and we stepped into a small courtyard. Two horses, saddled and bridled, stamped and jingled their harness bells. We squeezed between them and went into the house. The outer room was quite spacious, and was lit by a large rectangular hole in the flat roof. I followed Tashi through the door on the far side, into the room beyond.

The inner room was quite dark, lit only by a tiny window which looked on to the yard, but full of noise and laughter which fell silent for a moment as we entered, then resumed. As my eyes adjusted to the gloom, I could make out the shadowy forms of a dozen or so Tibetans squeezed on to the rug-covered benches which lined the walls. Someone took my pack and stowed it in a corner, while a space was made for me on one of the benches and a cup of chang was pushed into my hands.

'*Shea, shea*!'

I complied, largely because Tashi had her hand under my cup and was tipping it insistently. As soon as there was room, she topped it up again. I wondered how long this drinking party had been going on – a fair time, if the boisterous laughter was anything to go by. It was as if I had suddenly stepped back twenty years into Tibetan history. Everyone in the room was dressed in traditional homespun or sheepskin, men and women with their long hair braided with hanks of brightly coloured wool. Chunks of turquoise and coral gleamed from ears and throats in the dim light from the window. The air smelled of chang, mixed with the tang of smoke, butter and animals.

Everyone seemed to be enthusiastically asking questions at once, between exhortations to 'drink up'. Often, in the confusion, I found myself giving answers which did not necessarily fit the questions, but nobody seemed to mind. The chang jug passed round yet again, and someone seized my cup and topped it up.

'Good chang, eh?'

I laughed. They were looking forward to finding out what the stranger would do after drinking enough alcohol.

Someone asked, 'Where are you staying in Tingri?'

Tashi said, 'You can stay here.'

Once again, I found myself unable to answer. Much as I wanted to stay in this friendly and hospitable place, I had no way of knowing if it would get my hosts into serious trouble with the authorities. More to the point, I could not be sure that they themselves knew how to stay on the right side of what seemed to me to be a set of regulations which changed constantly, and furthermore at the authorities' own convenience. I was beginning to question the morality of trying to see more of Tibet and its people, if my very presence could put those people at risk.

One of the men stood up.

'You stay here,' he said, clumping his hand on my shoulder. Then he went out. I relaxed a little. He must have gone to report my presence. Surely if the authorities did not want me to stay here, they would simply order me to leave. I hoped it would be as simple as that.

There was a clattering at the outer door and a sheepskin-clad man in (I would guess) his sixties lurched into the room demanding chang. He looked as if he had already consumed more than enough, but was welcomed to the company. Someone, mischievously I suspect, made room for him next to me. He sat down, recovered his breath, and concentrated hard on keeping his cup steady as it was filled. Then he turned to me, looked me up and down appraisingly and put the cup carefully down on the low table.

'You have turquoise in your hair.'

'Some friends of mine put it there for a joke ... like *nama*.'

'So you are *nama*. Where is your *magpa*?'

I shook my head. '*Magpa mindu*'.'

He placed one hand on his heart, while the other made an expansive sweep that almost dislodged his chang cup.

'*I'll* be your *magpa*!'

The rest of his words were drowned in the howls of laughter from the rest of the company. I got the distinct impression that my suitor was a well-known performer when under the influence of chang.

'I, Mingma Dorje, will be a most wonderful *magpa*... '

There were noises outside and two army officers came into the room. One of them was evidently a man of some rank and importance; his uniform was well-cut and his manner authoritative. They both sat down and were given chang, but their attention quickly turned to me.

'Where is your permit?'

I handed them the crinkled remains of my letter. As I watched them frown over it, I realised they were able to read only a few of the characters. The smartly dressed one folded it with an air of satisfied importance and handed it back to me. Then the questions started. Who were my friends? Where were they? How did I get here? When was I leaving? I hesitated, confused as to which question to answer first. In an effort to make me understand, both soldiers repeated the questions more loudly, but as they were both talking at once and twice as fast I only became more confused than before.

Mingma Dorje decided that the time had come for him to take on the role of interpreter. He began an elaborate explanation of the questions, slurring his words and keeping his balance with difficulty. I could hear the gurgles and snorts of barely suppressed laughter from our fellow-drinkers, and found that I, too, was having difficulty in keeping a straight face for the benefit of the officials.

Mingma Dorje was beginning to enjoy himself. His rhetoric was becoming more and more enthusiastic, and he accompanied it with plenty of dramatic arm-waving. I caught the word *magpa* once or twice, and realised that my inebriated suitor had once more become carried away with his proposal of marriage. How on earth had I managed to get myself into a party in the middle of Tibet, being both proposed to and interrogated? I could hold out no longer, and broke down in a fit of giggling. Mingma Dorje stared at me with a funny, surprised look on his face, then collapsed sideways into my lap, while the rest of the company collapsed in uncontrollable mirth.

The two officers helped each other to their feet with difficulty, wiping tears of laughter from their eyes. One of them waved a weak hand as if to say, 'How can we deal with official business with all these crazies.' The other managed to stop laughing long enough to say, 'You stay here.'

After they had gone, order was slowly restored. Gradually it dawned on me that I had just been given official permission to stay here. Everyone seemed to approve of the decision. People were beginning to drift away. The inert Mingma Dorje was carried out, and the room became quiet once more. For the first time I was able to tell which people actually lived in this house. Tashi's only daughter, Chozom, had continued to live at home after she married, as Tashi had no surviving sons. Chozom and her husband Tsering had a two-year-old son, Norbu.

A quiet voice spoke from the shadowy corner by the window. 'Have you ever been to Kath-a-mandu?'

The words were Tibetan, but the inflexion was Nepali.

As I peered into the darkness, the speaker obligingly moved forward. The dusty light from the window revealed a lined, elf-like face and soft brown eyes framed by rumpled grey hair. His name was Sonam, and he was a cousin of Tashi's who now lived in exile in Nepal and was visiting for the first time for many years.

'How long does it take to get here from Kathmandu?' I asked.

'Oh, about one day by bus to the border, and then another day to here. But there is a bridge broken, and you have to walk for three days in between.'

His soft voice expressed no surprise or alarm at finding he had had to carry his luggage for three days through the mountains in the middle of a bus journey. I asked him if he knew my friend Samten and the brothers Ngawang and Kusho, who also lived in Kathmandu. Again, he expressed no surprise, although there are thousands of displaced Tibetans living in Nepal.

'Yes. I live a few doors away from their house in Boudnath. Like them, I also live by weaving carpets. I studied for ten years at Dza-Rong monastery with Kusho. Later Ngawang joined us and he was there for three years. When the soldiers came I escaped over the Nangpa La to Nepal. Later I discovered my friends had made it too.'

I wondered how he had taken to the noise and bustle of Kathmandu after the isolation of a mountain retreat. He gave the impression that it would take a great deal to disturb the quiet calm with which he surveyed the world.

Tashi took me on a tour of the house, which was more extensive than I had first thought. From the front courtyard, now empty of horses, a wooden door led to a larger courtyard at the side of the house. Around the perimeter of this were storage sheds, and shelter for the cow and the *dzo* (a cross between a yak and a cow), which were tethered to wooden stakes, chewing placidly. Stone steps led up to the flat roof where the fuel was stored, with one area walled off for a lavatory. Because of the dry atmosphere and the fact that it was used by only one family, there was no smell at all – a pleasant contrast to the Nyalam facilities! The outer room of the house seemed to be functioning as a repository for an assortment of household articles – buckets, flasks, brushwood, rugs, skins, straw trays from Nepal and half a dried goat. This latter Tashi took down, blew the dust off and inspected carefully all over. There followed a short discussion with Tsering regarding which bit to start on, after which he took it from her and began to chip away at a leg with a large knife.

'You like *thukpa*?' asked Tashi.

Thukpa is noodle soup flavoured with meat, vegetables, spices or anything else that happens to be around. I suddenly remembered how hungry I was.

'Oh yes. I like all Tibetan food . . . I think.'

We settled ourselves around the stove in the inner room. Chozom came in with an armful of dry yak-dung pancakes which she broke up and put on the stove, together with a few juniper twigs to aid combustion. The pot of noodles was put on to boil, while Tashi added the dried meat chips, herbs and the small onion she had been dicing.

The evening was fading now into darkness. Tashi lit an oil taper and the leaping flame held us together in a bowl of light in the centre of the room. We ate in a comfortable silence broken only by the crackling of the stove and the spluttering of the lamp. While we sipped our last bowl of salt tea, Tsering pulled a pile of heavy bedcovers out of their corner and began to arrange them on the stone benches around the walls, his shadow flickering with the unsteady flame before fleeing upwards to be swallowed in the deeper darkness of the soot-blackened ceiling.

I slid under the covers and sank into a fitful doze where I dreamed of being awakened by a crowd of soldiers and officials, all shouting and talking at once and hustling me away to a little concrete room where everyone was forbidden to speak to me. My eyes opened. The family were still preparing for bed, shadowy figures moving to soft whisperings and the rustling of blankets. Tsering was making his pillow somewhere behind my head, his evening mantra a scarcely audible whisper.

Reassured, I slipped deep into the silence of sleep. My mind, released from the earthly bounds of waking, flitted away from the darkened house to the courtyard where the sleeping cattle shuffled in their straw, and beyond, over the dusky plain to where the mountains shone white and cold beneath the stars.

The softly vibrating tones of mantra slipped into my dreams. I hung for a moment in that void between sleeping and waking, knowing nothing but myself and the sound. Then the day, layer by layer, announced itself. I remembered where I was and lay, eyes closed, listening to my new surroundings. Tsering was still chanting as he folded the bedcovers in the corner behind my head. I could hear the occasional murmur of voices as Tashi and Chozom began the day's chores. There was the rattle of the stove as the ashes were emptied, and the chink of the china bowls being taken down from their shelf.

It was time to join the day. I opened my eyes and found that Tashi was watching me quizzically, her head on one side, a cup and a flask in her hands.

'*Cha*?' she asked, and it was poured before I had time to answer. She set it on the table, then went back to the stove. 'Wait there, and I'll get you some hot water.' She ladled hot washing water into an enamelled bowl.

I felt lazy and spoiled, and had to admit I was enjoying it. I wriggled my toes inside the warm covers and reached for the butter tea. Because I was beginning to relax, I was becoming aware of how tense, how much on my guard I had been ever since leaving Colorado. The sudden contrast between the situations I had been experiencing and the friendly and caring atmosphere here was accentuated by my own gut reaction. These people were so open and unguarded I could feel intuitively that they were not out to get anything for themselves or to prove anything about themselves. The natural response to this was to become open myself, to let go of my guardedness.

What then? The question came with an almost physical shock. Without that carefully maintained ego-defence, what was left? I would be putting myself on the line as a person, laying fragile emotions open to being misunderstood, or trampled on. I recoiled from the feeling of vulnerability. Not yet, I told myself. After all, I had been here less than a day. Anything could still happen. Yet how was it they could be so unguarded with strangers and I could not? They had lived for twenty years within a system that had in only a few weeks made me feel extremely cautious, not to say nervous. Yet in an intangible, inexplicable way, they were free.

Sonam was sitting amid the rumpled covers on the bench, rubbing his head in an effort to wake himself up. Norbu was having a spoon rebellion. Tsering put the spoon carefully in the child's hand, then held out a bowl of tsampa mixed with tea. After a half-hearted effort to get some tsampa on to it, Norbu gave up in disgust, hurled the offending spoon across the room, and plunged his hand into the tsampa in order to get a good mouthful. Chozom took over, but with no more success. The carefully retrieved spoon once again became airborne, this time hitting the stove with a resounding clang.

'Bad boy!' remonstrated his mother, trying not to laugh.

Sonam fielded the spoon, grinned, and went outside.

I rooted in my pack for soap and towel, and carried the bowl of water outside. The back courtyard was bathed in morning sunshine. I stripped to the waist and washed while the *dzo* masticated placidly and stared at me with bovine boredom. The locals didn't seem to wash very much, but smelt of nothing worse than smoke and butter. I had heard that human skin reaches a kind of equilibrium if left alone. I wondered how long mine would take if I left it, but decided not to attempt the experiment.

Tashi came out and went up on to the roof for more fuel. I followed her, picking up one of the dry 'pancakes' and weighing it in my hands, surprised at how light it was.

'No, not those on that side. They've only been there for a week. It takes a month before they are dry enough to burn. These are good.'

She carried them inside. I stayed on the roof for a few minutes. The air was cool and fresh, and the distant mountains clear and sharp in the morning light. Already people were at work in the mud-holes at the edge of the village.

Down in the yard Chozom was milking the cow, hands moving rhythmically over the teats and one foot steadying the wooden bucket half full of creamy milk. Tashi brought out the calves' breakfast, buttermilk, tsampa and cooking oil warmed in an enamel bowl. At eighteen days old, the calves were doing well on it, pushing and shoving each other to get the first mouthful.

Inside, Norbu was sitting on Tsering's lap, eating tsampa with the spoon as if nothing has happened. Tashi was mixing salt tea and tsampa for breakfast.

'There's no sugar,' she apologised. I dug out the last of my supplies and we used that. Chozom came in with the bucket of milk and poured it into an earthenware churn with a chipped handle. She replaced the stopper and set the churn on a bundle of rags before rocking it rhythmically back and forth.

'More butter for the tea and tsampa,' grinned Tashi. 'Here, have some more.'

'Oh, no thanks, I'm really full.'

I received the top-up anyway. It seems that where Tibetan hospitality is concerned, even 'no' is taken to mean 'yes please'.

Two boys aged about sixteen came into the room carrying brimming water buckets on their backs by means of a leather strap held across their shoulders. Chozom helped them empty the water into the great copper storage tank which stood on a pedestal of rocks near the door. The smaller boy went straight out to fetch more water, but the taller one paused, watching us. He wore a battered woollen jacket, or *chuba*, breeches of heavy sheepskin and canvas Chinese shoes which were falling apart. His hands were roughened and scarred from years of hard labour but his face was delicate-featured, almost beautiful, like a girl's. Then he noticed that I was watching him. He lowered his eyes and went out.

'Who is he?'

'They are from Tragtze, about two hours from here. They are relatives of ours, come to stay while they work on the brick-making. It's government work, four *yuan* for a hundred bricks.'

Tashi peered into the butter churn, and seemed satisfied. She poured the contents into a bowl and began to collect the floating globules of butter with two wooden ladles. By the time the buttermilk was skimmed the ball of butter was the size of two fists. She slapped it back and forth between the ladles to squeeze out the rest of the milk, then put it into a clean bowl and covered it with a cloth. She put the ladles down with a flourish.

'Tea-with-milk?'

She put the buttermilk on to boil. I wondered when she would be satisfied that I had been sufficiently well fed. She searched through the jars and flasks that filled the shelves at the back of the room, and brought out a small jar of instant coffee, evidently a prized possession. I had not seen Tibetans making 'milk tea' before and was surprised to see her add a little coffee to the boiling milk, then some black tea and a spoonful of sugar. The result was certainly unusual, but quite pleasant to taste.

Sonam picked up my Tibetan language book and was chuckling to himself as he read out the lessons.

'The wooden table is in the house. Having eaten too much, I am ill. Sounds like your stories of Nyalam, doesn't it?'

I laughed. 'Oh, Nyalam. What terrible food! Can you read Nepali as well as Tibetan?'

He folded the book on his lap. 'Enough to get by in the city, but I don't read it very well. For most of us, it was a case of having to work to make a living as soon as we arrived in Nepal. There wasn't much time for study. When I have time after work, I still like to read *peja* at home in the evening. I enjoyed studying at Dza-Rong. It was a beautiful place.'

There was a wistful note in the soft voice, and I wondered if he had perhaps found life in the city a difficult contrast after all.

'I think I have a picture of Dza-Rong in one of my books,' I said, rummaging in my pack.

One of the books contained a description of life in pre-Chinese Tingri, reconstructed from the accounts of the many refugees now living in Nepal. I turned to the collection of old photographs in the centre of the book.

'Oh, yes – this is Dza-Rong.' Sonam's expression became animated for the first time. He began eagerly to examine the photographs. 'Here is the chörten, and Chomolongma behind. Look, this is my teacher, Trulzhig Rinpoche! When he was the lama of Dza-Rong many Sherpas would cross the Nangpa La and come to visit him. He founded monasteries in Solu-Khumbu, and after escaping from Dza-Rong went to live in Solu. Sometimes he visits Kathmandu, and his former students can go to see him. There are quite a few of us in Kathmandu now.' He paused, absorbed in his own thoughts. 'Not everyone got out in time...' His voice trailed off and he turned back to the photographs. The others had gathered round to look, and Tashi was peering over my shoulder.

'This is my lama, Pema Chogyal.' She took the book from me and touched it reverently to her head. 'He came here to meditate in the mountain places of Milarepa: Lachi, Chuwar and Kyi-rong. Then he built a gompa at Tzib-ri, not far from here.'

She passed the book to Tsering and Chozom.

'Do you ever go to Trulzhig Rinpoche's monastery in Solu?' I asked Sonam.

'Yes, I go there sometimes – wait a minute, here's a family that lives near me in Boudnath. Look, remember them? They used to live in Tingri.'

He passed the book to Tashi, who smiled as she recognised faces she had not seen for over twenty years. I found myself glancing from the photographs to their faces, caught up in their excitement at finding pictures of their friends and lamas. The book was eagerly searched until every photograph had been minutely examined. Sonam looked at me expectantly, but I had no more.

'I have a book about Milarepa,' I said, remembering Tashi's comment.

At first Sonam seemed disappointed that this was also in English and so impossible for him to read. As he looked through the plates of the paintings depicting Milarepa's life, his disappointment seemed forgotten in his concentration on deciphering the scenes. The paintings were in a style not unlike an elegant form of cartoon strip, with the central character portrayed several times, involved in different events in his life.

'Here is Milarepa meditating in a cave ... oh yes, and down here is where he goes to beg, and meets his aunt again – and she sets the dogs on him! Then she comes out herself and beats him with a tent pole ... '

Tashi stood up and walked over to the shelves at the back of the room. Reaching behind the pots and vacuum flasks she took out a small book hidden in the dark shadows behind the clutter.

She handed it to me without speaking, and Sonam helped me to spell out the faded letters on the title-page. I looked up and saw Tashi smiling as she watched me.

'So you have a Milarepa book also.'

It was hard to find words for such an unexpected surprise. Here I was, staying with a family which had kept the tradition alive through the turbulence of the past twenty years. How absurd it had been to think of searching for empty caves on the mountainside, and how deeply ingrained was the Western concept of tangible goals. Here in this Tibetan home was the *living* tradition, and suddenly I realised that to come upon the forgotten landmark that had once been one of Milarepa's caves would be no more illuminating than standing on the summit of a mountain.

The afternoon windstorm was getting up, shaking the doors and windows of the house. The light in the room dimmed as clouds blew across the sun. Chozom took out a pile of raw sheepswool and began to card it, the heavy carding combs rasping as they brushed against each other. Tashi was spinning the carded wool with a drop spindle, the movement of her fingers almost imperceptible in the fading light. I settled into a corner of the rug-covered bench with my diary. Sonam picked up the Tibetan volume of Milarepa and began to read, his soft lilting voice blending with the rhythmic brush, brush of the carding combs and the sound of the wind outside. I recognised the part of the story where Milarepa was inquiring of everyone he met along the road if they knew where lived the great lama Marpa who alone knew, so he had been told, the powerful teaching which leads to enlightenment.

> At the side of the road a tall and corpulent monk, with large eyes and an awesome look, was ploughing a field. I had scarcely seen him when I was filled with an unutterable joy and inconceivable bliss. Stunned for a moment by this vision, I remained motionless. Then I said, 'Master, I have heard that the learned Marpa the Translator, personal disciple of the glorious Naropa, dwells in this region. Where is his house?'

For a long time he looked at me from head to foot. Then he said, 'Who are you?'

I replied, 'I am a great sinner from the upper Tsang. Marpa is so renowned that I have come to beg for his teaching.'

'Very well, I shall arrange for you to meet Marpa. Meanwhile, plough the field.' He took from the ground the jar of beer which he had hidden under his hat and gave it to me. This beer was very refreshing and very good. 'Work hard,' he added, and went away ...

Sonam's voice drifted into the background as I dwelt on the story. It seemed to carry a hidden symbolism. The great Marpa did not usually do manual work, but on that particular day he went and ploughed a field some distance from his house. According to the custom of Tibetan hospitality, the farther one goes from one's house to meet an approaching guest to welcome him with beer, the greater the honour accorded that guest. Marpa had been told of Milarepa's coming in a dream, and so greeted him with great respect, in honour of his future attainments, without appearing to do so. In terms of people living in today's Tibet of army trucks and political meetings, this sort of encounter seemed very remote.

9

The Spy

Days in Tingri passed with the ease that comes of contentment. I found myself happy to become absorbed with the daily household routine. All the spinning and carding, the cooking and sleeping, the drinking and socialising, went on in this one dimly lit room, almost filled by its stove, shelves, benches and utensils. The atmosphere was always one of cheerful calm, the four adults and one child moving smoothly together, sharing the limited space with a profound sensitivity towards one another. I sensed the timelessness which had once prompted a Tibetan exile to say, 'In Tibet life may have been harder, but living it was easier.'

Sunlight was filtering through the dusty window, illuminating the china bowls on the low table. Chozom was lighting the stove, teasing a flame out of the juniper twigs and dried yak and sheep dung. Her face and hands were blackened with soot from tending the fire between her other chores. She always seemed to be busy, but never rushed, her quiet cheerfulness and patience making a comfortable background for her more talkative mother. She gathered a few glowing embers on to a small plate and carried it outside. I followed her. She set the plate down at the side of the doorstep and topped the embers with a sprig of green juniper which filled the air with a heavy, sweet smoke.

Tashi was coming in with the morning's milk. She followed my gaze to the smoking juniper and caught my questioning look.

'Thab Lha,' she said, making the sign in the air. She went into the house, leaving me breathing the sweet scent of an offering far older than any Buddhist ritual. The ancient Bön shamanism of pre-Buddhist Tibet recognised the juniper tree as the haunt of powerful spirits, making the smoke from its branches a fitting offering to Thab Lha, god of hearth and life-giving fire on this freezing desert plateau. When the Indian saint Padmasambhava, the 'Guru Rinpoche' of the Tibetans, brought the Buddhist teachings to this remote land, he used his powers to subdue the 'demons' (or negative forces) and make them work as protectors of the new doctrine.

What were these local 'demons' that Guru Rinpoche was said to have 'converted' to Buddhism? My Western sense of logic demanded an answer. There was something intangible here, something with which farmers and nomads must have an intuitive relationship to enable them to survive in this harsh landscape. Was it one of the local mountain gods that had guided me out of the blizzard, or was it a part of my own mind in another state of consciousness? These people seemed to regard the material and the mental universe as equally real, or even unreal. From such a viewpoint, the distinction between a local guardian and a state of mind became less clear. As a Westerner, I was used to believing only what I could measure or perceive with my senses, whereas here all the emphasis seemed to be on the training of the mind to transcend the senses. I found myself taking another look at ideas I had always dismissed as mere superstition. If technology developed a means of quantifying such things, then presumably they would become acceptable as scientific fact. I had often been told in my travels that the early Buddhists, far from dismissing earlier beliefs and existing sources of power, had sought to embrace and transform them in accordance with their own practice. Maybe Western science could usefully adopt a similar attitude.

It was no coincidence that the juniper smoke evoked memories of the incense burning in the dark temple of Tashi Lhunpo.

That day seemed so long ago now. Indeed, everything outside the calm island of Tashi's house had receded until it had become as unreal as a dream.

The boy from Tragtze was on his knees in the dirt of the courtyard, moulding the night's dung into pancakes to be spread out to dry in the sun. As I emerged from my reverie and my eyes focused on him, he looked up and smiled, brushing a tendril of hair from his face with one shoulder as his arms were caked to the elbows in wet dung. I wondered if I could maintain such a quiet dignity while doing a job like that; wondered, too, if such a thought had even occurred to him.

Inside the house, Tashi and Tsering were packing the spun wool into bundles for ease of transport. Eventually Sonam would be taking it back to Nepal to weave into carpets.

The stove was crackling and glowing now, and Chozom was boiling water for tea. When the leaves were steeped, she poured the brew through a strainer into the *dongmo*, shaped rather like a wooden butter churn, the wood held in place by bands of copper. She added salt and butter, and began to work the wooden plunger up and down to emulsify the fat. I offered to help, fascinated by the simple efficiency of this device. Chozom showed me how to put my foot into the leather strap to hold it steady, then I took the plunger in both hands and began to haul it up and down. Satisfactory gurgling sounds came from inside the churn, but the rhythm was difficult to maintain. Several times the plunger rose above the level of the tea, then flopped back down with a squelch that squirted hot butter tea over me and everything else within a five-foot radius. Chozom looked amused but not surprised, and I noticed that everyone had moved out of range before I started. Perhaps this was a common beginner's problem. It took several attempts and a fair amount of tea to perfect the technique.

Meanwhile Chozom had poured some water into a bowl and was carefully washing her sooty hands with soap. Then she took a pot of buttermilk which had almost boiled dry and added sugar from a new bag Tsering had brought in. With her hand, she began to mix the milk solids and the sugar together, squeezing the mixture out between her fingers on to a flat basketwork tray. When the tray was full, she carried it out to the courtyard at the rear and hooked it on to a line to dry in the sun.

'Once it's dry, we can store it for winter,' she explained.

There was a fire smoking in the corner of the yard with a pot of barley mash boiling, ready for making chang. Chozom carried the chang inside and poured it into earthenware jars, in which it would be left to ferment for three days before being ready for drinking. The jars were stowed in a warm corner of the room and covered with sheepskins and blankets. Among the sheepskins was a heavy sheepskin coat. I picked it up, surprised at its great size and weight.

'That's my winter coat,' Tsering said with a grin, looking across at me.

It was the weight of the coat more than the careful preparation and storage of food that brought home to me what Tibetan winters must be like. Even now, in May, nights brought frost and ice to the shallow stream across the plain, and the afternoon sunshine lost its meagre warmth once the afternoon windstorm got up. I knew that in winter the winds would be far more violent, howling down from the mountains as the jet stream lost altitude, bringing stinging snow and ice particles instead of dust. Winter in Tibet was traditionally a time in which to stable the livestock and gather indoors for hearthside chores, such as toasting and grinding barley for tsampa, or spinning and weaving. Even some of the monks and nuns would come home from their mountain retreats, and give some tutoring to the younger children. Not everyone, perhaps, was as stoic about sub-zero temperatures as Milarepa.

Sonam came in, kicking the dust from his shoes, and Chozom set out china bowls for tea. Sonam sat down and drank in silence before speaking.

'They didn't give me the permit. They say they have no authority for that.'

He had been to the commune offices to apply for a permit to travel to Lhasa. He paused, and then went on.

'They kept me in there a long time, asking questions.'

'What kind of questions?'

'They were asking how I arranged to meet you here, how

long I have known you in India, what work we are doing together. They think you are a spy.'

Ludicrous though the idea was, the news brought an uneasy clutch to the pit of my stomach. A more unlikely or less efficient spy would have been hard to find, with my haphazard knowledge of Tibetan, and a mop of hair that stood out like a bar of soap in a coal-scuttle, but they must be taking their suspicions quite seriously to go to the trouble of interrogating Sonam. I was shaken out of my comfortable complacency with a jolt. If things went any further, then as a foreigner I would probably be taken to the authorities in Peking. I felt reasonably sure they would see the absurdity of the whole suggestion; Sonam had no such protection if the local authorities wished to make their presence felt.

It had been so easy to allow myself to be lulled into forgetting the harsh reality of life in Tibet beyond these walls. Such was the natural ease of the atmosphere here, I had almost convinced myself that most ordinary Tibetan families lived contented lives, free from fear. The very existence of the Milarepa book, scarcely concealed here on the shelf, made the Chinese boast of religious freedom seem more genuine than the show for tourists in Lhasa, which I had assumed to be empty propaganda. Surely my perception of the system, I had begun to tell myself, had been coloured so far by a series of unfortunate encounters with a few uncaring and unscrupulous individual officials? Surely the authorities would never be so dishonest as to go back on their word once they had given permission for me to stay here?

All my old fears came crowding back. What right had I to go on a sightseeing jaunt round a country whose inhabitants could be put at risk by my presence? It was just too ridiculous to suggest I was a spy, but I had seen before how officials here were capable of mounting any story, true or false, if it suited their purposes.

'Sonam, they can't believe that, surely?'

He shrugged. 'I don't know. They want to see me again tomorrow.'

Tashi came in with a man wearing a green denim cap and

jacket. He sat down, and she poured him a cup of chang. It seemed like a good time to go for a walk.

I stepped outside, breathing the cold air and trying to relax the knot of nervous apprehension our new visitor had re-tied for me. I squeezed through the half-open wooden door of the courtyard into the dusty street. A large hairy pig was sunning itself by the white adobe wall. It opened one eye, decided I was too unusual to be tolerated, and trundled off without a backward glance. If only all those who felt threatened by the presence of a stranger could be so pragmatic.

Little snatches of conversation were falling into place, things I had scarcely noticed at the time because my mind gave them no context. I had seen the sacks of barley stacked in one of the storerooms at the back of the house, and wondered if the family cultivated the land as well as keeping their few animals.

'Are you *trel-pa*?' I had asked Tsering.

'Oh no, not *trel-pa*, we are *shing-pa*,' he had answered hastily.

They did not usually bother to correct my inaccurate Tibetan, but the word I had used implied a kind of middle class – farmers who inherited their leased farms and who, despite the heavy taxes, were usually prosperous and respected citizens. Not all Tibetans were tied to their land, but those without land were usually the poorer, and certainly lacked social prestige. Tsering's hurried correction, *shing-pa*, means 'one who does the work of farming'. Everyone had become a worker-farmer now, even though the *trel-pa* had been the 'slaves of the feudal system' the Chinese had come to liberate.

In the late Sixties, when the Chinese set up communes all across Tibet, a few families classed as 'upper or middle class' were purposely not permitted to join. As the communes had appropriated all the fertile land and the water supplies, these groups were intended to be an example of how much better life was within the commune. This may have been the reason Tashi's family still lived on the fringes of commune society. Another group of 'outsiders' was created when the labour camps were disbanded in 1979, but the family seemed too well established to fall into that more recent category.

I had taken a circuit of the old village, my feet occasionally kicking against a piece of dried bone or hoof abandoned by the dogs in the soft white sand. The boys from Tragtze were standing knee-deep in muddy water on the brick-making site. Splashes of mud had dried white on their clothes and faces. They smiled and waved, then bent again to their work. A group of villagers heading home after a morning's brick-making stopped to look me up and down inquisitively.

'Are you the *inji* staying in Tashi's house?' asked one woman.

'That's right. Do you live in Tingri also?'

'We do,' she said, indicating those nearest her, 'but they are from Tragtze.'

The people from Tragtze smiled and nodded, but volunteered no further information. We all stared at each other happily for a few minutes, and examined each other's clothes and jewellery. I passed my camera around and showed them how to use the zoom lens and focus. Their open curiosity was as keen as my own, and I suffered none of the self-consciousness I had been taught to feel for staring or being stared at.

More people were walking over from the brick site, splattered with white clay, some carrying straw baskets on their backs. Walking quietly at the back of the group was a beautiful, olive-skinned girl with wide dark eyes and high cheekbones. She looked Tibetan yet not Tibetan. Puzzled, I turned to one of the villagers.

'Where does she come from?'

'She is from here, from Tingri Gangar.' Then he understood what I meant. 'She is Tibetan, but she is Kazara.'

Of course, that explained what was so strangely familiar about her. Kazaras are the descendants of visiting Newari traders from Kathmandu who had taken Tibetan wives or mistresses. The blending of Newari and Tibetan features gave the girl from the work party her dark beauty. Kazara women had been much sought after for wives by wealthy Tibetans in the trading heyday of Tingri Gangar. The girl looked shyly in our direction and hurried off down a side street.

Some women were walking towards the village, in single file, dark against the sunlit plain. They were carrying water from the river in heavy buckets on their backs. Every drop of water in the village arrived in this way, and was emptied into the great copper water-tanks in the houses.

They noticed the blonde stranger watching them, and, curious, came over to talk, oblivious of their burdens as they stood chatting.

'Oh look, she's wearing Tibetan boots!'

'I wonder if she speaks Tibetan?'

'Where did you get those boots?'

'From some farmers on Shishapangma.'

'She does speak Tibetan!'

'Look, you can see your boots come from a different village from ours. The colours are different.'

I looked. Yes, there was a difference. Tingri boots favoured more red and green. Mine were mainly red and black. These women's boots, like the rest of their clothes, were well worn and carefully darned in many places, but still looked colourful and attractive.

Then they noticed my necklace.

'That's a nice one. Where did you get it?'

'My Tibetan friend in Namche Bazar gave it to me.'

There was much nudging and giggling at this. I discovered later that I had used a word that is understood as 'boyfriend' rather than 'companion'. When it became evident that I was not going to volunteer further details about my 'friend' in Namche, they began to display their own jewellery, reaching inside their collars to pull out their bridal necklaces. My single stone was a humble thing compared to these. One *zi* was almost twice the size of mine, and had three eyes instead of two. This, I knew, was a rarity, worth a lot of money and luckier than a common two-eyed stone. Some of the other stones were striped or spotted in patterns the like of which I had never seen in Nepal.

'I've been to Namche Bazar,' volunteered an older woman. 'We went there trading with many yaks.'

I was interested, but not surprised. Tibetan women are every bit as active and adventurous as their menfolk, being equal partners in the perilous journeys involved in trading, and often the more astute when it comes to hard bargaining.

'When was the last time you were in Namche Bazar?'

'Oh, many years ago now. But before, I went many times.' She grinned. 'They drink too much chang in Namche Bazar!'

I could agree with that. But they had healthy enough appetites for it here in Tingri. I went back into the house. The man with the green jacket had gone.

'Tashi, who is he?'

'*Pon-po*,' she said flatly,

'He works in the office, for the government,' explained Sonam. '*Mi-chen-po*. Big man.'

'Is he watching me?'

'Oh, no. He comes here all the time.' She grinned. 'For the chang!'

Perhaps I had been over-reacting. I sat down on the bench and joined the others in their drinking.

There was a minor commotion in the outer room and a large woman (also *pon-po*) strode through the door, her corpulence encased in padded olive-green denim, her hair stuffed into a matching cap. She sat, heavily, and was given chang.

'Who's that?' she said, pointing at me. Tashi explained briefly.

'Where is your permit?'

She stabbed her finger in my direction again. I handed her the remnants of Wu's letter. She read it easily, then frowned and glared at me.

'Who wrote this?'

'Big-man from Peking.'

She handed it back in silence, apparently satisfied. I was unable to follow the details of the rest of her conversation with Tashi and Tsering, but was relieved that at least it did not concern me. From time to time she would break off and address me, abruptly, raising her voice and pointing.

'Hey, *pu-mo*.'

This form of address was technically correct, as she had ascertained that I was not married, but the term is mainly used as a diminutive for smaller girls, and her overbearing manner gave it a certain aggressiveness.

'Hey, *pu-mo*. Those boots are no good. These are good.'

She indicated her own Chinese-made shoes of black plastic, then resumed her conversation with the others.

'Hey, *pu-mo*. Your hair is no good. You should braid it. It's getting full of dust.'

Tashi fetched some strands of blue and red wool, took my comb, and braided the wool into my hair. The *pon-po* looked appraisingly at the results and nodded approvingly.

'That's better.'

She finished her chang and left, a little unsteadily.

Sonam emerged from his dark corner.

'You all right, Sonam? You're not saying much.'

'I don't say much when there are *pon-po* around. They are very big . . . and I am . . . very small.'

In this case, he might have meant it literally as well as metaphorically.

Chozom and Tsering were gathering ingredients for supper. Rice went on to boil, and Tsering brought in some eggs from next door's chickens. Tashi beat them in a bowl for an omelette. Tsering was crushing chillies for sauce. Sonam searched his bags and brought out another small Nepalese onion, which Tsering cut up. The tense atmosphere relaxed, and Sonam sat back and picked up my book.

'What's the Tibetan word for vegetables?' I asked in Nepali.

'*Tsaa*. And that is *tsong*,' he said, pointing to the onion.

'What about the vegetables Milarepa lived on when he was in the cave?'

'*Sa-bo*.'

'We say "nettles".'

'He boiled them in a pot,' said Tashi, dropping the eggs into a pot of hot oil and spooning in some cold water.

'And one day the pot broke.' The whole family knew the story, and were taking cues from each other.

'It rolled away down the hill and broke,' expanded Sonam, demonstrating graphically with his hands.

'And when it broke, the green inside the pot from boiling the nettles came out shaped like a pot.'

'And the green pot-shape is in Tashi Lhunpo monastery.'

'Is it?'

I paused. 'Well, that's what my book says, but when I was in Tashi Lhunpo I didn't see it.'

Sonam searched the pages of the family Milarepa and read the 'Song of the Breaking of the Pot' while Tashi served supper.

> I owned a pot
> Containing all my worldly riches
> And at the same time, I did not have it.
> With this loss
> I gained the realisation
> Of the impermanence of things.
> My humble pot becomes my teacher
> In the very moment of its breaking.

An undercurrent of uneasy tension now seemed to permeate the comfortable routine of Tashi's house. I could not tell if the atmosphere had changed or if the change in my own attitude now allowed me to perceive a caution which had been there all along. Sonam was questioned again, and sent back, but there were no new developments. Perhaps I should comply with regulations and request transport to Lhasa. I walked over to the government compound.

Outside the large gates, a group of men were sitting in the dust, their bags and bundles around them. One scrambled to his feet and smiled broadly, flashing his gold teeth in the sun.

'You going to Nyalam, Kathmandu?' He spoke the first English I had heard since arriving in Tingri, heavily accented, and sounding more strange and foreign than Tibetan.

'No, other way. Shigatze.'

'Oh. I live in Kathmandu. I've got a shop. You wanna buy *chuba*? Very good quality. Yak.'

The hard-sell syndrome seemed as out of place in Tingri as the language. I wished him a good journey back to Kathmandu.

The fat *pon-po* came out of the compound and began a tirade of rapid and unintelligible Tibetan.

'Is there a truck to Shigatze?'

I was delivered another flood of incomprehensible language. Maybe she had switched to Chinese. I had no great desire to leave, only to ensure that my presence did not bring trouble to Tashi's family. Perhaps it would be worth waiting to see if my request to leave would put the officials' minds at rest.

'Oh well, thank you very much anyway,' I said politely in English, and walked away.

I took a different route back through the old part of the village and found myself picking a way through the rubble of a large construction site. The freshly made adobe bricks were being trundled over here on heavy carts, and a number of new houses were rising from their foundations. I stood back from the busy scene, and then noticed something I had previously missed: a large gap could be seen amid the clustered houses of the village, cutting a swathe through the tiered buildings, right in line with where the gompa had been. It was as if some of whatever had been aimed at the gompa all those years ago had fallen short of its target, and felled the houses instead.

Back in Tashi's inner room, I asked, 'What broke all the houses in the middle of the village?'

Nobody answered. Everyone suddenly seemed very busy and preoccupied. There were, perhaps, some subjects which were better left alone. Sonam broke the awkward silence.

'Come, I'll show you the gompa of Pema Chogyal.'

We went outside and climbed the steps to the roof.

'He had a gompa in the Tzib-ri Mountains, to the north, there at Shiri-da. He was a great teacher, many people came.'

An eloquent sweep of the arm encompassed all the villages scattered at the edges of the plain. I screwed up my eyes and squinted against the sunlight but could not see anything resembling a gompa.

'Oh, there's nothing there now,' said Sonam. 'But that's how it used to be.' He went back into the house.

The next-door neighbour was on his roof, collecting fuel. He called a greeting and waved, then descended out of sight.

Clouds were spilling over the Himalaya. Sudden gusts of wind caught the prayer flags above the houses and filled the air with stinging sand.

A few moments after I had settled back into my corner of the inner room, the neighbour appeared at the door, holding a wooden jar of chang, complete with a dab of fresh butter on the rim. At his side was a stocky, red-robed figure whose shaven head shone dully in the dim light from the window. They sat down, and the jug of chang was passed round.

Tashi was explaining the presence of the neighbour.

'He is our *gan-ye*. He brings chang one day, we bring chang the next. We work together.'

I had come across these reciprocation friendships among the Sherpas of Nepal. Such a friend would not only help with the harvest and house repairs, but would also provide the kind of social support which in the West now comes almost entirely from the impersonal ministerings of the Social Services. It seemed there was still a place for this kind of support within the commune system.

I turned my attention to the neighbour's companion, surprised to see someone in robes outside a monastery. I turned to Tashi.

'Is he a lama?'

'Not exactly. He is *ser-kyim*. There are not many of them left. Just in a few villages to the south of here.'

The *ser-kyim* of Tibet, I knew, had a role similar to the married farmer-priests of the Sherpa villages across the border. As well as cultivating land, they had been able to read the *peja*, and could perform the complex household rituals which are an essential part of Buddhist life in these highlands.

This *ser-kyim* was a lively, extrovert character, obviously enjoying his chang and the tale of the strange foreigner, grinning across at me during pauses in the story. Then he drained his cup and got up to leave.

I was disappointed. His open friendliness had promised a lively conversation and I was curious to learn how he and his fellow *ser-kyim* had adapted to modern Tibet.

Tashi caught my look of disappointment.

'He has a long way to travel to his village,' she explained. 'He lives near Chuwar.'

Chuwar. The place of pilgrimage, where the Master had

passed into Nirvana to the accompaniment of 'miraculous signs which filled the sky with lights and colours'. For his devotees, he had left a marble slab carved with the four sacred syllables. This had been enshrined in the temple which had been built on the site.

'Is the chörten still at Chuwar?' I asked Sonam.

He shook his head. 'Nothing left now,' he said slowly.

I had expected as much. I had already lost interest in searching for a broken ruin. What I was really looking for was less tangible, elusive to the point where I could not put a name to it. I could only hope I would recognise it when it appeared.

The next day I went back to the office. The government compound was deserted and silent. Outside, an old man leading a horse stopped and, interpreting my vacant look, pointed to the flat grassy area over by the river.

'*Pon-po.*'

A group of them were picnicking on the grass. The plump woman was there, looking quite festive in a red sweater embroidered with flowers, and with her long pigtails flying free. Her mood had mellowed to match her looks, and she spoke carefully, so that I could understand.

'We would offer you some tea, but we've just drunk it all.'

'That's all right. Any trucks to Shigatze?'

'Not today. There were three yesterday, but you missed them.'

'Oh dear. Well, never mind. I'll wait until tomorrow.'

There was nothing more to say. I paid my respects and departed. At least if the authorities had been seriously concerned about the supposed spy in their midst, someone would have come over and made sure I was packed safely aboard one of those trucks.

Sonam was sorting through his luggage. He had decided to ride to Shegar the following day in the hope of getting his Lhasa permit there. I was impressed by the amount he had with him, all of which he had carried on his back for three days through the mountains. Out of the bags came chillies and onions, mixed in with lengths of Indian cotton and white kataks. Then came handfuls of Nepalese candy, sickly-sweet, a bundle of gaudy plastic tea-strainers and a quilted nylon jacket for Norbu. He repacked two leather saddlebags with minimal travelling luggage for his ride to Shegar.

We slept late the next morning, and were inundated with visitors from Tragtze before any of us were out of bed. Chozom dressed quickly and brought round salt tea kept hot overnight in a painted Chinese vacuum flask. The outer room was full of the bags and bundles the visitors had brought to trade. Some of them were going to look for work at the brick-making. Three horses were tethered in the yard, and the cow was wedged into her corner looking uncomfortable and crowded. One of the calves, seeking either more space or extra food, wandered through the open door into the outer room, and had to be evicted from among the bags of wool and barley.

The *gan-ye* neighbour arrived with yet another horse, for Sonam's journey to Shegar; Tsering helped him to strap the saddlebags over the wooden saddle. To protect the horse from the hard saddle, a richly coloured woollen rug was draped over the animal's back. Then, to protect the rider from the hard saddle, another, matching rug was draped over the top. These, together with the silver harness bells, made the mount look as if it had come straight from some nomadic tribesman of the steppes, rather than next door.

Sonam led the laden animal out of the courtyard to where the street widened a little. He swung himself cautiously into the saddle, then turned to bid his goodbyes. Before he could speak, there was the sound of thudding hoofs, and a rider reined his galloping horse in a spray of flying sand.

There were smiles and shouts of recognition. He and Sonam dismounted and embraced each other. Everyone walked back to the house to drink chang. There were two more horses tethered in the yard.

Sonam and the stranger had known each other from childhood to Sonam's exile. The newcomer was a trader. He had been to Nepal and India many times in the old days. Now, not so much, he said, and changed the subject. He and Sonam were soon deep in conversation. I watched from my corner, fascinated. It was impossible to guess at his age – dark, sun-dried skin weathered like old leather against the brilliance of the coral and turquoise at his ears and throat. His clothes were worn and patched, and his greying pigtails braided with dust and red wool. There was something wild and untamed about him, a rider who fitted with the trappings of his horse. There was no way someone like this could remain quietly inconspicuous and pay lip-service to the Party line. He must surely haunt the mountains on the fringes of habitation for the greater part of the year. I wondered how he had heard of Sonam's return.

There were loud voices in the outer room, and Tsering came in with two men. The taller of the two had a clipped moustache and a blue and red down jacket; the other was small and quiet, inconspicuous in his baggy worker's khaki. The tall one was talking loudly, continuously. Somehow he reminded me of a world that was separate from this one, the details of which I could not quite remember.

Tsering was looking at me expectantly, and I heard the tall man say, 'I thought you said she spoke Tibetan.'

Tsering just smiled nervously, and looked at me again. Then the man spoke a word I recognised. 'Pemba.'

The missing pieces of my memory were falling into place. Down jackets, climbing expeditions, loud people, liaison officers, Pemba. Somehow he had discovered where I was and sent these people to fetch me.

Down Jacket seemed convinced that speaking quickly and shouting was as effective as speaking slowly and clearly, so to save everyone's eardrums, Tsering translated into intelligible Tibetan for me.

'This is the driver for the Japanese Shishapangma expedition. Pemba has sent them to fetch you. They have come in a big truck. There is also a small car, but maybe it has already gone to Shigatze. This truck is going to Lha-tze tonight, Shigatze tomorrow.'

There were too many thoughts clamouring for attention at

Tashi Lhunpo.

The deserted fort at Gyantze.

Desecrated wall paintings being restored in the gateway of the Panchen Lama's Summer Palace.

once. How did Pemba know where I was? How did he make contact with an expedition on the other side of the mountain? Presumably anything that happened in these villages was passed on to the authorities by telephone. There was no question but that I would have to leave; to stay would be to bring Pemba's attention on Tashi and her family, and he was not the gentlest of men.

I nodded vacantly to the driver and slowly began to put my belongings in my pack. Tashi took my hand and led me outside to where the truck was parked at the edge of the village.

'Is it all right for you? If it's too bumpy you could stay until a proper truck comes for you. This one, you have to ride in the back, on top of the gear.'

I looked at her anxious face.

'No, I'd better go. I would love to stay, but Pemba might get angry if I don't go with the people he sent, and it could be trouble.'

We went back to the house.

Sonam was sitting in the straw of the rear courtyard behind the *dzo*, talking to the trader. Evidently Down Jacket had been too much for them.

'Too many big people?'

That wry smile. 'We are just . . . very small people.'

'Goodbye Sonam.'

He raised his hands in the Nepali salutation.

'Perhaps you will come to Boudnath one day.'

Inside, I finished packing my things. Down Jacket was pacing up and down, in a hurry to leave, ostentatiously glancing at a flashy wristwatch.

It was too sudden. My mind could not adjust to leaving like this. Chozom clasped my hands without speaking, then turned and went outside. I paused.

'Goodbye Tashi.'

And then the tears were running down my face and we were crying and hugging each other. Suddenly she seemed so small and frail; it was only her personality which had filled the house with such warmth and vitality.

Down Jacket was clucking impatiently. I stumbled into the

outer room to collect my pack. A scene of frenzied activity met my gaze. Pasang, one of the men from Tragtze, had decided to take advantage of the ride to do some trading in Lha-tze, and Tsering was hauling some extra sacks of barley out of the storeroom for him to take along.

Then the whole house emptied of people and we poured through the narrow streets to the waiting truck. Pasang and his barley sacks disappeared into the back, and then he was leaning out again, scrawny, muscled arms reaching for me and my pack. I scrambled up, and immediately the tarp was pulled down and secured. I caught one last glimpse of Tashi's anxious face among the crowd, and then everything was grey and dim among the boxes and baskets of the Japanese expedition.

After a series of violent jolts we were off, Tingri receding invisibly in the sunlight outside. In an effort not to think about the loss of Tashi and her family, I tried to talk to Pasang about trading. Get a Tibetan trader on his favourite subject, and you can be assured of an entertaining ride. He was going to stay in Lha-tze, and we were just discussing the possibilities of trading some wool for a piece of nylon climbing rope I had in my pack when the truck stopped. The tarp was pulled back, and searing sunlight forced its way into the dim recesses where we were crouching.

Imperatively, Down Jacket waved for me to get out, and Pasang passed down my pack. I blinked my eyes to focus on what it was that everyone else was staring at. The empty desert and barren mountains rippled in the heat haze.

Then I saw it.

Coming down the road, looking as alien as an off-planet space cruiser, was the Japanese minibus.

10

Japanese Bus

Everything in the minibus, from cookies to passengers, had been inported from Japan in mint condition. Sunburned noses were the only giveaway that the crisply attired climbers had been on a mountain at all. The Expedition Leader, a stocky, serious man with greying hair, was busying himself with large quantities of cine equipment.

For the first time, I was able to see the real Chinese Tourist System in action. At each appropriate piece of scenery the minibus would halt, windows would snap open, lenses would protrude, shutters would click, and then the whole vehicle would be hermetically sealed once more as the passengers retreated into their dust-filtering face-masks. I looked down at myself. A generous amount of soot and dust had attached itself to my clothes and skin during my sojourn in Tingri, rendering everything a fairly uniform brownish colour a couple of shades darker than the desert plateau through which we were travelling. The Japanese had been generous to allow such a creature into these sterile confines.

'Elen-san, do have Japanese cookie.'

The cookie packet was decorated with pictures of bone china teacups and a plate piled with cookies, bringing an unexpected wave of homesickness. Suddenly I was back in rural England, an eager five-year-old, perched on the edge of my chair and clutching a pink-roses teacup in both hands, eyeing the cookie plate and wondering when it would be polite to ask for another one. Old Mrs Peckover would invite me to tea once a week in her little Cotswold cottage with the box-tree hedge and the buddleia fluttering with butterflies. My plans for dodging the System and going off exploring as soon as we reached Shegar began to waver. I longed to be back in familiar surroundings, with people whose reactions I could anticipate, where I could relax because I knew the rules, as everyone does in their own society. Out here I had to be constantly alert, weighing up each new situation, trying to decide which way to jump. Learning about Tibet and, even more, discovering how Tibetans live and think was exciting and challenging, but there was more involved and more at stake than I had first imagined. I was tired. The spring flowers would be in profusion in England now, and I began to realise how strong were the roots and traditions I was born to, as they began to reassert themselves in a mind which had been trying hard to align itself with a different culture. I felt adrift in a sea of disjointed images, trying desperately to rearrange them into a comfortable pattern. 'What am I?' the chaos demanded. Too tired to contemplate such abstractions, I pushed the thoughts back into an obscure corner of my mind, to be dealt with later.

It seemed to me that this group of climbers was smaller than when we had first met in Lhasa. The Leader noticed me looking round.

'One friend dead. He fell from ridge. We shall miss him.'

There was that sadness mingled with acceptance that is so Japanese. Death with honour. The Samurai mountaineer.

The climber sitting behind me leaned forward.

'How long you stay in Lhasa?'

'Don't know. It's very expensive.'

'You think so? Really not expensive at all.'

I fell silent. We were living in different worlds.

Spring had done little to lay the dust in the streets of Shegar. We stepped out of the bus in the familiar hotel compound and had to close our eyes against the choking cloud whipped up by the afternoon windstorm. The cheerful hotel keeper made no comment at my presence. The hotel was empty except for our party.

I sat in the cold concrete room watching the naked low-wattage light bulb swaying in the draught, sending eye-straining shadows flitting back and forth across the walls. This seemed a chilly and cheerless place after the warmth and friendliness of Tashi's house. The window and door opened directly on to the compound, and the searching wind brought dust and grit in through the gaps and cracks. Black clouds loomed over the mountains and stretched dark fingers towards the town. I wondered what was happening to the remaining climbers. As I watched the clouds my unease grew, prickling at the nape of my neck and sending shivers across my skin. I tried to dismiss the feeling as the product of lack of news combined with someone else's tragedy, but the restless feeling persisted and I knew I would sleep little that night.

There was a polite and insistent knocking at the door.

'Elen-san, supper.'

Reheated canned food. I had no appetite anyway. The Japanese were enjoying themselves, toasting their Chinese hosts who would then return the toast. The proceedings became even more inebriated when they switched from beer to 'mao-tais'. I slunk quietly back to my cold room.

There, I lay awake for a long time, wondering if I would be able to find the energy to dodge the System again. My mind flitted from one possibility to another, counting off the days I had left, and wondering if I would meet up with the rest of the expedition in Lhasa. Maybe the Everest team would be coming out at about the same time. It would be good to see Pete and Joe again, and to hear about their experiences. Suddenly I just wanted to take the easy option and sit in the Japanese bus all the way to Lhasa, to allow myself to be shepherded into the hotel until everyone arrived. I could already hear the shrill complaints when the others saw my astronomical hotel bill added on to their overstrained budget, and I did not have enough money with me for even one night at tourist rates. The easy option was out of the question, yet alternative plans were impossible to formulate with such an inadequate knowledge of the System. I would just have to wait and see what turned up.

The bus departed punctually early the next morning and, luckily for Japanese heads, sped smoothly over the dirt roads. The speed and motion were a remarkable contrast to our lumbering truck on the outward journey. The plateau was still barren and desolate, brown and gold sand and rock etched sharp against each other in the thin clear air, with here and there a tuft of spiky winter grass bent in the chill breeze. Apart from the occasional black speck of a lammergeier wheeling against the deep blue of the sky, the plain was quiet and empty, with no wildlife to be seen. I recalled Heinrich Harrer's descriptions of the great herds of wild asses, the marmot colonies and the flocks of wild geese seen throughout Tibet. The Tibetans, being Buddhists, recognised all living beings, including animals, to be interrelated through their countless rebirths, and avoided the taking of life for fear of being reborn themselves into a suffering existence.

It seemed that reports of Chinese hunting parties bagging huge quantities of game were true: a repetition of the buffalo hunts by English and European settlers in North America.

The rocks twisted themselves into buttresses and pinnacles on either side of the road, while perched on the top of almost every spire were the ruins of some temple or hermitage. It was not difficult to believe that, out of three and a half thousand monasteries and temples in Tibet, only nine had survived the onslaught of the Cultural Revolution. I wondered if the famous tower built by Milarepa at Lhobrak, south of Lhasa, had suffered similar destruction. Not that the tower itself was of any great importance: it was the act of building it out of devotion to his teacher that made one of the most powerful and moving episodes of Milarepa's story. Marpa, knowing that Milarepa was not yet ready to receive initiation and teachings, first set him to build a series of towers, which he then had to tear down when half-finished and rebuild elsewhere.

This time we went to the top of the mountain to the north

and the Lama said to me, 'Great Magician, the other day I was drunk and did not give you good direction. Build a sturdy tower here.'

I replied, 'To tear down something while it is being built makes me miserable and is a waste of your wealth. Please think carefully beforehand!'

The lama replied, 'Today I am not drunk. I have thought about it very carefully . . .'

And so the building and demolition went on until Milarepa's back became covered in sores from hauling the earth and stones from place to place. Every time he went and asked for initiation and teachings, the lama would pretend to be angry, and threw him out.

I said, 'I rendered you homage by building the tower for your son. You promised to give me initiation and instruction. That is why I am here.'

'You made a little tower that isn't even as thick as my arm. It is hardly worth the Doctrine which I, with great difficulty, brought all the way from India. If you have the price of my teaching, give it to me. Otherwise do not stay here among the initiates of the secret teaching.'

Speaking thus, the lama slapped me, grabbed me by the hair, and threw me out. I wanted to die and I wept the whole night. The lama's wife came to console me.

Although the compassionate wife of the lama and several other teachers tried to give Milarepa instruction, he was unable to benefit by it as he was not yet ready to learn. Throughout all his trials, Milarepa showed no sign of resentment against his lama. In the end, when he was about to kill himself in despair, Marpa relented and gave him the teachings. He had finally let go of all his aspirations and preconceptions; his mind had become open, and ready to learn.

Milarepa now withdrew to places of mountain solitude to meditate on the Path that leads to Enlightenment. He had lost everything in the material sense, and was often reviled by those he met, such as the young girls of Tingri, but he considered himself the most fortunate of men, having acquired spiritual wealth beyond imagining.

In appreciating the peace of mind which often accompanies time spent in mountain solitude, the mountaineer is sometimes tempted to make a facile equation with the ascetic practices of hermits like Milarepa. I had myself experienced this peace, but knew all too well that this alone was just a temporary 'high', without foundation. Marco Pallis, Himalayan mountaineer of the Thirties turned Tibetan scholar, expressed this contrast in his conversation with the Lama of Lachhen.

> One day he [the Lama] suddenly asked, 'Why did you go up to the Zemu and try to climb snow mountains?'
>
> ... I made a lame answer: 'We love to go to wild places for their solitude, to avoid the bustle of town life.'
>
> 'You will never find it thus,' he replied. 'You have no idea how to seek it. It cannot be won by such methods. It will not be obtained nor acquired nor gained nor procured nor encompassed. The solitude to seek is the concentration of your own heart. If you have once found it, it will not matter where you are.'

Pallis replied by quoting from Milarepa's songs:

> 'Obeisance at the feet of Marpa the Translator
> May he grant me strength to persevere in my mountain retreat?'

But knowing in his heart that mountains are the means and not the end, he asked the lama:

> 'Tell me truly, can anything be learned about solitude without a teacher?'
>
> 'It cannot.'
>
> 'So it seems a study of the sacred books by itself won't reveal the way to it?'
>
> 'It will not reveal it ...

Without milk you won't make butter
Without barley you won't brew beer . . .
Without meditation you won't attain Buddhahood.'

In this context, the teacher gives not only technical instruction and guidance to his pupil but, by initiating him into the practice, provides the subtle inspiration which sets the mind on the path of meditation.

At about 16,000 feet, on the crest of a windswept pass, the driver pulled over and stopped. As if at an unspoken command, all the Japanese got out and dispersed over the hillside where they squatted on the barren ground, picking up rocks and smashing them against other rocks. Perplexed, I walked over to the nearest group.

'Fossils,' explained the Leader, diligently scooping them into a large plastic bag. I put two small fossils into my pocket to take home for Doug's daughter, who was an enthusiastic collector, then wandered over to where a group of Tibetans were taking a chang break by the prayer flags which marked the top of the pass. Their donkey was taking a break too, searching minutely for the occasional spiky blade of grass among the dry rocks.

The man offered me chang.

'Thank you. Where are you going?'

'Lha-tze. We came from Shegar.'

But the official five minutes were up, and the driver was shouting impatiently for us to get back in the bus. I reached it in time to find him throwing the glass from a broken vacuum flask on to the side of the road.

'That's terrible,' I said suddenly in English, looking at the pile of splintered glass on the ground.

Chinese and Japanese alike stared uncomprehendingly at me. I knelt down, and slowly and deliberately began to bury the glass under a pile of rocks. After a pause, one of the Japanese came over to help. The driver swallowed his exasperation and retreated into the bus.

The designated lunch stop turned out to be a dusty and windswept field, into which the cardboard box containing the hotel's official packed lunch was carried. Everyone paused, looking from the dust to their own immaculate clothes, circling like cats looking for a place to sit. Amused at being the only one with nothing to lose, I plonked myself happily down in the dirt and reached for a sandwich. The Japanese followed my example. Only the Chinese driver and the interpreter squatted fastidiously on their toes throughout the meal.

The Expedition Leader was leaping about energetically brandishing a large butterfly net. The driver and interpreter took no notice, pausing in their eating to glance at their watches from time to time.

The rest of the journey to Shigatze was as smooth and uneventful as watching a TV travel commercial. The flustered official at the tourist hotel, who protested that he had no advance warning of my arrival, retreated to his office and slammed the door. The Expedition Leader offered me a chair. Half an hour later an interpreter arrived from the Ministry of Tourism on his bicycle.

'This is most irregular. Where have you come from?'

Hope and interest were immediately rekindled by this comment. If communications were less efficient than I had feared, then perhaps there would be a chance to drop out of sight of the System once again before I reached Lhasa.

'I am returning to Lhasa from Shishapangma.'

'Where is the rest of your group?'

'On Shishapangma.'

'Ah.'

He recovered his composure and found me a room. Evidently this kind of thing was considered most untidy. As I was now back in the System, the expedition would be charged the equivalent of £40 per night for my stay here. This, I suspected, would make it easy to persuade the interpreter that I was too tired to be able to continue to Lhasa the next day with the Japanese. I was not disappointed. Now it remained only to wait for an opportunity to fade into anonymity again.

The next morning the Japanese climbed tidily back into their minibus, the door snapped shut and the vehicle disappeared in a cloud of ochre dust.

As a concession to my new surroundings, I decided to try to remove at least some of the layers of accumulated soot and dust. I poured the contents of the room's vacuum flask into an enamel bowl, stripped, and began to scrub.

'Oh, ah, good morning, excuse me.'

I turned and found myself face to face with a small and embarrassed Chinese.

'Ooh! How did you get in? Go away!' I squeaked, in English, in a reasonable imitation of outraged modesty. The Chinese fled.

An hour later he returned, knocking cautiously at the door before entering.

'You have been sent a guide from the Ministry of Tourism. I have brought him here.'

He ushered in his companion. It was Cho.

There followed a long and rather dull interrogation about my presence, reason for travel, location of group, and ETA in Lhasa. This I eventually recognised as Cho's curiosity rather than a requirement for official reports. I became flippant, regaling him with graphic descriptions of the Nayalam maggots in order to study his fastidious disapproval. If I had hoped to persuade him to avoid my company, I was doomed to disappointment. Cho became my shadow for the duration of my stay in Shigatze. This was partly from a sense of duty, but also because it entitled him to eat at the hotel. Apparently the food was better there than elsewhere. Poor Cho. Detailed to spend the next few years here, he found himself away from his wife and family, in a country where he disliked the altitude, the climate and the food, with people who did not wash, and whose language he did not understand. Not surprisingly, perhaps, he tried to persuade me to stay until the team returned from the mountain, with himself as official guide. Only the assurance that I would be delighted to stay, but did not have enough money to pay for the hotel, persuaded him that it might be less trouble to get rid of me after all.

'But we cannot let you travel by truck. It is too uncomfortable. You must wait here until there is a bus. It leaves on Wednesday. It stops in Gyantze and reaches Lhasa the next day.'

He seemed to have overlooked the fact that I had already travelled several hundred miles across Tibet by truck, but Gyantze sounded interesting so I did not argue.

'Now it is time for lunch.'

There was a group of American tourists in the dining-room, but Cho and I were shown to a separate table, as seemed to be the rule here. During the meal I asked Cho to interpret for me for the first and last time during my stay in Shigatze.

'Would you ask the cook to bring us some butter?'

'There is no butter,' he said, without looking up.

I stared at him in disbelief. 'There is no butter in Tibet?' I repeated slowly and deliberately.

He stared back in even greater disbelief.

'You don't eat *yak* butter, do you?' he asked, with a mixture of incredulity and horror. Only now did I begin to understand how great was the Chinese dislike of Tibetan food, to the point where they preferred to eat the stale and often unattractive imports from mainland China.

After the meal two of the Americans came over to talk. They had paid $8,000 each for a package tour of Tibet, and their bus was moving on towards Everest Base Camp the next day.

As they left the dining hall Cho said, 'They are *properly* organised. They have *proper* transport.'

'Oh, Cho, stop being so stuffy.'

I seized a large feather duster from the window sill and pursued him with it. It is difficult to maintain dignity when being menaced by such a ludicrous object. Cho looked pained.

'You have strange customs in your country.'

'Come on, let's go to Tashi Lhunpo and the Summer Palace.'

'It will have to be specially arranged. It is too late today.'

'Well, off you go and specially arrange it then. We can go first thing tomorrow. I'm going to have a nap.'

Cho eyed me suspiciously and left.

I went down to the market in the old town.

The jostle and chatter of Tibetans bargaining and selling mingled with the buzz of the flies in the meat market. Large chunks of flesh and bone lay on bloody slabs and hides, while here and there were whole dried sheep, their legs spliced into a sitting position, looking like a row of begging dogs waiting to be sold. In old Tibet, butchery had been a prerequisite of the Tibetan Muslims; for Buddhists the taking of life is regarded as having serious karmic consequences in the future. In a high, desert country like Tibet it would have been impossible for the population to survive without using meat, and Tibetans, ever practical, had come to the compromise that it was acceptable to eat meat if it had already been killed by someone else, and not specifically for oneself. I wondered how many Tibetans who had been won over to Communism had left their old beliefs far enough behind to take on the lucrative profession of butchery.

I wandered between the stalls of plastic shoes and trinkets, denim shoes and hats, Chinese noodles and vacuum flasks. A few individuals pursued me with pieces of their antique jewellery for sale. Beautiful though the pieces were, they were beyond my price range.

Neither the market nor the range of goods it offered was extensive, and I soon found myself heading towards the great cluster of buildings dominating the town that was Tashi Lhunpo. Knowing it was useless to try to get in without a guide, I joined the straggle of pilgrims, a few dogs and a goat on their circumambulation of the monastery walls. Perched on the rocky hillside above was a small shrine housing a row of prayer wheels, each inscribed with the mantra OM MANI PADME HUM. Everyone filed past, on the left as is the custom, and each spun the wheels with his right hand to release the mantra into the air, and to gain spiritual merit from so doing.

From here the path became steeper, twisting up the hillside on which the monastery was built. I fell into step with a family of five when we all had to slow down behind the man with the goat.

'You have nice Tibetan boots,' said one of the young women.

'Thank you. I bought them from some farmers. But I really need a *chuba* to go with them. Like that one.' I pointed to the handsome black and silver trimmed jacket worn by the young man I judged to be her brother.

'*Tsong*!' He clasped the wool of the article he had just declared was for sale as if to show it off to best advantage. We bargained for a while, until it became evident that I was not going to offer the amount of cash he wanted. Then he noticed my watch, and began to appraise its value eagerly. His mother called over, warning him not to take it until he was sure it was working properly, so he waited until the well-dressed Tibetan behind us had caught up. He studied it carefully. Yes, it told the same time as his own, and yes, it was still ticking, so it must be all right. Hands trembling with excitement, the young man handed me the *chuba*, and strapped the watch to his wrist. The rest of the family had gathered round to look, smiling their satisfaction at a successful trade. Then they took out their beads again, and resumed their pilgrimage.

I draped the *chuba* over my shoulders and followed them. I had been in Tibet long enough to appreciate the naturalness of pausing in the middle of an act of devotion to do a bit of good trading, in the same way that I had heard Tibetans repeating mantras as they worked or before they slept. They do not seem to have separated the spiritual world from everyday life in the way we have in the West.

The upper part of the trail was flanked by small shrines topped with prayer flags. Pilgrims had left offerings of tsampa, and there were several stray dogs hanging around waiting for their next meal. Others were curled up asleep on sunny ledges and niches in the rock.

One of the rocks was marked with a hole the same size and shape as a human head, and each pilgrim would kneel and, bowing, place his head into the recess. One thin and bony old woman knelt and bowed, but was too weak to rise to her feet again, whether from starvation or sickness I could not tell. Two of the men came over, lifted her gently by the arms and sent her tottering slowly on her way again.

We passed into the cold shadows behind the great white wall on the west side of the monastery, the slim stone obelisk rising a hundred feet above our heads.

'On days of celebration they used to hang great prayer flags from this wall,' explained my friend with the new watch.

We emerged from behind the wall and were looking down on the golden-roofed warren that was the gompa. The remains of the old town clustered around the foot of the west side of the monastery, while the corrugated iron roofs of the new section stretched in squares out on to the farmland. Beyond the flat river valley the brown hills of the plateau stretched away to the now-distant Himalaya, still shrouded in dark clouds. I shivered involuntarily. It would be good to have some news of the expedition, but Cho had insisted he had heard nothing. I turned my steps down the hill.

Next morning Cho's knock awakened me from an elusive dream. I scrambled into my clothes and hurried across the chilly courtyard to the equally chilly dining hall. Cho was already eating.

'Good morning.'

'Hi. Summer Palace?'

'Well – '

'Good.'

The two miles of dry dirt track to the Summer Palace were lined with slender willow trees just into spring leaf. All across the flat river valley the fields were furrowed and newly planted. A group of peasants were eating together, sitting in the ploughed field, passing food and jokes, and laughing.

Cho was still twittering about the Summer Palace being closed.

'The Panchen Lama is in Peking at the moment.'

He had been in Peking for the past eighteen years, but I had heard rumours that he had been given permission for a return visit to Tibet. As if to confirm this, it was clear that the Summer Palace was undergoing extensive renovations. It was now resplendent in a very fresh coat of yellow paint, while across the front of the main building were hung new white banners with the symbol of the Endless Knot emblazoned in deep blue. The red-painted doors in the perimeter wall were firmly shut.

'I told you it would be closed,' Cho said smugly.

As if he had uttered the proper incantation, the doors opened to let out two sturdy women wheeling barrows of rubble. I grabbed Cho's hand and pulled him inside before the doors swung shut again.

'Ask someone if we can look round.'

Cho's look spoke volumes, but I was unabashed. Finding himself in the position of being inside without permission, he either had to get permission or leave. He glared at me a moment longer, then turned to the official-looking Tibetan standing near the doorway and spoke a few words of rapid Chinese. The Tibetan shrugged and waved us inside.

An old man was perched on a rickety wooden scaffold, painstakingly repainting the minute details of a huge mural of two golden tigers. The scars and burns in the wall were being smoothed over with new plaster and the blank spaces in the picture sketched in.

'Are you painting all this by yourself?'

He smiled. 'Oh no. I have helpers.'

He indicated a group of grubby, paint-spattered boys working on another scaffold across the courtyard. The drawings over there had been completed, and the children were filling in the green and white of two snow lions with bright paints and fine brushes. Delighted with the distraction, they scrambled down from their perch, demanding photographs of themselves, the painting and everything else. As soon as my camera pointed in the direction of the building the official from the gate stepped in front of the lens, shouting angrily that photographs were forbidden. The children immediately swarmed all over him, hugging and teasing and dragging him across to pose with them. He tried to push them away, shouting and ordering them back to work. They would have none of it, and continued to plague him until at last his face relaxed into a smile, and he began to preen and pose for the camera with the motley crowd still swarming round his feet. I was impressed by the transformation they had wrought on him so surely and so knowingly.

Cho was getting restless.

'They are busy with repairs. We will be late for lunch.'

'Never mind lunch!'

One look at Cho's horror-stricken face reminded me that it

was my turn to concede a victory to him. The closing door framed a last glimpse of the Summer Palace with the official trying to round up the children and shoo them back on to their scaffold.

We were not late for lunch, to Cho's obvious relief.

The American tourists had left, with the exception of a 75-year-old Californian grandmother who was having altitude problems. She had been ushered to a separate table to eat alone, so I invited her to join us.

'Thank you. It's so nice to have some company. I am so disappointed I haven't gotten to see Everest Base Camp, but I'm really not well you know.'

'Never mind. There's plenty to do here. Have you been to the monastery? We're going this afternoon.'

I looked meaningfully at Cho.

'Oh, is there one? How interesting. Is it far?'

'It is too far to go this afternoon,' said Cho hastily.

'Tomorrow morning then.'

'Oh, that would be so nice,' said the American lady happily. 'Then I can have a nap.'

Cho's attitude was obviously perfect for most tourists. It was his misfortune to be assigned to someone like me.

It took us forty minutes the following morning to cover the half-mile to the monastery. The Californian lady moved slowly, leaning on her stick, and I thought it fortunate she had not tried to reach Base Camp.

'It's just the altitude you know, my dear. When I lived up in the Sierras we did some pretty rugged things.'

An old man in rough homespun approached us.

'How old is *mo-lag*?'

He was impressed by my answer. 'I'm sixty-eight,' he told us.

He saluted her, and went his way.

Grannie was pleased. 'I wonder if there's anyone here as old as I am?'

'I'll keep a lookout,' I promised.

Cho had arrived with another guide for Grannie. Perhaps this was the slack season. Once inside the monastery the two guides wandered round ringing the bells hanging from the colonnades, mimicking the monks with their rosaries, and giggling. It was easy to slip away down the twisting cobbled paths between the tall buildings.

The main temple must have sustained some damage in the Cultural Revolution, for it was now bristling with scaffolding, and the sounds of repair work drifted from within. The courtyard outside was busy with carpenters and builders cutting, sawing and carving to replace the ornate roof timbers. A few monks in patched red robes were gathering wood shavings into baskets and carrying them to the kitchens for use as kindling. They waved me over to one of the smaller temples which was resonating with the boom of drums and the clash of cymbals.

Inside the shadowy room, about a dozen monks were seated cross-legged on low benches, chanting with the beat of their instruments. A great golden Buddha statue glowed in the flickering light of the butter lamps, an illusion of light and flame. An old woman entered the room, leading a blind old man. Slowly, they walked towards the Buddha, then stopped and bowed, touching their foreheads to the cold stone below the golden feet. The woman went around the butter lamps, topping them up with liquid butter from a Chinese vacuum flask, leaving the man slowly doing his prostrations. I stayed for a while after the couple had gone, listening to the chanting ebb and flow, until the sound and the light seemed to blend into a shimmering golden humming that became part of the temple and everything in it. This was not music in the ordinary sense of the word, but a chanted pattern for an inner visualisation, a kind of blueprint for group meditation. I left the monks, their eyes half-closed in concentration, and, picking my way between the boots and shoes by the temple doorway, stepped into the sunlight outside.

In the centre of the flagged stone courtyard, a tall prayer flag rose almost as high as the three-storey temple complex which surrounded it on four sides. I wondered how far the wooden flagpole had been carried to reach here – the nearest forests were on the monsoon side of the Himalaya. A pilgrim clad in sheepskins paused to make an offering of tsampa at the base of the pole, eagerly watched by a long-haired, off-white dog.

Around the four sides of the courtyard, the walls were painted with the thousand Buddhas who had promised to renounce Nirvana and return to help the beings still struggling in the cycle of existence. Buddha means 'enlightened one', and the many paintings and figures in the temples represent aspects of enlightened mind. Although no expert on Tibetan iconography, I could recognise Chenrezig, the Bodhisattva of Compassion, whose mantra OM MANI PADME HUM was once to be found carved and painted everywhere in Tibet. The Bodhisattva is depicted as a beautiful white prince, with a thousand arms radiating like a halo round his body. Each of his thousand hands has an eye in the centre of the palm, with which to see all the suffering in the universe. He has eleven faces because, it is said, he vowed before his teacher Amitabha, the Buddha of Light:

> May I never cease to strive for the happiness of all beings. If I should ever think of my own happiness, may my head be cracked into ten pieces, and may my body be split into a thousand parts, like the petals of a lotus.

Then he travelled throughout the six realms of Samsara, teaching the Dharma by means of the six-syllable mantra OM MANI PADME HUM. When he gazed out over the land and saw that he had not helped even one hundredth of the beings to enter the bliss of liberation, he thought – 'What is the use? I can do nothing for them. It is better for me to be happy and peaceful myself.' Whereupon his head cracked into ten pieces, and his body split into a thousand parts. In agony, he cried out to Amitabha, who transformed the shattered body into a thousand hands, and restored his heads, giving him ten faces, then placed himself on top of the ten-faced head, making eleven in all.

The fangs and claws and flames to be seen in many of the paintings represent not devils but powerful means to righteous action. The dagger cuts through ignorance and the corpses of ego and pride are trampled underfoot. Even peaceful Chenrezig can appear as the fierce Mahakala, with a fiery energy to get things done. It was this kind of dynamic energy which Milarepa

Chenrezig

had to develop and use in order to transform his own mind in the space of a single lifetime.

In the smaller shrine-rooms, as well as the main meditation hall, a variety of offerings had been left before the Buddha statues by the monks and the pilgrims, from traditional coins and tsampa to the more modern imported rice, needles and safety-pins. It all spilled over the bowls and on to the altar cloths, as spontaneous as the act which had placed it there. Perhaps not all those who made offerings had the knowledge to express that it is the act of offering, rather than the needs of the recipient, that is the essence of this practice, but not one of them would even consider helping themselves to the wealth so temptingly displayed.

The old couple from the temple were walking slowly across the courtyard. The woman seemed hesitant at first, then asked, 'Have you a picture of the Dalai Lama? Is he coming back to Tibet?'

It was not the first time I had been asked these questions, and I was sure it would not be the last. I had to repeat the same answer as before, that I was sorry, but I had no pictures, and I did not know if the Dalai Lama would come back to Tibet. The couple shuffled off down one of the narrow alleyways.

One of the monks nodded in my direction and called a greeting.

'Tashideleg. When did you come back to Shigatze?'

I recognised him as the monk who had been detailed to show us round on our first visit. If he still had the same duties, then Cho would not be far behind, but perhaps I had time for one question.

'I want to ask you about Milarepa's cooking pot.'

He thought for a minute, then frowned.

'Who?'

'Milarepa,' I repeated slowly. Names are always the most difficult to communicate when your pronunciation is a bit odd, because it is impossible to guess from the context, as it is with most other words.

The monk was thinking again; then his severe expression broke into a smile.

'Ah, Milarepa. Yes, he meditated in caves, and cooked nettles in a pot.'

'Yes, but is the green nettle pot from inside the pot kept here in Tashi Lhunpo?'

He shook his head. 'No, it is not here.'

I was already laughing quietly at myself. How long would it be before I would stop needing some tangible evidence of Milarepa's existence?

Cho was standing at the edge of the courtyard, motioning that it was time to leave. The American lady was hobbling carefully down the uneven cobbles to the main gate, leaning on her stick.

'Well, that was most interesting. These two young men were most informative. I hope we won't be late for lunch.'

An old Tibetan woman walked with us for a while before peering into Grannie's face with radiant curiosity.

'How old is *mo-lag*?'

'I'm seventy,' she said, when I told her.

I fell a few paces behind, enjoying the two old ladies' silent delight in each other's company. Cho did not seem comfortable about us having our own conversations without him in between as translator, and was edging closer as we walked.

'What is she saying?' he asked me in English, then, without waiting for a reply, he grabbed the woman by the arm and asked her himself in rapid Chinese. She turned her head away, wriggled her arm out of his grasp and scuttled off down a side-street.

Over lunch, Grannie said she was worried about stamps.

'I've written so many postcards home, and if I don't mail them soon I'll be back before they are! But I really don't know if I'll be able to get stamps in this little village.'

'Actually, Shigatze is the second city of Tibet. I'm sure it'll have a post office somewhere. Hey, Cho, why don't you take us down to the post office?'

Cho looked considerably more enthusiastic at the prospect of the post office than he had at the suggestion of the monastery or the Summer Palace. It was, in fact, only a few blocks away from the hotel – an echoing, single-roomed concrete building smelling faintly of urine. A long counter running the length of the building had several pigeonholes labelled in Chinese. Being unable to read the signs made little difference, as there was only one person on duty, and everyone was queueing at the same pigeonhole. There were about a dozen post office workers altogether, but the remainder did not seem to be doing much. Shigatze's public telephone stood in a cubicle in the corner. Through the glass panel in the door I could see a small and earnest Chinese shouting into the receiver. After listening intently for a reply, he stuck his head out of the door and called over to one of the post office staff, who busied himself with the telephone equipment behind the counter. This performance was still being repeated by the time Grannie had bought her stamps and we returned to the hotel.

A group of Swiss tourists was in the hotel dining hall that evening. Grannie and I were still eating in splendid isolation at our own tin table, but after the meal one of the Swiss women came over to chat. She spoke English and, like Grannie, had been ill in Lhasa. Soon they were swopping tales about the local hospitals.

'Of course they're not up to the standards we're used to, but they're better than nothing. The problem is training these people to use them. Did you know, most of the local Tibetans won't even go to a hospital? Think how many lives could be saved . . . but then, re-educating these people is going to take a long time. The Chinese doctor was telling us all about it.'

Grannie was nodding assent. 'Well, you've only got to see them in those temples. I went down with my guide this afternoon. They're all into voodoo, all that bowing and so forth to those statues . . . '

What could Cho have been telling her?

I was puzzled by the Tibetan aversion to hospitals. In Nepal, the Tibetans I knew had never expressed any fear or reluctance when speaking of any visit to hospital. It was not until afterwards, when reading the report to the International Commission of Jurists, that I found the same story repeated by one after another of the Tibetans who had escaped, and began to understand the basis for their avoidance of Chinese hospitals:

The Chinese told the Tibetans they were dull and should have better blood in them. Their race was inferior and like animals, and a better race would be produced by giving injections.

Statement no.39.
Doctors arrived in Doi in the second Tibetan month of 1956. They announced that the people were to be given medicine to make them strong ... a list of names was prepared and his [the witness's] own name was included. He was called inside and the first thing that happened was an examination of his reproductory organs ... then a blood sample was taken from his arm. A rectal examination by means of a finger was then carried out and he saw in front of him a piece of glass in a basin. When the finger was agitated he ejaculated a fluid on to the glass which was then taken away. Immediately afterwards he was bound to a chair with his back arched and supported and he could see his own penis. Very thin forceps were then inserted inside his urethra. This instrument he described as being tapered and capable of being opened and closed like scissors. It was kept in some kind of fluid. As it went further inside the pain became intense and he saw the instrument inserted about two and a half to three inches. Then with the pain, he could not look any more but felt the instrument going further inside. The forceps were opened. He felt great pain and fainted.

When he recovered consciousness, he had been set free and saw tiny puncture marks on each side of his groin with a yellow stain on each ... The Chinese warned him, on pain of his head, not to say anything of what had happened ... at home he remained in bed for a month suffering pain in the genital organs and in the upper part of his body ... he became absent-minded ... and suffered from split vision... Since undergoing this treatment he has had no intercourse at all, no sexual urges, and no erection ...

His wife was sent for two weeks after him ... She was bound in a chair and some kind of bladder was inserted inside the vagina and inflated. When this was taken out, a piece of flesh was pulled to the opening of the vagina, a yellow substance and a white powder were applied to this piece of flesh ... She told her husband she had no sexual feelings and although her menstrual cycle prior to this treatment was normal, she ceased entirely to menstruate afterwards ... witnesses told of other men and women who had received this treatment dying shortly afterwards.

International Commission of Jurists; *Geneva 1960*

There was only one bus in the flat space designated as a bus station, the engine coughing and revving and filling the air with dust and diesel fumes. The passengers were crowded by the vehicle, pushing and shoving for precedence, although the door remained firmly shut. It was well before breakfast time, and Cho had been uncharacteristically late. I had met him halfway to the bus station wheeling his bicycle between the dusty potholes. He accompanied me in silence, stepping aside discreetly to place me between himself and the milling crowd around the bus.

The driver, a stout woman in green coveralls, had switched her attention from the engine to the passengers. She opened the door and stepped outside, while a heaving sea of khaki and green pushed and shoved its way up the narrow steps. Cho handed my ticket to the driver, then waved a hand graciously to indicate that I should join the mêlée and haul my pack on board, while he stepped hastily out of the fray.

'I have instructed the driver to take you to the tourist office in Lhasa.'

The driver did not look grateful for this extra responsibility.

I sat down in one of the front seats which had extra legroom, but my comfort was short-lived. It transpired that both tickets and seats had corresponding numbers, and the khaki-clad owner of the ticket for my seat arrived and began to shout abuse at me. I smiled blankly back at him. Evidently this was the wrong technique, for he then threw his luggage (a couple of heavy boxes) on top of me, perched on the seat beside me, and began digging me viciously in the ribs with his elbow. As he was considerably bigger than I was, there was little alternative but to retreat hastily to the 'good place' Cho had reserved for me at the back of the bus, now occupied by a man so fat that he spread across the double seat, leaving barely four inches at the edge for me. Maybe I should have argued with Cho and gone by truck.

All the other occupants of the bus were soldiers or denim-clad commune workers, probably because the fare, at 17 *yuan*, was beyond the pocket of most individual Tibetans. These people would have their fares paid by their particular government organisation.

There was a burst of argument from the front of the bus. A young man with blond hair and a backpack had wedged himself in a corner at the front, there being no spare seats, and was being harangued by the bus driver. He was smiling, replying carefully in American-accented Chinese and refusing to budge. I wondered if he would fare better than I had, and cheered inwardly when the driver gave up and drove off.

The journey was bumpy, dusty and smoky. The American and I were the only people on board who were not chain-smoking cheap Chinese cigarettes. It seemed a long way to Gyantze.

11

After Younghusband

The Chinese Hotel was nearly a mile out of town, a smaller and more run-down version of the one at Shigatze. The single-storey concrete-with-corrugated-iron-roof buildings were set on three sides of a square around a dirt courtyard, with several army trucks parked to one side. I joined the queue of people heading for a small window set in a wall where a man in the office behind was examining everyone's papers and handing out room numbers.

'Been here before?' It was the blond American.

'No. You?'

'Couple of weeks ago on my way out of Lhasa. The people here are really friendly, but the food's terrible.'

'Can't be worse than in Nyalam!'

'We could have a wager on that.' He smiled wryly.

'How come you're not with a tour group?'

'I came in through Hong Kong and got travel permits from town to town in China. Then I heard you could get permits to Lhasa at a place in Mongolia, so I took the four-day train ride up there, got the permit and hitch-hiked to Lhasa. One or two people who had learned enough Chinese managed to do it, but there's no getting permits further than Lhasa. I was lucky to get as far as Shigatze without one, and I've been trying to get out for days, but just got turned back every time. So I'll go back to Lhasa and Chengdu now.'

'How did you learn Chinese?'

He grinned. 'Survival and a book. All I could say at first was "woh-sah-bei-dah-shur-shen", which means "I am a student from Peking", and nobody could understand why I couldn't speak any more Chinese than that. But once they'd decided I was just stupid, everything was okay.'

We were almost at the ticket window. I was peering over the shoulders of the people in front, trying to see what papers they were presenting, and wondering what the office would make of my letter.

'Do you want me to fix up a room? The dormitory's cheap, but you need your own padlock or your stuff disappears.'

Rob had obviously made his mark here, for he was welcomed with smiles and handshakes. We were shown to the dormitory nearest to the outside water-pump. No one asked to see my papers, for which I was relieved. The water from the pump was freezing cold, modifying my plans to wash off the dust from the bus journey.

We joined the other passengers for supper in the concrete dining hall. It was hard to believe, but Rob was right. The food was worse than in Nyalam. Watery, greasy soup with a few pieces of tofu floating in it, and a pile of tasteless, transparent noodles adorned by a spoonful of green-black vegetables which had obviously been dead for some time. Everything was cold. Knowing what the inside of the rice bowl would be like, I tried bread, but it was grey and rock-hard. Rob was eating very slowly, then looked up from his plate. The look on my face must have been as funny as that on his, and we both burst out laughing.

'You win the bet.'

'Breakfast elsewhere?'

'Definitely.'

I half-awakened in the pre-dawn darkness to the hysterical screech of the klaxon as the bus made ready to leave. I could hear the driver looking for me, her questioning voice irritable with early-morning work and unwanted responsibilities. I stayed where I was. She soon gave up, glad to be rid of me no doubt, and the bus roared off in the direction of Lhasa. I did not move until a shaft of dusty sunlight forced its way through the grimy window at the end of the room.

'Come on, breakfast!'

The shapeless bundle of covers on the bed by the window began to move, and Rob's tousled blond head appeared.

'So you didn't get whisked off to Lhasa then?'

There was a knock at the door. Rob let in a middle-aged, grey-haired man with a shabby khaki jacket draped over his shoulders. He sat, smiling through broken teeth, and made intermittent conversation in Chinese.

'He's from next door,' explained Rob. 'Seems like he lives here. Very friendly, always coming round to tell you something or invite you somewhere. Unfortunately, he has no sense of time and comes round at all hours of the day or night. But he means well.'

The family who ran the hotel and various children had gathered meanwhile on the sunny doorstep.

'I know what they're waiting for.'

Rob brought out a small harmonica and played a few bars. Appreciative clapping from the audience, and the harmonica was passed round and shared.

'They'll remember this, too.'

In his pack he had a pair of plastic glasses with a Groucho Marx false nose and moustache attached. He put these on and terrorised the children with them, then handed them over for the children to play with. We managed to clear everyone out of the room, and Rob padlocked the door. The delighted shrieks and squeals followed us across the compound.

'Do you travel around with that thing?'

'Oh, yes. Everybody loves it. I've got some other things too. I've a weird sense of humour I suppose, but I make lots of friends.'

The road ran between rows of willows, fresh green in spring leaf. There was no traffic except for a few peasants walking to work with their hoes across their shoulders. As we neared the town the fort came into view, perched on its rock high above the willows, looking as impregnable as when Sir Francis Younghusband first saw it, in the April of 1904.

The British invasion of Tibet in 1904 seemed to establish, more than anything else, that neither side had the faintest idea of what the other wanted. Younghusband, described by Peter Fleming as 'an efficient, hardworking officer with a deep sense of dedication', came to the conclusion that the Tibetans were 'hopeless soldiers'. After several exasperating attempts to negotiate a treaty, he thought Tibetan attitudes 'more futile and inept than intentionally hostile'. The Tibetans, having neither the material equipment nor the spiritual inclination for fighting, simply wanted to be left alone.

The walls of the fort were skilfully blended into the rock on which they were built, leaving no purchase for hands or feet. The smooth stonework defeated my skills as a rock-climber, even without the additional hazard of defenders hurling rocks from above.

Initially, Younghusband was saved the trouble of forcing an entry. As he approached the dzong at the head of his force, he was met by the dzong-pen, or commandant, an ageing and unwarlike character who explained regretfully that he could not surrender the fort as this would land him in deep trouble with the Dalai Lama. On the other hand, he could not defend it, as all his soldiers had run away. He suggested that Younghusband and his army could, perhaps, simply ignore the fort's existence and continue their business elsewhere. This, of course, did not comply with the established British code of how a military campaign should be conducted, and the fort was occupied and searched the following day. However, the British did not remain in occupation. Recognising that their force was too small to defend the water supply, they encamped at the hamlet of Chang Lo, about a thousand yards away by the river, and waited for authorisation from the British Government to continue to Lhasa.

That the Mission stayed in Gyantze until 14 July was due in part to the indecisiveness of a weak government, but more to the personal and political manoeuvrings of individuals in the corridors of Whitehall. The fact that a band of stalwart Englishmen were tramping across the Tibetan plateau at all was largely due to the determination of the Viceroy of India, Lord Curzon, to establish contact with the Dalai Lama in Lhasa. All his letters had been returned unopened, and he had finally persuaded his government to sanction an expeditionary force on the grounds that it was vital to curb Russian expansionism and influence in Lhasa. The suspicion of Russian designs on Tibet centred on a Mongolian monk from Drepung monastery named Dorjieff, who was from one of the outlying Russian territories and who seemed to enjoy the confidence of both the Dalai Lama and the Tsar.

The official reason for the expedition was the refusal of the Tibetans to comply with the treaty Britain had concluded with China over frontiers and free trade. China claimed suzerainty over Tibet, but at that time was unable to enforce the claim beyond stationing an Amban, or delegate, in Lhasa. The Tibetans detested their Chinese overlords, refused to recognise the treaty, and took a perverse delight in tearing down frontier posts and grazing their yaks on the wrong side of the border.

It was on these rather shaky grounds that the expedition was despatched to secure a treaty to which the Tibetans would adhere. Younghusband left Siliguri with detachments of Sikhs, Gurkhas, Pathans and a regiment of British soldiers, all over six foot, to impress the Tibetans: 'I will say we only sent small men with our guns.' They lost a total of 7,321 pack animals and 88 porters on the long haul from tropical Sikkim over the Himalayan passes into Tibet.

On the way to Gyantze the expedition encountered a large number of poorly armed Tibetans at Guru, who simply stood and watched the British march past. An attempt to take their antique guns from them resulted in scuffles; shots were fired, the British artillery opened up, and 300 Tibetans were killed, with no British casualties. As soon as the Tibetans saw the British fire-power, they had turned and walked slowly away, even though they were still in range of the guns. One of the gunners wrote, 'I got so sick of the slaughter I ceased to fire, though the General's order was to make as big a bag as possible.' It was not the sort of glorious battle the British had hoped for.

At no time did the invaders seem really to understand the kind of country they had entered. They found admirable sport and food-supply in the large numbers of wild birds in the area, which had no fear of man owing to Buddhist Tibetans never harming them. For the most devout Tibetans, the taking of life, either animal or human, would have such severe karmic consequences that it was debatably a better choice to allow your enemy to kill you. The balance between the preservation of this life and concern for the next varied with individuals, but it was never a factor the British took into account during the campaign. Most of the participants wanted to distinguish themselves 'for King and country', and to be recognised and rewarded at home after an exciting adventure. Modern climbing expeditions seem to share this last aim with the military expeditions on which they were originally modelled.

During their three months in Gyantze the British army found the Tibetans to be extremely friendly, hospitable and eager to trade. A bazaar grew up around the British encampment. The new Chinese Amban in Lhasa sent regular messages that he was 'anxious to hasten to the frontier and discuss with you all matters requiring settlement', but as the Dalai Lama refused point-blank to provide him with transport his progress was slow, to say the least. (It had taken him over a year to reach Lhasa.)

Several other aspects of the expedition had the good qualities of a farce. During the latter part of their three-month sojourn, the force was technically besieged by large numbers of Tibetans gathering in the area, strengthening the fort and so on. In spite of this, Post Office engineers were left unhampered in their work to extend the military telegraph line to Gyantze. Legend attributes this to the chief engineer's reply, on being asked what the lines were for, that the British did not know Tibet and had only poor maps. They were constantly getting lost, and were afraid it would be as difficult to get out of the country as it had been getting in! Since they were anxious to leave as soon as their business was finished, the line was to show them the way out. The Tibetans left the line intact.

Eventually negotiations got under way between Younghusband, the Panchen Lama from Shigatze, the Grand Secretary

The roof of the Potala in Lhasa. Women repairing the walkway have left a baby (right) under the ornately painted golden pagodas which shelter the pinnacles of chortens to successive Dalai Lamas.

Pilgrim with a prayer wheel, one of thousands who travel great distances to visit the holy city of Lhasa.

Rioting and burning in the streets of Lhasa in March 1989. (A tourist's photograph supplied by Jane Moore.)

and the Tongsa Penlop of Bhutan, who had offered to mediate. The discussions came to their usual inconclusive end. In Younghusband's words, it was 'like throwing butter at a granite rock'. The Tibetans ignored the ultimatum to clear the fort, and on 6 July the British finally tackled the daunting walls of Gyantze dzong. They threw into the affray the combined force of the Mounted Infantry, the Gurkhas, Sikhs, Pathans and two antique seven-pounder guns named Bubble and Squeak. A hole began to appear at the base of the wall, the Gurkhas climbed up the rock and through the hole, and the fort was properly taken.

Younghusband subsequently made his way to Lhasa, and once again found himself with a long wait before Whitehall's dithering and Tibetan obstructiveness could be resolved. He was told that the Dalai Lama was in 'retreat' in the religious sense, but in fact the head of the Tibetan government was in hasty retreat in the direction of Mongolia. Finally, the treaty was signed in the Potala, with the Ganden Tri-Rinpoche affixing the seal of the Dalai Lama. 'Done in quintuplicate at Lhasa this 7th day of September in the year of our Lord 1904, corresponding with the Tibetan date, the 27th of the seventh month of the Wood Dragon year.' The 'Thibetans' seemed unable to take the solemn British dignitaries seriously and giggled throughout the proceedings. The Chinese Amban (later described by one of his own countrymen as 'a cowardly and incompetent poltroon') nevertheless proved sufficiently adept to use the presence of the British to strengthen the Chinese position in Lhasa. When, in 1910, the Dalai Lama fled from the Chinese army to India, the British government recognised the Chinese administration set up in Lhasa. Sir Charles Bell, appointed as mentor to the exiled god-king, commented, 'The Tibetans were abandoned to Chinese aggression, for which the British Military Expedition to Lhasa and subsequent retreat were primarily responsible.'

It was the internal struggles of the revolution which recalled the Chinese troops from Lhasa, and the Dalai Lama returned to his capital in 1912. During the next three and a half decades, Tibet enjoyed an emerging independence, the thirteenth Dalai

Lama died, and his reincarnation was recognised and installed in 1940. The Tibetans, having discovered what the telegraph was for, extended the line to Lhasa. Bell became British Agent in Gyantze, according to Younghusband's treaty, and later moved to Lhasa. The Red Chinese arrived in 1951, enjoying, no doubt, the same ease of advance as the British had done.

Younghusband himself, returning from Tibet with hopes of recognition and reward for his success, was doomed to disappointment. Changes in Whitehall's policies in the meantime had resulted in his Convention becoming a political embarrassment on the international scene. It was convenient to make Younghusband the scapegoat, and he received the minimum decoration possible and a minor posting to Kashmir. After the initial disappointment he seemed contented enough. In 1910 he resigned from the Government of India's service to devote his energies to religion. Tibet had left its mark on him. Fleming describes him as having a 'deep, mystical love of all wild and empty places and especially of mountains ... ' His generation saw the heart of Asia as possessing a mystic, hidden quality, even though they were not themselves sure exactly what it was. The expedition, for the most part, failed to recognise the qualities which fascinated them even when in Tibet itself; having finally reached the Forbidden City most of them were immediately bored and eager to get home again. Doubtless many of them, like the returning mountaineers who had regaled me with adventure stories, would forget their disillusionment upon their return, and immediately start re-creating the mystique.

Younghusband had noticed the cheerful serenity of the Tibetans as well as the wild beauty of their land. Although he left no record of studying their philosophy at the time of the campaign, something of that inner peace must have come through to him intuitively. Looking back on Lhasa on his homeward journey, he says, 'I was insensibly suffused with an almost intoxicating sense of elation and goodwill. This exhilaration of the moment grew and grew until it thrilled through me with overpowering intensity. Never again could I think evil, or ever again be at enmity with any man. All nature and all humanity were bathed in a rosy glowing radiancy ...'

In 1933 Younghusband founded the World Congress of Faiths, so that the leaders of most of the world's religions could get together to establish common ideals of love and unity. He later became President of the Royal Geographical Society and helped to sponsor some of the early Everest expeditions. After his death a friend remembered him as 'the happiest person I have ever come across'. With him was buried his most treasured possession, a small image of the Buddha, given him by the Tri-Rinpoche in Lhasa.

The helpful neighbour was standing in the hotel doorway, his face shadowy in the uncertain light of the low-watt bulb.

'He's inviting us to a movie,' Rob translated. The two chang-houses in town had supplied similar fodder to that in the hotel, and any distraction from the thought of food was welcome. We accepted. The fee was 3 *fen* (100 *fen* equal 1 *yuan*), about the cheapest movie I would ever see.

A large concrete building with a corrugated-iron roof and dirt floor probably served as a kind of village hall for political meetings. The conversion to cinema was effected by the population arriving with their own wooden stools and handing their 3 *fen* to a fat woman perched by a rickety metal table at the door. A large sheet had been hung at one end of the hall, and the projector perched on a bench in the centre. Two children were immediately dispossessed of their seats by our friend, and we rather guiltily sat down. Not understanding Chinese proved to be no disadvantage, as the dialogue was inaudible and in any case the audience talked loudly the whole way through. The scratchy pictures and melodramatic music were designed to tell their own story. The plot followed the trials and adventures of a beautiful Mongolian Boadicea and her four-and-a-half-hour campaign against an evil, red-haired Russian who took delight in torturing women, putting whole villages to fire and sword, and shooting babies in their cradles. The camera dwelt lovingly on the graphic details. I felt perhaps the original showing of the film had been intended for the northern borders.

'I wonder if they knew people would be sitting on hard seats when they made this movie?' commented Rob ruefully, half-way through hour number three.

The quest for edible food was resumed the following morning, with new tactics. Rob had had experience of the newly emerging free market in China.

'Once people have done their quota for the commune, they're allowed to sell any of their own produce on the free market. It's a new government incentive to increase productivity. So we should be able to buy veggies and eggs in the town.' He laughed. 'I came across some pretty amusing examples of free trade in China. Now that it's legal, whereas before it had been illegal, most of the Chinese peasants assume they can sell anything there's a demand for. You can buy student cards, official travel documents, things like that – just over the counter.'

'Is it easy to travel independently in mainland China?'

He laughed again. 'It's an exercise in patience. People in shops will tell you they haven't got what you're asking for – even when it's sitting there in front of both of you. And in hotels you'll be told they don't have a room, when you know they're almost empty. So you just sit and wait, and wait, and insist, and in the end they give you a room. The longest I've waited was two and a half days!'

I thought of the Shishapangma expedition's long negotiations with the CMA and could see the similarity in tactics.

'Have you found Tibet much different?'

'I haven't really had much of a chance to travel around – only Lhasa and Shigatze. I don't speak any Tibetan, so I've mainly been in contact with Chinese officials and government workers who can speak Chinese. They've been pretty pleasant, once you accept that most of them lie, all the time.'

'Oh, so it's not just my imagination!'

'I think it's just the way they go about things. Confusing for us, but they seem to consider it quite normal. The few times I did get to meet the top man of a commune or office, "he" was a woman, always Chinese, and an idealist who really seemed to believe in what she was doing. Further down the ranks there's not much incentive for anyone to care about anything.'

I said, 'Most of the Tibetan government workers seem far less pleasant than the village people who are living much as they always did.'

'I think that figures once you've had some experience of the Han Chinese out here. They still consider the Tibetans to be inferior. So a government man abandons his old beliefs and society, and can't be fully trusted by his old friends. But he's not accepted as an equal by the Hans – so he's nowhere. Very sad really.'

We crossed to the other side of the rocky spur on which the fort stood, and followed the dirt road which was the main street of the old town. An elderly couple were sitting in the dust on a street corner, working as they gossiped with a group of their friends who had gathered to chat. The old man was drilling holes in a strip of wood using a hand drill which he spun with a small bow, while the woman was cutting a spiral from a piece of leather to make a thong. Both gave the impression that their hands were working automatically while their minds were on their gossip.

'Does anyone have eggs or potatoes to sell?'

Their prices were outrageous. I dismissed them with a laugh and a wave of the hand. The bargaining continued for the proper length of time, until it seemed I had passed the test, and then an only slightly exaggerated price was easily agreed upon. Rob was told to wait at the corner until someone returned with potatoes, while a young woman took me through the winding streets to her house to collect some eggs.

She stopped at a high wall on the edge of the old town and pushed open the heavy wooden door. We stepped into an enclosed courtyard surrounded by sheds and storerooms similar to those in Tingri. A wooden ladder led to a mud-surfaced platform in front of three upstairs rooms. Waiting by the door was her son Panden, a quiet, well-mannered ten-year-old, who waved me to sit down and brought me tea which he topped up attentively. I smiled as I thought of the contrast between him and the wild antics of Phurbu's son. But then, Gyantze was the third city of Tibet, and it was only to be expected that there would be a comparatively sophisticated population.

Panden's mother was showing off the improvements to the house.

'The new stove is waiting to be put in, but the walls have to be plastered first.' As yet the walls were surfaced only with rippled mud, awaiting the final white plaster. 'My husband's a builder, so he's able to do most of the work himself.'

There was a commotion outside in the street.

'Your friend's here,' she said, without looking up.

I went out on to the front porch and craned through the tiny window that overlooked the narrow street. A flowing crowd of people had washed Rob along and deposited him outside the gate. Panden ran down to let him in. He arrived at the door a little breathless.

'I wasn't sure what was happening at first when they started dragging me down here. They're certainly helpful.'

The crowd hovered for a moment, to see if there would be any further entertainment, then began to disperse. Panden and his mother sold us four eggs and we went down to the city's chang-house to find someone to cook them.

The door of the chang-house opened directly on to the road, the noise made by the occupants being its only advertisement. Inside, about a dozen commune workers were passing round cigarettes and a large jug of chang.

'Come and sit with us! Have some chang, have a cigarette.'

We opted for tea, syrupy with lavish amounts of imported sugar. Already the room was beginning to fill up with curious spectators. I wondered how Younghusband's garrison and Post Office engineers had managed to move without tripping over inquisitive Tibetans. Those who could not make it through the packed doorway were reduced to peering in at the wire-mesh covered windows. A smart young man, whose green jacket was hanging open to reveal a well-fitting leather jacket beneath, edged over to us from a nearby bench, offered cigarettes, and spoke to Rob in Chinese. From time to time he would pause, so that Rob could translate for me. It seemed that the young Tibetan had a good job at the government offices, having received a Chinese education. Until recently, only Chinese had been taught in the schools which the government had set up. I found it hard to believe that this young Tibetan could not speak his native language but, whatever the reason, he would not acknowledge any questions I directed at him in Tibetan, confining his conversation to the Chinese he spoke with his friends or with Rob. He had found favour with his employers, and so had been granted permits to buy luxury goods such as the clothes he was wearing. He also had a radio.

The girl serving tea and chang was picking her way through a human obstacle course, trying to find out who was buying, and evicting those who were not. I took our eggs and potatoes round to the kitchen and asked if they could be cooked. My hopes faded as I looked around at the perplexed expressions on the cooks' faces. Then a plump woman began to smile.

'Of course! Come and sit down.'

After a peremptory scrub, the potatoes were dropped into a pot of hot water and the eggs into hot oil. A man was sitting by the door, his khaki jacket hung on the back of a chair. He watched the proceedings for a while, then produced a small onion and diced it into the omelette – a gesture I fully appreciated now I knew how rare onions were in Tibet. He came over and sat down at the table.

'How long have you been in Tibet?'

'About three months.'

'Have you been to Dharamsala and seen the Dalai Lama? Is he coming back to Tibet?'

That question again. If only I knew how to answer it.

'I haven't seen him, so I don't know if he's coming or not.'

The plump woman came over, wiping her hands on her apron. 'Maybe you have his picture?' I shook my head, making a mental note to bring several dozen if ever I came back.

'Have you seen Gyantze monastery? You must go and see it today. The lama is my friend. You will like it there.'

The man reached inside a canvas bag hanging on the back of the chair and took out a paperback in Tibetan script. It was of the kind produced by the Chinese-Tibetan publishing company at Koko-nor on the eastern borders of Tibet. He pushed it across the table so that I could attempt to read some of the text.

'Have you seen this book before? It is a book of Dharma, but in some places it is changed.' He paused. 'There are many things in Tibet that have changed. I suppose I have too.'

He fell silent for a while, calloused hands resting on the open book. I wondered who or what he had been before becoming a commune worker. Most of the literate Tibetans had been monks, and he was unlikely to have been taught to read Tibetan by the Chinese.

'Were you a monk before the Chinese came?' I asked.

He shook his head. 'All that is finished. These days I work for the government. I suppose I am becoming Chinese. In the early days, Tibetans had to change their minds about many things. For those slow to change there was *thamzing*.' His eyes narrowed as if remembering an old pain. 'It was ... very effective.'

We sat for a while in silence in the dimly lit kitchen, while the women clattered around in the firelight, moving pots and pans and scooping barley from a hopper to brew for chang. Maybe he had been a monk, or maybe an educated aristocrat, although few of either had survived the revolutionary purges. It seemed unlikely that younger Tibetans would be aware of the changes that had been made in the reprinting of old books, having nothing to compare them with. Some of the changes are no doubt quite subtle, although others are obvious and have been pointed out by Tibetans living in exile who have obtained copies of these books. Dharma itself, for example, is described in the Chinese edition as 'a system whereby external objects are mistakenly perceived by imputation, and whereby the significance of human nature is lost by a belief in gods and the supreme jewel and the Creator of the world, leading to a hope for heaven and a future life.' The correct description of Dharma (a Sanskrit word meaning, literally, 'that which holds') refers to 'special realisations that hold us back from taking unfortunate rebirths in the future, and from experiencing in this life the fears and sufferings that arise as a result of our own unwholesome actions and delusions, such as anger, desirous attachment and ignorance'. For example, the direct, intuitive realisation of emptiness, the ultimate nature of all that exists, is but one that will eliminate suffering. In the light of the Chinese comment on a 'Creator', it is interesting to look to an eighth-century Buddhist text, the *Shantideva-Bodhisattvacharyavatara* ('A Guide to the Bodhisattva's Way of Life'): 'From beginningless time, all happiness and suffering have been produced by wholesome and unwholesome actions respectively. We cannot find any object that is produced by a permanent god.'

Tibetans in exile became greatly concerned that the sacred texts were being rewritten and their meaning perverted, and began reprinting them in India in their original form, with the intention of smuggling copies back into Tibet so that people would have the means of checking the validity of editions produced locally. If those printed by the Chinese gain credibility, they feel, then the last of their religion will be eaten away at its heart. It would be as if all Bibles in the West were destroyed and replaced with a new edition whose meaning had been subtly changed, with vital parts left out. There are even those who say this has happened already.

The plump woman brought over the tea and food, and I rejoined Rob in the outer room. We ate slowly, savouring the feast. Afterwards I left Rob to his conversation and went to bid goodbye to our cooks. They refused money for anything but the tea. The service, they insisted, was hospitality.

Outside, I stood blinking in the sunlight for a moment and then walked up to the monastery. The buildings stood clustered about the base of the hill, while on the flat space in front stood the huge terraced chörten known as the Kumbum, the Golden Temple of the Hundred Thousand Buddhas. The mandala-shaped lower tiers were linked by connecting stairways, so that a circumambulation of the stupa became an ascending spiral – the inner, spiritual path of a meditator passing through higher stages of consciousness, manifested as a physical journey. Each tier had many doorways, leading into small, windowless chapels containing frescoes and statues. Above, the way led out on to a circular terrace, the equivalent of the dome of the smaller stupas I had seen in Nepal and representing the noble eightfold path and the powers of higher knowledge. Within the golden spire of the chörten stood the figure of Buddha. He symbolises the final state of enlightenment.

I walked up the rocky hillside behind the chörten and came

The Kumbum

to the back of the half-repaired monastery. A straggle of children followed and became my guides, showing me a small doorway set in a rough stone wall. They must have been used to swarming up and down the passages like mice, because they found their way unerringly through the darkened maze of corridors until we were in the main temple in the heart of the palace. The statues were covered with dust, lit only by a few butter lamps. There was a soft cold silence in here, in contrast to the activity of Tashi Lhunpo. A narrow stairway led from one side of the temple to a small upper room. The window was large by Tibetan standards, and sunlight streamed in. Two monks were sitting at a low table, printing long slender pages of texts by laying the paper on to a carved woodblock which had been covered with ink. They worked steadily, as a team, one inking the block with a roller dipped in a tray at his side, while the other laid on the paper and smoothed it with a clean roller. The old books had used parchment inked with soot mixed with butter, but here the paper was modern, although the ink looked remarkably like soot and butter.

The printers looked up and smiled a welcome, beckoning me

over to look at their work. One took advantage of the pause to top up their cups from the vacuum flask of butter tea which stood among the inks and rollers on the table. The other held out the slim page for me to look at. I stumbled through the first two lines, not understanding what I was reading. The old monk chuckled as I pronounced letters which were supposed to be silent, or missed a stop and ran two syllables together. Tibetan texts are remarkably complex, as there are dots between each syllable and a stroke at the end of a sentence – but many words are made up of two or more syllables and you have to judge from the context where each word starts and finishes. The complexities of spelling seem to be comparable with English in their ability to confuse the beginner; Tibetan has fewer exceptions to its rules, but there are more rules. Moreover, many syllables have silent prefixes or suffixes, and still more have letters piled on top of or underneath each other, so that the word becomes cruciform rather than linear. Textual Tibetan is archaic, and differs greatly from the conversational language – both of which contain different words which must be used depending on the level of importance of the person being addressed or referred to. For instance, if referring to a respected lama, not only would any action he performed require the honorific form of the verb, but his pen or even his dog would require a different word from the common one. I had initially felt great embarrassment when trying to make conversation with lamas, because my command of the honorific form was practically non-existent, and I felt I was being as disrespectful as someone who addressed the Queen as 'guv', or something similar. However, none of them had ever seemed to mind, and their cheerful encouragement had made me realise that the problem was in my mind, not theirs.

The two old printers were enjoying their tea and my efforts. One of them handed me a page as I stood up to go. I folded it carefully into my pocket, then left a few coins as an offering on the little shrine by the window. They called me back, and one of them reached inside his robe and brought out a smaller, folded paper, printed with script that was finer, and older than the ones they were making.

'Keep this safe,' he said. 'It is a prayer of Tsong Khapa. It is very precious.' He gave me the paper and waved for me to go. The two monks bent again to their work, absorbed and undistracted, as if nothing had happened.

I left by the main door of the temple. In the great porch, about a dozen Tibetans were working to restore and rebuild the twenty-foot high statues which sat two to each side of the door. The figures were being built up stage by stage with clay and plaster, which would later be painted in the same brilliant colours as the fragments of the originals which still remained. I looked around at the rest of the huge crumbling temple and wondered how long it would take them to rebuild all of it. The Tibetans did not seem particularly over-awed by the prospect. They were laughing and talking together as they worked, passing round the inevitable jug of chang, and yet working with speed and enthusiasm.

'How do we know how long it will take? We just work, and bit by bit it gets done.'

'It's the same with Ganden. The Tibetans find the money and start the work, and the Chinese say, "Who is paying you? Where is this idea from?" And we say, well, we are just doing it, you know ... And they don't stop us, and they like to say they are restoring the gompas ... '

It was as if the whole of Tibet were undergoing the ordeal of the towers. Perhaps it was not whether they finished the temple that mattered, but the personal commitment to keep rebuilding what had been torn down, and what, with a change of government and the stroke of a pen, could be destroyed again. I found I was watching the faces of the builders as they worked, rather than the faces of the statues which were emerging from their hands.

I walked slowly back to the dilapidated hotel. The evening light deepened to a rich red glow as the sun sank, silhouetting the crag and its fort black against the flame-red sky. Tibet had become a Dali landscape of colour and light, as unreal and intangible as it had been before I ever came here.

PART THREE

The City

What you write with ink, in small black letters,
Can all be lost
Through the work of a single drop of water,
But what is written in your mind,
Is there for eternity.

Tsangyang Gyatso,
the sixth Dalai Lama

12

Lhasa: Heaven and Earth

Hitch-hiking to Lhasa was a slow business. It took until three o'clock the following afternoon before a Liberation Army truck stopped and the cheerful Chinese driver threw his kit behind the seat and waved us aboard.

The noisy vehicle ploughed its way up and down the gradients in the single-track dirt road, running well despite the alarming sounds coming from the engine. At every available stream or spring the driver would pull over and stop, throw water over the engine and top up the radiator. At first I assumed this was to humour the idiosyncrasies of this particular vehicle, but we soon found ourselves joining queues of identical trucks at each water stop. Some were loaded with dusty but lively passengers, others empty but for the solitary driver.

'They're all the same design,' Rob commented cheerfully. 'The gas line goes real close to the block and over-heats.'

I wondered if it was a potentially explosive combination, but as there was nothing I could do about it, it seemed better to think about something else. A waving truckload of Tibetans sailed past us at the next water stop.

'I expect we'll pass it further up the pass, broken down,' Rob observed drily.

It had stopped in the middle of the narrow road when we

caught up, forcing us to stop too. The diminutive Chinese driver grinned and lit a cigarette, unconcerned about speed and schedules, and the various hiccups in the transport system. The truck in front lurched off – and ours refused to start. The driver grinned philosophically, and plodded off with a jerrycan for more water to throw over the engine.

It was evening by the time the rippling blue expanse of the Yamdok Tso came into sight.

'Nagartze tonight, Lhasa tomorrow,' chirped the driver. He swung his insignificant weight hard against the wheel, and turned the truck into the compound of the army barracks just beyond the village.

'You like fresh fish?' he enquired, and went off to the kitchen without waiting for an answer. Rob and I waited in the almost empty mess hall, where a few soldiers still lingered, and a handful of mangy mongrels were cleaning up the scraps from the floor. We were instantly cornered by an enthusiastic Chinese corporal with a teach-yourself-English book.

'Please to pronounce this?' he piped, pointing to a page of sentences. Rob moved with the corporal to one of the tables. I stood watching for a moment, trying to clear my head of the truck's vibrations. Suddenly I was struck violently on the back of the leg. It did not seem that I had fallen, but I became dimly aware that I was lying on the floor, and that the screams I could hear echoing on the high tin roof were my own. Rob was elbowing his way between the soldiers who had gathered round, staring dumbly.

'Here, get over to this chair.' He was dragging me across the room.

'What happened?' I was still dazed.

'One of the clean-up dogs was strolling past, and it suddenly went berserk and bit you. Let's have a look. Maybe it didn't break the skin . . . Oh *shit*.' Four deep puncture wounds dripped blood on to the dirty floor. 'I guess we should check the dog out, in case of rabies. It was a pretty big one – got you four inches above the knee. Shouldn't be too hard to spot.'

Rob disappeared in pursuit of the dog. I sat on the edge of the cold metal chair trying to remember what I knew about rabies. It wasn't much, mainly gruesome stories of madness and death, although I recalled something about two weeks' grace before having to start the antidote shots. The soldiers were still staring blankly when Rob returned.

'No chance. Could be any of a dozen out there. Hey, you all right?'

The shock reaction was starting; an increasing tightness around my head, which soon spread to my whole body. Even my lungs felt cramped and it became increasingly difficult to breathe. I wanted to faint, but felt that if I did I would surely stop breathing. Rob was holding me on to the chair. I tried to grab hold of his arm, but found that my hands had stiffened into useless claws. Through the fading and reappearing images of the empty mess hall I could hear Rob's broken Chinese.

'She is sick, she needs to lie down . . .'

The Chinese medical orderly arrived carrying a green canvas bag with a red cross painted on it. He began to swab at the wounds busily with a tuft of cotton wool soaked in hydrogen peroxide which fizzed nastily as it came in contact with the blood.

'She is sick, do you have a bed somewhere. . . ?'

'Excuse me, please to pronounce this. . . ?'

The camp commander arrived. 'Please, show me your passport.'

'She is sick . . .'

'Please, is this word correct?'

Eventually Rob managed to satisfy the commander with his passport and I was carried to one of the bunkrooms and deposited on a bunk. The medical orderly followed and there completed his interrupted bandaging job. Rob shooed out the inevitable spectators, my head began to clear and the little Chinese driver arrived with supper. The commander returned to address me in sing-song English.

'We worried for your health. Better you go to Lhasa tonight. No big hospital here. We take you.'

He turned to our driver and gave him the good news that, instead of going to bed, he was about to drive all night until he reached Lhasa. The driver took it in his usual philosophical way, grinned and shrugged, and went out to his waiting truck. We were escorted by the commander, who shook our hands and wished us a good journey. Even the spectating crowd emerged from its collective trance and produced smiles and waves. I found myself wishing we could have stayed longer. They all seemed rather nice.

The moon was rising over the Yamdok Tso. Rob and I took turns at feeding the driver peppermints to keep him awake. After his head had slumped over the wheel a couple of times, he swallowed a small white pill and then seemed all right. I wondered if he would ever pick up hitch-hiking foreigners again. Rob gave him directions to the Chinese hotel, as he had left some of his luggage there, and we were dropped in downtown Lhasa at two a.m.

'I stayed here last time. Just let me do the talking, and there should be no problem.'

With some difficulty, Rob eventually roused the bleary-eyed receptionist, who was not used to having people arrive in the middle of the night. I parked myself as inconspicuously as possible on a bench in the foyer, wondering vaguely why the cheap Chinese hotel was more imposing than the supposedly luxurious Tourist Hotel. Maybe this one even had hot running water, although it was perhaps better not to get one's hopes up too quickly.

Rob was still talking to the receptionist, speaking, I suspected, rather worse Chinese than usual. She looked suitably confused, glanced at our passports, wrote our names on a list, and led us up the stairs to the third floor. I was still wondering what she would do with the names on the list, when she began pounding on a door to wake up the occupants of the room. We groped our way between the half-dozen beds, while the person who had opened the door was already burrowing back into warm blankets again.

In spite of the tiredness, I did not sleep for a while. Things had been happening too quickly, and I felt impelled to go over the situation. I had already decided to wait until I reached England before starting any rabies shots, as I still had a suspicion that the Chinese might use water rather than admit they did not have the exact remedy. The rest of the expedition was due back from the mountain in five days' time. It remained only for me to keep out of the expensive Tourist Hotel. Would I be able to summon the energy to go on dodging the System for long enough?

I wondered if the officials were as aware of my lies as I was of theirs, or if the practice had become so habitual for them that truth had become synonymous with maximum profit. My own methods of dealing with their customs were no more pleasing than the arguments and frustrations of the expedition's direct confrontations. I began to see why lying is so high on the Buddhist list of 'negative actions'. After changing the facts around often enough, you begin to doubt which story is true, and the resulting confusion eats into your spirit. Were any of us ever true to ourselves, let alone to others? How easy it had been to accuse Doug of carefully editing snippets of philosophy, selected and arranged to support an egocentric view of the world, and how much harder it was to admit to doing so myself.

Quite why I chose this moment of exhaustion to arrive at such a realisation I was not sure, but it brought me crashing down from my carefully maintained self-confidence. I was nothing but a collection of attitudes and conceits. I knew nothing, and even if I did learn anything worth while, how could I be sure I was not immediately distorting it to suit myself? Suddenly I saw that what I had been avoiding was the *commitment* to anything I might learn, whether or not it suited my ambition or ego.

Slowly the confusion and dissatisfaction began to subside. Letting go of it all left me feeling relaxed and free. A strange calm swept over me. Nothing else mattered but that I was here, in the fabled city of Lhasa, unfettered by meetings, arguments, bored companions or preconceptions, and I had at least five days in which to explore.

We were at the Lhasa hospital early the next morning. My leg was sore and awkward, but nothing like as painful as I had expected it to be after seeing the ugly black blotches caused by internal bleeding. Rob talked to the Chinese doctor and I talked to the Tibetan doctor, and between us and a Chinese medical dictionary we managed to convey the problem. They sent me off down a corridor, where I joined a line of Tibetans waiting for tetanus and antibiotic injections.

The wounded Tibetans were cheerful enough, showing off their injuries to each other. Some of the damage was gruesome, often the result of injudicious use of farm or factory machinery. My own wound was very unexciting by comparison, but the Tibetans were generous with their sympathy none the less.

The hospital equipment and treatment were simple but functional; the doctors were caring and concerned, and far more sincere than the officials who deal with tourists. Perhaps, gradually, the ghosts of past horrors would die and more Tibetans would begin to use the hospitals. By the time I left, I felt that perhaps I had been too hasty in my earlier suspicions, although I was still inclined to wait until I got home before starting the rabies shots.

A deputation from the Tourist Office greeted us coolly in the hotel foyer when we returned. The interpreter was a neat young Chinese lady by the name of Pan.

'Where is the rest of your group? Why are you not staying at the Tourist Hotel?'

I paused, knowing there was more to come. Throughout the interrogation I tried to look blank, as if I was unaware that there was supposed to be a difference between the two hotels.

'You should move to the Tourist Hotel. You will not be comfortable here.'

'Really, I am most comfortable here. This hotel is much nicer than the Tourist Hotel.'

What both sides were delicately refraining from mentioning was the price – 3 *yuan* instead of 250. I kept insisting that my injuries required frequent visits each day to the hospital, which might inconvenience their bus driver. The Chinese hotel was only a couple of blocks from the hospital, walking distance, even with a sore leg. It was also only a couple of blocks from the Potala, but I avoided mentioning that, for it was hardly a convincing argument from someone who was supposed to be severely incapacitated. In the end they seemed to decide I might be more trouble than I was worth, and gave up. Attention immediately turned to Rob.

'Where are you staying? Where is the rest of your party? Please show your student papers.'

Rob suddenly remembered he was late for an important appointment and disappeared hastily into the back streets of Lhasa. I shrugged.

'I don't know who he is, I just met him at the hospital. Perhaps he's staying at the Tourist Hotel?'

The officials bustled out, evidently not wanting to become involved in any more problems than they already had. They assured me they would return with a reservation for a flight out without delay. At 3 *yuan* a night, I was sure they meant it.

'Make sure I also have connecting reservations out of Chengdu and Peking,' I called after them.

'Yes, of course,' someone called back, without conviction.

As soon as the coast was clear, I set off to explore Lhasa.

It was one of the strangest cities I had ever visited – a juxtaposition of medieval splendour and proletarian uniformity, as if someone had mixed up the pieces of two separate jigsaws and then put them together without looking. Unable to read Chinese or complicated Tibetan, I could not discern the function of the various schools, colleges, offices, factories and government headquarters which were housed in the modern buildings that comprised the greater part of downtown Lhasa. Few were higher than three storeys, while away from the city centre stood the standard single-storey concrete and tin roof models which could be seen all over Tibet.

On the way to the Barkhor, I turned a corner and found I had stepped into a piece of the other jigsaw. The buildings here were of stone, three storeys high, with their walls and windows tapered towards the top. All the houses were in a poor state of repair, and it was questionable if the ban on maintenance had been lifted in time to save them. A scattering of market stalls around the periphery were selling anything from tea to Chinese shoes, and over one doorway a small sign announced *sa-kang* ('restaurant'), but it was closed. The throng of pilgrims must have been on the move since the day we first arrived in Lhasa, three months ago. An old man wearing heavy sheepskin clothes sat at the side of the road reading prayers from a faded *peja*, while the passers-by dropped coins into the cloth bag spread out on the ground beside him.

I walked back through the straight concrete streets towards the Potala. Two or three stone carvers had found themselves niches in the base of the rock on which the palace was built, and were carving small stones with the mantra OM MANI PADME HUM to sell to the devout, or to the tourists. Behind the great rock was an area of wooded parkland enclosing a small lake. A little temple stood on an island in the lake, built by the sixth Dalai Lama, one of the more controversial figures in Tibetan history.

It was the fifth Dalai Lama who instigated the building of the Potala, and he died before it was completed. Fearing that enthusiasm for the building's completion would wane when the death became known, the chief minister kept it a secret until everything had been finished. By the time the reincarnation of the Dalai Lama was found he was twelve years old, and had become used to the adventurous life of a young Tibetan peasant. He never completely settled to the quiet monastic life expected of a Dalai Lama, and used to sneak out of the great palace at night to visit his girlfriends. The Chinese Ambans tried to discredit him, and to replace him with their own candidate, and he died prematurely and under mysterious circumstances. The Tibetans, however, succeeded in establishing their own choice as his successor. I felt the sixth Dalai Lama was a rather sad figure, yet a very moving one, living in the world both of the common man and of the religious recluse. Whether one believes that he was a Buddha acting in enlightened but mysterious ways, or a young man struggling to fulfil his destiny, there can be no doubt that Tsangyang Gyatso forged a link between the seemingly unattainable purity of the other Dalai Lamas and the outlook and emotions of the common people. The poetry he wrote reflects his struggle to reconcile the two.

In meditation I think of my teacher.
I see his face come before me
But the face is that of my lover.

Some nomads were camped in the woods by the lake. Two of them were walking over to receive a blessing from the old monk reading prayers at the side of the path leading down from the rear of the Potala. At his side was a little bowl of melted butter and a soft grass brush. Each in turn dropped a coin on to the piece of cloth at the monk's side, folded his hands together, and bowed, whereupon he received a dab of butter and a blessing on his crown.

I ran into Rob at the Chinese Friendship Store. Apart from a small vegetable market at the side of the road, it was the nearest thing to a shopping centre either of us had found in the city. The usual range of Chinese manufactured goods was displayed, together with a few Tibetan felt boots and striped aprons. I bought a pair of black Chinese slippers to use in Peking, where my Tibetan boots would probably raise too many eyebrows. I had already identified with the local people in wanting to remain as inconspicuous as possible.

Back at the hotel, Rob managed to procure some copies of the *China Reconstructs* magazine. Printed in English, it was obviously intended to present a picture of China to the outside world rather than offer information for home consumption. I leafed through a few copies to find articles on Tibet. There were glowing accounts of how industrialisation and productivity were increasing, glossy colour pictures of modern hospitals, and much emphasis placed on the traditions of China's 'colourful minorities'. Reading this sort of thing in Tibet, and comparing it with the view from the hotel window, brought a strange sense of unreality to the images thus superimposed. In a 'commune school', a class of spotlessly clean Tibetan children sat at their desks, wearing equally spotless traditional clothes and hats of wool, silk and brocade in bright colours. Outside in the dusty streets, the children ran home from school, grubbily mischievous, in their blue denim trousers and jackets – not a felt boot or fur-trimmed hat in sight! I had assumed the authorities took a pride in their uniformity and would want to present themselves as they were. Perhaps, after all, there was some truth in the rumour that the 'monks' in the monasteries spent most of their time working in the fields and were recalled to dress up in their robes and chant their *pujas* only when a large party of tourists was due.

I had seen photographs of the exhibition of clay models in the Tibetan Revolutionary museum in Lhasa, depicting the alleged sufferings experienced under the old system in Tibet. The models were of people having their hands cut off, eyes gouged out by their feudal landlords, or their babies buried alive as part of the religious rituals in monasteries. Photographs of skull-cups and thighbone trumpets were exhibited as evidence that people were done away with in order to obtain their bones for ritual instruments. Many Westerners no doubt found this evidence convincing, not realising that Tibetans have always displayed a matter-of-fact attitude towards death. Once a dead person's consciousness has departed for its next life, the body is regarded as being of no further use, and as a last act of Buddhist generosity it is given back to one of the four elements: fire, water, earth or air. Tibet being a dry, rocky country with a shortage of firewood, air burial is the most practical and widely practised. This involves cutting up the corpse and mixing it with tsampa, to be eaten by the birds. (Large flocks of vultures hang around near all Tibetan burial grounds.) The method is chosen by astrological divination, which might also reveal that it would be auspicious to use certain bones for ritual instruments. To Tibetans, this idea is neither ghoulish nor sinister, but a very practical reminder that our present human lifetime is impermanent, and that it would be very short-sighted to allow ourselves to be distracted by the business and pleasure of this life alone.

Han Suyin, one of the first Western writers to be allowed to visit Lhasa since the Communist takeover, interviewed a number of Tibetans working for the Chinese administration in 1975, and quotes in her book, *Lhasa, the Open City*, many stories of hardship and atrocity along the lines depicted in the clay models, and similar to Pemba's own story. Yet, with so many supposedly actual examples to draw upon, I wondered why the propagandists had needed to resort to artists' impressions when photographs would have been far more convincing. Harrer's observations after seven years in Tibet seem to indicate that the government was too slack rather than too harsh, and that bandits were more to be feared than administrators, the more so because of the lack of modern communications.

It is difficult to equate Han Suyin's claim that there was a good deal of starvation before the Chinese arrived with her assertion that at the time only 5 per cent of fertile land was under cultivation. It would have taken a huge and efficient army to keep hordes of starving peasants from wresting a living from the 95 per cent of idle land – an army which, all too clearly, Tibet did not possess before the Chinese incursion.

Both Heinrich Harrer and Han Suyin comment on the large numbers of beggars in Lhasa: in fact, the Tibetan government rounded them all up and offered them good wages to work on Harrer's canal-building project. Within a week, they had all run away – to resume the easier and more lucrative profession of begging!

The Dalai Lama himself was described by the Chinese as a pleasure-seeking lama who loved women, gold and silver, and who 'sacrificed a human heart, liver or arm every time he read a scripture'. Are we to assume that the thousands of Tibetans who followed him over the Himalaya, and later flocked to Dharamsala, where the Dalai Lama's government reformed in exile, did so in their eagerness to donate arms and livers for his nefarious purposes? My own time in Dharamsala revealed no echo of the 'hell on earth' attributed by the Chinese to the old regime in Tibet.

If 'slaves' were as desperately oppressed as the Chinese made out, why was there no peasant uprising? Tibetans proved themselves capable of such uprising in the revolt of 1959, against the Chinese. The Tibetan government had no strong army or police to keep them down, as the ease of invasion by both the British and the Red Army indicates. There was no historical evidence of famines before Chinese occupation. The great granaries of the monasteries provided a kind of social security for the population in times of poor harvest. The old Tibetan government's real shortcoming was that it had become over-comfortable and slack.

It was not only Heinrich Harrer who was able to slip through the controls of an inefficient government and reach Lhasa. At the end of the nineteenth century a number of 'pundits' were dispatched as spies from British India to map Tibet, measure distances and so on. Most of them travelled as wandering pilgrims, counting paces on their rosaries and hiding their records in prayer-wheels. It was probably the remoteness of Lhasa, combined with the unwarlike attitude of the Tibetans, which made it so easy for the Red Chinese to gain a good hold in the country. The first arrivals were, by all accounts, well disciplined, and worked in the fields with the peasants. They offered the Tibetans good jobs building the new military roads, and paid well. There was no interference with the old order, or with religion, and many Tibetans simply went along with the new system, as it had the nominal backing of the old central government which they had never seen.

The Tibetan government itself was outmoded in political and military terms, and would have been unable to withstand pressure from any large twentieth-century power. Exiled lamas express the situation in spiritual terms, saying that the collective good karma of Tibet had simply run out, and the merit that caused the teachings to come to their country had been expended. There were not enough highly developed practitioners with the spiritual powers to protect Tibet as in the past. The Buddha-dharma, they say, is not static. It moves and flows, according to the karma of the people who hold it. Just as it was destroyed in India and remained safe in Tibet, so it has now been destroyed in Tibet, and carried to many other countries by exiled Tibetans. Whether it will take root and grow will depend entirely on the actions of the beings in those countries.

Pan had made my flight reservation for 6 July. I would have

liked to stay one more day, to see if celebrations would be allowed on the Dalai Lama's birthday, but the remainder of the expedition was due back, and it seemed pointless to argue. Where were they – Doug and Alex and Roger? I made a series of fruitless telephone calls to the Tourist Office, unable to shake off the persistent premonition of disaster creeping insidiously up my spine every time I looked across towards the mountains. I could have saved the effort. The bored voice on the end of the telephone knew nothing, and cared less. If only the Everest expedition had reached Lhasa by now, they might have had some news; but no, the bored voice had no information of a Chris Bonington being there, nor any of my own team members.

I was told I could have my taxi-fare to the airport reduced to £50 if I was willing to share with a passenger from the Tourist Hotel. I hastily agreed, wondering what the original fare had been. Rob was flying to Chengdu to catch a connection to Shanghai, so I suggested he might try his luck with the jeep too.

Our jeep was one hour late. The Chinese tourist guide frowned hard at Rob.

'There is only supposed to be one extra passenger.'

'Oh no,' I said casually. 'Two, you know.'

He had only one receipt with him, so decided to avoid any trouble by pretending Rob didn't exist. I handed over money for one and the two of us slid into the back seat. The other passenger, seated in front, was Chris Bonington.

'Oh, hello Chris. Where's the rest of your team?'

'They're a few days behind. They've been packing up Base Camp.'

He seemed tired and tense. He had seen nothing of Doug and the others. The noise of the jeep precluded much conversation, and Rob was not eager to explain his presence in case the guide overheard.

We were in the same hotel in Chengdu as the American Everest team. One of the men was hobbling about with pieces of wood under the cut-away front of his plastic double boots to take the weight off his frostbitten toes. Everyone was subdued and quiet. One of the women climbers, Marty Hoey, had fallen from the fixed ropes high on the mountain. The loss had touched all of them, taken the gloss off the adventure. They had not reached the summit.

The tourist package included a meal at a restaurant serving traditional spicy Szechwan food. By this time the guides assigned to the Americans from the Chengdu Tourist Office assumed Rob was with Chris and me, while those assigned to us took it that he was with the Americans. Rob himself was enjoying his first glimpse of the Chinese five-star tourist package – quite a contrast to the rest of his five-month journey from Hong Kong. He was catching the flight out to Shanghai the following day, with the idea of eventually making his way to Bangkok. I wondered what the Thais would make of the Groucho Marx false nose and the harmonica.

The following day I went round to the Tourist Office to find out about my reservation to Peking. The staff were polite, and smiling, but they were very sorry, they had received no message that I was coming, they could not possibly get a reservation to Peking for at least five days.

'So sorry, you will have to stay here.'

I smiled my best plastic smile and tried a new tack.

'I must get back for my rabies shots or I may die.'

There was an amused snicker from one of the officials.

'I don't think Chengdu is so bad! A few days here won't kill you.'

Their expressions changed rapidly when I offered to bite the interpreter, and a seat was found for me instantly.

Then they wanted 20 *yuan* cancellation fee for cancelling my original flight. I thanked providence and Rob for his parting gift of the Chinese Airlines regulation book, and quoted them the correct fee of 4 *yuan*. From the looks on their faces, this was something I wasn't supposed to know. They agreed to 4, but frustration had turned into a savage desire to win outright. If they had no message of my arrival, how could they have booked a flight in the first place? There was some consultation, then a smile and an assurance that they had decided to waive the cancellation fee. I felt no satisfaction in the victory, only bitterness that I had been reduced to playing such games.

Chris and I were on the same flight to Peking. He sat in

silence for a few minutes, and then spoke quietly, looking at his hands.

'Pete and Joe are dead.'

All I could think of at first was the utter loneliness in his face.

'Oh Chris, how could you travel alone without anyone to talk to?'

'I couldn't say anything before. There were too many people listening. I have to relay the news back home before it gets leaked to the press. Marty's mother heard about her daughter's death on the radio. I don't want that to happen to Maria or Hilary.'

'I wish I knew where Doug and the others are.'

'Hey, don't you worry. There just *can't* be any more.'

There was little else to say. Any words would have seemed inadequate. That morning Chris was not an adventurer or a mountain climber. He was just a man grieving the loss of his friends, a loss that had left him open, unguarded. Through the pain in his eyes, I felt I was looking into his soul.

I knew it would be a while before I could really believe it. Perhaps it was too sudden, or perhaps I was too exhausted, too drained of feeling to be able to react. It was just academic information that there were two friends I wouldn't be seeing any more. Deep down something remained stubbornly convinced that they would be there in the pub next Saturday, swapping pints and jokes, and going on about what an epic place Tibet was. As it sank in, I began to feel indignant. This was taking climbing too far. It was such a waste. But I knew that half of the lure was the risk – watching yourself balanced precariously between triumph and disaster.

Chris was whisked away in a car as soon as we stepped out into Peking airport. Once again, I was not expected, and it was a while before the disgruntled officials could set the system in motion and find transport and a hotel room.

'So sorry, so strange they assured you in Lhasa your flight out of Peking was confirmed. We have heard nothing, we were not expecting you. So sorry, all flights out of Peking are full for the next week ... unless you would like to buy a ticket on Chinese Airlines, cash? Then you can leave tonight.'

I called John at the British Embassy and interrupted his afternoon swim. He stood dripping on the Embassy floor and reassured me down the crackly telephone line. After fifteen minutes he called back to say that the PIA flight the following day was only a quarter full; then he repeated the news in Chinese for the official who took the phone from me. An hour later I was informed by the Tourist Office that they had managed to find me a seat on tomorrow's flight after all. I felt helpless and angry. Exhaustion and the growing fear that I would not get back in time for the shots had sapped the last of my resilience to the tactics of the faceless System. It seemed that they saw in my predicament and my fear only a useful lever to prise more money out of me. They seemed incapable of human emotions, such as sympathy for someone needing help.

A group of acupuncturists staying in the same hotel stuck needles in my hands, arms and ears, but even acupuncture cannot heal such complete exhaustion. The group comprised students from Europe, undertaking a three-month course in acupuncture in the country of its origin. They were bitter and disappointed, and were leaving early, feeling they were just Great White Cows to be milked of their money. I thought of our cheerful Chinese truck driver and wished that I could break out of the System's net of officialdom and discover the rest of the real Chinese people.

There was enough time before the evening flight for just one sightseeing tour in Peking. With difficulty, I persuaded my guide that we should follow him up the long paved avenue to the Buddhist temple in Peking. It had been impeccably restored; not a lick of paint was out of place. Outside each building was a notice in Chinese and English saying photography was forbidden inside the buildings. The guide watched me intently to ensure I committed no breach of the rules. Inside, the paintings and statues had been beautifully restored, and were walled off with glass to prevent anyone from touching or damaging them. The shrine was decorated with dusty plastic flowers. There were no offerings spread out here, only a Plexiglas collection box with a slot in the top to prevent people from stealing the money. There were no pilgrims, only guided parties, the guides intoning dates and measurements. For the first time, there was no need for the guide to hustle me back for lunch. I turned to go. I could feel no life in this sterile building.

As I walked down the avenue to the beautifully repainted main gate, I felt an overwhelming sadness for the Chinese people. A whole history of wisdom and learning wiped out in a single generation. And they didn't even understand what it was they had lost. Now, like America with her Indians, the government is crying 'shame', and trying to put the pieces back, not understanding that painted tepees or temples for tourists to stare at do not make a culture or a source of knowledge.

I could still hear the guide's voice expounding the scale and accuracy of the restoration work . . . but what do they have? A painted temple, preserved with glass and railings, measured by builders, documented by historians, a museum of artefacts and plastic flowers. Soon this crystalline death would spread to the last corners of Tibet. But not just yet.

13

Turning of the Wheel

Three years later, looking back on a journey and a country which marked a turning point in my life, I find my mind filled with a kaleidoscope of superimposed images, thoughts and emotions. Anxiety and exhaustion alternate with curiosity and the elation of discovery. The flat-roofed houses of Tingri, the chang parties, the exotically bridled horses, recall a fleeting glimpse of life in Old Tibet; a teaching without words, a mirage that will fade rather than crumble.

The images change, and I am in Lhasa again, back in the jostling, laughing, lively crowd of Tibetans circumambulating the Jokhang. Prayer-wheels click round to the rhythm of the cries of the chang-sellers and the shuffle of felt boots and canvas shoes on the uneven street. I step around a group of women doing prostrations outside the main doorway, stretching their arms out to move one more bead on the rosary. Inside the temple, a thousand butter lamps flicker and burn, illuminating the shadowy gold faces of the Buddhas with a shimmering glow.

I am laughing with a gap-toothed woman with dust and turquoise in her hair and a Chinese vacuum flask of melted butter in her hand. She is laughing at the butter lamps, at how shocked the Chinese are at the outrageous waste of food, at how they collect it up every evening and take it down to the People's Commune to be eaten. And how, every morning, it is back, burning in the temple.

I am standing at the side of the road out of Lhasa with the dry wind blowing dust into my hair. Hitch-hiking is easy today; the truck driver stops out of curiosity. I am only going the five miles to Drepung.

The monastery stands behind a grove of low willows, backing on to a bare hulk of rock and scree. The tall buildings block out the sun in the narrow dirt streets that climb steeply between them, linking terrace with terrace. These narrow streets are a labyrinth on the hillside, and they are so quiet after the elbowing, jostling crowd in the Barkhor. The sound of a kicked stone echoes and rattles from the high walls as it rolls down the steep slope. Every now and then I catch a glimpse of a solitary red-robed figure walking across the sunlit space at the end of an alleyway, and once a little group of sheepskin-clad pilgrims emerged from the shadows into the courtyard where I was sitting, only to scuttle away again at the sight of a stranger. The temples are painted deep red, while the other buildings are painted white. Patches of sunlight fall between the heavy red pillars at the front of the main temple. In the shaded colonnade, the wall of the temple is covered with huge painted figures. The four kings, who are the guardians of the four directions, sit two on either side of the doorway, as they do in temples all across the Himalaya, from Sikkim to Ladakh.

The red-painted doors stand slightly ajar. Inside, the great hall lies silent and empty, the faded silk hangings on the pillars shining dully in the dusty sunlight filtering through small windows set high in the walls. A few lamps burn in dark corners in front of the shrines. An old monk is sweeping the floor, moving slowly between the long cushions laid on one side of the hall. More than half the floor is bare marble. There are not enough monks now to fill the hall at *puja* time. Another old man comes in. He is wearing rough black homespun. He moves from lamp to lamp, topping up the liquid butter from a vacuum flask.

There are small chapels leading off from the main temple hall. The old monk puts away his broom and goes into one of them to tend the lamps. I follow, pausing to let my eyes adjust to the shadowy interior. I look over my shoulder, and behind me. On either side of the doorway stand two black wrathful deities, towering twenty feet above me, fangs bared, knives and daggers in their claws. The painted plaster and stone shifts and moves in the uncertain half-light of the butter lamps, and it is hard to feel easy in such a terrifying presence. My neck prickles as I turn my back on them again, and it is an effort to remind myself that their victims are greed, anger, pride and all other obstacles to omniscient mind.

Beside the shrine in front of me sits a massive stone figure in a yellow robe. The knees are somewhere above my head. The face, far above, glows in the light of the lamps, yet seems to have a radiance of its own. I have seen him before in other temples, the features stylised and rigid. Suddenly I feel that the sculptor knew the man he was portraying, knew his humour and warmth as well as the greatness of his mind and his teaching. A little smile creases the corners of his mouth, and his eyes are gazing into an eternity that could be outside, or within himself – it is impossible to tell. The old monk follows my gaze, pausing in his mantras to answer my unspoken question.

'*Om mani padme hum*, *om mani padme hum*, *om mani*... yes, that is Tsong Khapa, *om mani padme hum*... '

The old monk moves slowly into the next chapel. I follow. Another red-robed figure is sitting on the cushioned bench at the back of the shadowy room. Perhaps he is in his fifties; it is difficult to tell. His face is fine-boned and his long slanting eyes are clear and alert. I can sense a presence about him, even before the old monk bows respectfully before continuing his duties with the lamps. The Geshe smiles.

'Sit down.'

His manner is unhurried; he does not seem surprised to see me. He might have been waiting for me, or for anything, in this dimly lit room beneath the golden Buddhas. He asks how long

I have been in Tibet, and I answer three months. Then he asks why I have come, and I hesitate. Suddenly I feel that if I could explain what it is I am seeking here, I would already have found it. Yet he seems to understand my confusion as well as any explanation I might have given. He smiles, and points to my camera.

'Why don't you take pictures of the Buddhas? You can show them to your friends in England, and one day you may come to understand them.' He laughs and whispers conspiratorially: 'You had better be quick, before the *pon-po* see you and ask you for money!'

So I take photographs of every statue and painting that has enough light, while the Geshe nods encouragement and approval. It seems strange to have such freedom after the restrictions in the other temples; I remember how one official had smashed my camera into my face as I tried to photograph a wall painting.

I come back to my seat by the Geshe.

'You have paintings like this in England?'

'Not many. Some photographs.'

I pulled the Milarepa book out of my bag and show him the picture plates. He examines the book carefully.

'This is English script?'

'It is the story of Milarepa in English.'

He nods again, more to himself than to me, and touches the book reverently to his head. He pauses, then speaks again thoughtfully.

'There is a prophecy, made by Guru Rinpoche when he first came to Tibet. He said, "When the Iron Bird flies, and horses run on wheels, the Tibetan people will be scattered like ants across the world, and the Dharma will come to the land of the Red Man."'

The Geshe hands the book back to me, and sits in silence. Slowly, I begin to smile. I know what he is saying. Not that I have wasted my time here. Any search is a journey, a fulfilment in itself, a process of learning. But he is telling me that the 'secrets', the teachings of Tibet, have already moved on, and I can find what I am looking for at home.

All Tibet needed to do was open my eyes so that I knew how to look.

I am standing in front of the Potala Palace, the heart of Old Tibet, temple of the Dalai Lamas, the 'meeting place of heaven and earth'. The wide stone staircase zig-zags up the face of the stone pinnacle on which the temple is built, and today it is thronged with pilgrims from all over Tibet. I squeeze into the slow-moving mass of people, and let them carry me with them up the rough stone steps. Two old women start teasing me because my leg is still sore and I am limping. They walk either side of me, grab my backside, and haul me up the steps with them. Half-way up, the steps take a hairpin bend, and at the corner is a porch in one of the buildings which grows out of the rock. A monk is sitting on the floor of the porch, turning a huge prayer-wheel, the mantra OM MANI PADME HUM repeated over and over in gold letters.

The stream of people is being swallowed up into a dark doorway surrounded by brilliant painted carvings which accentuate the darkness inside. The noisy, chattering mass of humanity shuffles along the dark corridors until it spews out into the sunlight of the inner courtyard. Now the line of people winds itself like a snake on the open gravel, waiting for the bottleneck at the bottom of the steep wooden staircase on the far side to ease. There is a government official standing at the foot of the steps selling tickets, the familiar khaki jacket and trousers standing out amongst the black homespun and sheepskin of the pilgrims.

It is a long climb to the roof. The wooden staircases are more like ladders, and the twisting corridors are sometimes pitch black. The roof is flat, with the golden roofs dotted around like pagodas, standing above the chörtens of the Dalai Lamas which stand three storeys below, with the tall spires rising up to the roof. A baby is parked, asleep under the Buddha-paintings on one of the pagodas. Near by, a group of women sways, singing on the flat rooftop, pounding the roof with heavy sticks. A man breaks away from a party of guided tourists to ask me a question.

'Excuse me, but could you tell me what religious ritual those women are performing?'

I look again at the group of women. 'Looks to me like they're fixing the roof.'

He gives me the look he must reserve for philistines and the terminally irreverent, and rejoins his group. I walk over to the women, and ask the nearest one what they are doing.

'We're fixing the roof,' she says, with some surprise.

Another group of white faces wanders past in the wake of a Chinese guide.

'And now I will take you down to the dungeons where the Dalai Lamas tortured their prisoners . . .'

'Wonder where the Chinese tortured theirs?' mutters a voice from the back, and the group shuffles off towards the stairway.

The line of pilgrims snakes its way around the levels and terraces of the rooftop. On the corner of a small chapel a heavy bell hangs beneath a golden lion's head. Each pilgrim rings the bell as the line files past, and the chatter and laughter and murmur of mantras is orchestrated by the constant rhythmic dong, dong, dong of the bell.

The line is swallowed up into the dark labyrinth of corridors and staircases. Around courtyards and colonnades there are statues or wall paintings to be touched with the head or hand. So many people are carrying flasks of butter for the lamps it is inevitable that the paintings have acquired a black greasy patch at about shoulder height. No matter, their purpose is to illustrate intangible ideas, and to serve as a focal point for mind and devotion. When the picture becomes sufficiently badly defaced, some of the monks will be able to earn themselves spiritual merit by repainting it. It seems to be a twentieth-century idea that an old painting is an antique art treasure to be preserved, rather than a living tradition to be perpetuated. Here and there, some of the restored paintings and statues have already been walled off with wire netting to prevent pilgrims touching them.

I pause by a wall painting of the 'wheel of life', faded yet still beautiful. The jostling throng shuffle and rustle past, adding

The Wheel of Life

their fingerprints to the thousands that have gone before, at the base of the picture. The picture is a diagram of the Buddhist universe, and the mental states which are its causation. Or, as one Tibetan had cryptically expressed it, 'a diagram of Samsara and how to get out of it'. In the centre, a pig, a cockerel and a snake follow each other round in never-ending circles; these are ignorance, attachment and hatred following upon each other. Around these, the wheel is divided into six parts or 'realms', which correspond both to states of mind in this life and to the state to which one may be reborn in the next. The realms are graphically portrayed. For example, the 'hungry ghosts' have rapaciously large and hungry bellies, but inadequately tiny mouths and throats, so that they can never be satisfied – a devastatingly accurate portrayal of a greedy mind! The outer circle contains the 'twelve links of dependent arising'; everything arises in dependence upon causes – and creates further effects, thus returning to the theme of the emptiness of inherent existence. It is the direct realisation of this emptiness through meditation that is the key to escaping from the cycle of birth and death portrayed in the wheel. In case one might still remain attached to the more attractive aspects of this cyclic existence, one is reminded that these, too, are only temporary, by the fact that Yama, the Lord of Death, holds the wheel in his claws.

I photograph the Wheel, hoping I will gradually understand more of it as time goes on. One of the *pon-po*, a bulky Tibetan wearing government khaki, appears as if from nowhere and shouts at me for taking photos. I hurriedly put the camera in its case, and visit one of the nearby shrine rooms. The exit from the room is down an almost-vertical ladder to the courtyard twenty feet below. I wait in line as those in front cautiously take to the ladder, its handrail slippery with butter. A heavily built tourist photographs the shrine before easing his weight on to the steep ladder, and I hear the sharp intake of breath behind me as the *pon-po* expresses his disapproval. As I approach the top of the ladder, I am pushed violently from behind. I step back in panic colliding with the *pon-po* who pushed me. He grabs my wrist, twisting my arm viciously behind my back, and tries to smash my camera against the wall with his other hand.

The pilgrims back off, afraid to interfere. I try to struggle free, but he is too strong; it is frightening how strong he is – and suddenly I am certain he is going to push me off the ledge into the courtyard below. Because of my awareness that I am still in a temple, I have remained silent through all this, but now I am too alarmed to maintain such niceties and begin to yell at him, in English and broken Tibetan, to get his filthy hands off. He must have been momentarily unsure of himself, because I feel his grip relax a little, and by suddenly ducking under his arm, I am able to twist around and get my wrist free. I make my escape, shakily, down the ladder.

My attacker leans out above me and calls to his colleague, who runs out into the courtyard, reaches up, grabs my ankle and yanks me off the ladder. My injured leg is weak, and slips off the rung, but by hanging on with my hands I am able to stop myself crashing to the ground. Three more khaki-clad figures appear from somewhere, and the four of them grab me roughly and push me up against the wall before I can recover my balance. They are not interested in my camera; it is my body, especially my breasts, at which the punches are aimed. I realise, with a stab of fear, that everyone is too afraid of them to intervene, afraid of their power. No one steps forward to help me. These men have a free hand to do what they want and make their excuses afterwards. They have recognised that I am alone and do not have the protection of a tour group, that I am small and obviously limping. An ideal victim.

Suddenly the pushing and kicking stops, and the four men back off into the shadows. The large American, who unwittingly provoked the attack by taking a photograph, returns to see what all the commotion is about. Like any bullies, the *pon-po* like to have the odds well in their favour.

'Hey, you okay? What was all that about?'

'I think they objected to you taking that photograph, but took it out on me because I'm smaller. I'm just bruised and shaky, it was all too quick for me to get seriously damaged.'

He looks around, but my attackers seem to have disappeared.

'Looks like they've gone anyhow. You gonna be okay?'

'Oh yes, I'm fine now.'

He hurries off to rejoin his group, and I continue my wanderings.

The four of them are waiting for me at the end of the next corridor.

'Hey!' I call over my shoulder to the imaginary American who is somewhere behind me. I see the men falter a little, but it's clear the respite won't last for long.

'Excuse me, perhaps I can help?'

The small, white-haired Cantonese tourist speaks perfect English. He has a small camera slung over his shoulder. He offers to mediate, and begins to reason with the men, like a kindly schoolmaster lecturing the playground bullies. I lean against the wall, shaken and uncertain what to do. Unprovoked attacks by humans are more disturbing than those by dogs. The pilgrims, filing past, are taking in what is happening. A woman comes over and clasps my hands in hers before continuing on her way, and then they are all coming to me, wringing my hands, smiling encouragement, clasping me on the shoulder. Not a word is spoken, or needed. I am overwhelmed by such sympathy from complete strangers. The elderly Cantonese returns.

'I have suggested that as you are taking no more photos, it would be as well to let you continue in peace. It would be unfortunate if you made complaints to the Tourist Office. I think they see this point of view. I wish you a good visit.'

The Cantonese melts into the crowd as quietly as he came.

In the next great candlelit temple I pause to collect my thoughts and calm myself down, surprised that the euphoria I had felt at being here had been so fragile, so easily shattered. There had been nothing personal about the attack, yet how surely my ego had felt threatened! I stand for a while, letting my mind drift with the shimmering golden light from the lamps, watching the pilgrims doing their prostrations before the shrine.

Slowly, the peaceful golden atmosphere soaks in, and the tension eases. I rejoin the slowly moving line, moving into the next passage and hallway. We are standing before the great white chörtens of the Dalai Lamas, their golden spires disappearing into the shadows of the hall where, three storeys above, they are crowned by the golden pagodas on the roof. This is the heart of the Potala, a repository of the relics of a past greatness, a place of power and energy for the devout. A voice behind speaks, in English.

'That is the chörten of the fifth Dalai Lama.'

'Oh, you speak English!' I am delighted.

He replies in Tibetan.

'No. I can only say, "That is the chörten of the fifth Dalai Lama." It's my job. I sit here and say it to the tourists. It's a nice job. I can sit in the temple and read my book.'

On his lap is a book, on the life and teachings of Tsong Khapa. I stumble through the phrases of the title, and he corrects the mistakes, chuckling softly to himself. I turn to go.

'I read very poorly.'

He catches my hand, pressing the book into it. There are tears in his eyes.

'Take it to your country. Learn to read it, share it. It is finished here.'

Postscript

When the rest of the Shishapangma expedition arrived back in England, I learned that Doug, Alex and Roger had reached the summit with Nick ferrying loads to the lower camps. I thought for a while my premonitions had been for other friends, but I was wrong. Two months later I wrote my contribution for Alex's expedition book, looking forward to his abrasive comments when he returned from Annapurna. Suddenly I found myself thinking: He's not going to read it. He was hit by a rock and fell 800 feet to his death. Perhaps opening your heart to the world in writing a book depletes the finely tuned energy necessary to survive the hardest climbs.

Now, as I come to the end of this book, I learn that Roger has been killed while guiding in the Alps. So many deaths leave you numb; the sport has become a battlefield. All you can do is remember friends when they were still alive, doing what they wanted and doing it well, and wish only that the cost had not been so high.

In Tibet, the authorities honoured their agreement that I could stay in Tingri, and I learned from Sonam later that Tashi and her family suffered no recriminations.

Now the Chinese have thrown open the borders of Tibet, and 'yak-burgers' are being sold to the throngs of tourists in the streets of Lhasa. The Tibet that we experienced is gone, a fading memory re-created with photographs and letters on a page. As in Milarepa's poetry, to live with an awareness of impermanence would be a gift indeed.

GLOSSARY

Tibetan Buddhism

Because Tibetan Buddhism was imported from India, the basic terms may be in Sanskrit (Sans.) or in Tibetan (Tib.).

Chörten (Tib.), *Stupa* (Sans.): a religious monument, each section of which represents one of the five elements

Dharma (Sans.): the ethical precepts of Buddhism

Geshe (Tib.): a holder of advanced learning, resembling a Doctor of Divinity

Gompa (Tib.): a place for meditation; monastery or temple

Jangchub Sempa (Tib.), *Bodhisattva* (Sans.): one who is striving to attain enlightenment for the sake of others

Karma (Sans.): the process of actions being followed by an inevitable result: action and reaction; cause and effect

Kor-wa (Tib.), *Samsara* (Sans.): cyclic existence

Lama (Tib.), *Guru* (Sans.): a teacher or spiritual guide; *Dalai Lama*, Lama who is an Ocean of Wisdom

Nyingmapa (Tib.): the oldest sect of Buddhism in Tibet; followers of Guru Rinpoche's original teachings

Peja (Tib.): loose-leaf parchment books of Buddhist scriptures

Puja (Sans.): a ceremony involving meditation and recitation of prayers

Acknowledgments

I should like to thank Mr Phunsok Wangyal, Office of H.H. the Dalai Lama, for checking this manuscript, and Tony Colwell for his insight and understanding above and beyond the call of editorial duty. I am also grateful to the teachers and students of the Manjushri Institute for Buddhist Studies for their help and support in the writing of this book, and in particular to Jim Belither, Anila Helen Dearnley, Robert S. Kenmuir, Keith Milton, Elizabeth Roberts, Liza Tubb, Yeshe Wangchuck, Tessa Winterbotham and Philip Wood. Thanks above all for the patience and compassion of Geshe Kelsang Gyatso and Geshe Konchog Tsewang.

Bibliography

The following books have been quoted or consulted in the preparation of this text

Avedon, John E: *In Exile from the Land of Snows*, Wisdom Publications, London, 1984

Aziz, Barbara: *Tibetan Frontier Families*, Vikas Publishing House, New Delhi, 1978

Chang, Garma C.C. (trans.): *The Hundred Thousand Songs of Milarepa* (vols 1 and 2), Shambhala Publications, Boulder, Colorado, and London, 1962

Fleming, Peter: *Bayonets to Lhasa*, Rupert Hart-Davis, London, 1961

Gashi, Tsering Dorje: *New Tibet*, Information Office of the Dalai Lama, Dharamsala, India, 1980

Han Suyin: *Lhasa, the Open City*, Jonathan Cape, London, 1977

Harrer, Heinrich: *Seven Years in Tibet*, Rupert Hart-Davis, London, 1953

——: *Return to Tibet*, Weidenfeld & Nicolson, London, 1984

Holzel, Tom, and Audrey Salkeld: *The Mystery of Mallory and Irvine*, Jonathan Cape, London, 1986

Kelsang Gyatso, Geshe: *Buddhism in the Tibetan Tradition*, Routledge & Kegan Paul, London, 1984
——: *Meaningful to Behold*, Tharpa Publications, Conishead Priory, Ulverston, Cumbria, 1986
Lhalungpa, Lobsang P. (trans.): *The Life of Milarepa*, Paladin (paperback), Granada, London, 1979
MacGregor, John: *Tibet – a Chronicle of Exploration*, Routledge & Kegan Paul, London, 1970
Neel, Alexandra David: *Initiations and Initiates in Tibet*, Rider, London, 1970
Norbu, Dawa: *Red Star Over Tibet*, Collins, London, 1974
Norbu, Thubten Jigme, and Colin Turnbull: *Tibet, its History, Religion and People*, Chatto & Windus, London, 1969
Pallis, Marco: *Peaks and Lamas*, Cassell, London, 1939
Richardson, Hugh E.: *Tibet and its History*, Shambhala Publications, Boulder, Colorado, and London, 1962
Richardson, Hugh E., and David Snellgrove: *A Cultural History of Tibet*, Weidenfeld & Nicolson, London, 1968
Scott, Doug, and Alex MacIntyre; *The Shishapangma Expedition*, Granada, London, 1984
Shantideva: *A Guide to the Bodhisattva's Way of Life* (trans. Stephen Batchelor), Library of Tibetan Works and Archives, Dharamsala, India, 1979
Taring, Rinchen Dolma: *Daughter of Tibet*, John Murray, London, 1970
The Third Dalai Lama: *Essence of Refined Gold*, Tushita Books, Dharamsala, India, 1978
Tsondru, Yeshe: *The Essence of Nectar*, Library of Tibetan Works and Archives, Dharamsala, India, 1979
Unsworth, Walt: *Everest* (a history to 1980), Allen Lane, London, 1981

Paper quoted:

Report to the International Commission of Jurists – *Tibet and the Chinese People's Republic*, Geneva (6 rue de Mont de Sion), 1960